The Elusive Covenant

Advances in Semiotics

General Editor, Thomas A. Sebeok

THE ELUSIVE COVENANT

A Structural-Semiotic Reading of Genesis

TERRY J. PREWITT

INDIANA UNIVERSITY PRESS

Bloomington and Indianapolis

The paper used in this publication meets the minimum requirements of American
National Standard for Information Sciences—Permanence of Paper for Printed
Library Materials, ANSI Z39.48-1984.

Manufactured in the United States of America

Library of Congress Cataloging-in-Publication Data
Prewitt, Terry J. (Terry James)
The elusive covenant : a structural-semiotic reading of Genesis / Terry J. Prewitt.
p.   cm. — (Advances in semiotics)
ISBN 0-253-34599-5 (alk. paper)
1. Bible. O.T. Genesis—Criticism, interpretation, etc.
2. Structuralism (Literary analysis)—Case studies.   3. Semiotics—
Case studies.   I. Title.   II. Series.
BS1235.2.P74   1990
222'.1106—dc20   89-46325
1 2 3 4 5 94 93 92 91 90   CIP

CONTENTS

87212

To my parents,
and to Rachel, Electra, and Jennifer

FIGURES AND TABLES

PREFACE

The ideas for this book have been floating unformed or partially formed in various manuscripts, since about 1979 when Stanley and Jane Johnson, Dori Penny, Karen Haworth, and I jokingly placed "Genesis" on a *triskelion,* the somewhat inscrutable version of Greimas's "semiotic square" introduced in Lévi-Strauss's essay "Do Dual Organizations Exist." What began in jest quickly came around to more serious pursuit. I had already begun to work closely with John Gammie, my mentor in biblical studies at the University of Tulsa. His patience and colleagueship from 1977 through 1981 offered one of the most rewarding periods of learning I have experienced. Out of that endeavor came the initial drafts which underpin the present chapters of this book.

The transformations of this text have been many. First, much of the material was originally written in the form of papers. Their integration, including rewriting of published material, has been a slow process, further hampered by my other academic commitments. The manuscript in its present form was created by rewriting and expansion to meet criticisms by my colleagues of a somewhat shorter version finished in 1985. To Arthur Doerr, James Dyehouse, and Mary Rogers, as well as to Thomas Sebeok and readers at Indiana University, I must express a deep debt of gratitude. Their encouragement and criticisms gave me the primary direction of 1988, the year I was finally able to return to the project intensively. This opportunity was provided by the National Endowment for the Humanities Seminar, "Biblical Law in Historical Perspective," offered by David Daube and Calum Carmichael at the University of California, Berkeley. Finally, critical reading of my submission manuscript by Robert A. Oden, Jr., was particularly helpful in guiding my final textual revisions.

My experience in the seminar on biblical law, in addition to providing time for writing and research, was filled with new and challenging perspectives on the text offered in the lectures of Professors Daube and Carmichael. The key benefit of the seminar as a whole for this book has been expansion of my reference to Torah materials outside Genesis, especially the legal materials of Exodus and Deuteronomy. I believe this was an absolutely essential ingredient to enable the fullest appreciation of the social constructs in Genesis, and for the methodological escape from a purely internal structural analysis of the text. In this effort, I am also indebted to all of the other seminar participants, especially John Kampen, Shirley Castelnuovo, Ronald Knox, Pavle Batinic, Jacqueline Boley, Anne Griffiths, and Debra Zeifman. Special thanks is deserved by Calum Carmichael for his critical comments on the manuscripts and his help with many provisional readings of scripture.

Earlier comments by colleagues on particular issues of analysis must also be cited here. Michael Carroll provided some of the most challenging criticism of my initial papers on Genesis and greatly supported my impetus toward this book-length work. A similar role was played by John Gammie, Daniel Patte, and John Deely, each of whom provided substantive and theoretical bases for elements of analysis. Gary Shank and the brothers at St. Meinrad Archabbey, Indiana, contributed to this work through their comments and bibliographic sharing during a trip to the St. Meinrad community in 1984. Thomas Eggebean, Pastor of the First Presbyterian Church in Sapulpa, Oklahoma, stimulated my interest in developing a reasonably "popular" discussion of kinship interests in Genesis; in the end, this book only partially satisfies that aim, but I hope it will meet the interests and needs of at least some lay readers.

Finally, I want to thank several colleagues and students in Pensacola and Tulsa for their intellectual and practical supports toward this work. Robert Armstrong, Jay Knaack, Sam Matthews, and Bruce Dunn have all contributed greatly to my development of philosophical and technical perspective toward text analysis. Mary Rogers has been a constant source of both criticism and support and, above all, academic example. R. E. Lee, Ron Evans, and the many other members of University Toastmasters in Pensacola have also helped me give more popular direction to my ideas and their expressions. Students in seminars at Tulsa and the University of West Florida have also provided criticism and the context for exploration of hypotheses about the text. A special note of thanks goes to several of these students: Joe Dees, Ray Dupree, Tyrone Ealum, Dorothy Gaston, Diane Hudson, Patricia Jackson, Peter Kennedy, Declan Patterson, Gary Raney, Lynn Snyder, and Louise Walsh. Also in Pensacola, Karen Haworth and Debra Joy worked on text preparation for the various drafts leading toward this manuscript. Karen also prepared all of the final illustrations appearing in the book. The final manuscript was prepared by Cherry Starkweather at the Office of Grants and Contracts at the University of West Florida. I must also recognize again the support of the National Endowment for the Humanities summer seminar program, the University of California at Berkeley, and especially The Flora Lamson Hewlett Library of the Graduate Theological Union for resource supports. To my fellow residents at International House during the summer of 1988, too, I extend thanks for the environment for work and social communion they created.

The Elusive Covenant

1

GENEALOGIES

Personal genealogical study has become a popular endeavor in our society during recent decades. Finding information on our backgrounds can be a relatively simple task. We can obtain details of family relations by referring to volumes of records in census, cemetery, birth, and military archives, but the work is usually tedious, as the records were originally kept for purposes other than family reconstruction, and they are found mainly where the people in question lived, worked, and died. In ancient times, many of the relationships we meticulously record and casually forget would simply have been remembered. In fact, people of traditional cultures today are sometimes shocked at someone from another culture who cannot trace ancestors back several generations or relate independent lines of relatives descended from common ancestry.

These two orientations to genealogy, depth of ancestry and breadth of recognition as kin, go hand in hand.[1] Such reckoning, in addition to being important among people with oral traditions, is incorporated into the early written traditions of state-level systems in the Near East and other parts of the world. The advantages of written genealogy rest mainly in potentials for the creation of more sweeping and enduring connections, though independent traditions within early literate societies still follow many of the conventions found in oral tradition. The number of generations a person traces may depend upon how important recollection is to asserting rights and meeting obligations in an extended family context. The depth of genealogical recollection may also relate to the legitimation of leadership in such an extended family. Both of these concerns—rights and legitimation—are central to the genealogical materials of Genesis.[2] It is too simple to say, however, that the Genesis genealogies are mere family records. Indeed, it is doubtful that they are *actual* family records at all. We find in Genesis several kinds of "formula" texts which are offered, evidently, to systematize the supposed relationships between the principal patriarchs of Israel and the known peoples of the ancient Near Eastern world.[3] In addition, the names in the genealogies can sometimes be related as much to places as to the persons with whom they are commonly associated.[4] One may choose between understanding names as representing individuals, or as representing local groups who are linked to a common ancestor. The most developed patriarchal characters, moreover, are quite idealized in the depictions through which they are brought to us. The social level upon which the relationships of Genesis rest is well beyond that of the basic family or even the extended family. It involves groups of

1

large size and diverse history. In this context, then, we may understand the genealogy in Genesis as essentially political. The ties presented in the several genealogical texts provide a structure for a popular history.[5]

These observations help us understand why the relationships between diverse peoples are presented in the terms of family systems. In one sense, the family ties cannot be denied, while in another they are merely a framework asserted to make the conflicts and contrasts among groups seem culturally correct or historically valid. The relationships of early theological circles to this political-historical context are also important, since the development of natural and contractual relationships with *Yahweh* undergirds the whole genealogical structure.

In addition to political-geographic, historical, and theological functions of genealogical material, two other important purposes of genealogy exist in Genesis. First, kinship information included in narratives can relate to a legal context. Such instances provide a social background for illumination of laws set down in the Torah, forming an important element in what David Daube calls "legal legends."[6] Genesis seems especially rich with this kind of narrative, stories functioning as precursors of later legal pronouncements of Jewish law.[7] Second, we must keep in mind that genealogies are part of the larger narrative construction in the Torah, and so may serve literary functions within the whole construction. Robert Wilson has presented many illustrations of this kind of genealogical purpose in Genesis, and we shall view several instances where literary functions occur alongside other motivations for the inclusion of genealogical material.[8]

My purpose in this chapter is not to develop an exhaustive inventory of genealogical materials by function. In fact, Wilson's work already covers much of that ground. Rather, I offer a particular reading of the Genesis genealogies and some associated material from elsewhere in the Torah, drawing heavily from modern kinship theory and the techniques of literary-structural analysis. My form of argument departs somewhat from much of the traditional approach to the text. Specifically, for over a century biblical scholars have pursued a reductionist method directed toward the identification of sources and textual layers attributable to diverse authors and redactors.[9] The critique of this method in recent decades has been built on several grounds. First, some source analyses resulted in gratuitous association of short passages, even individual words, with particular "authors," working almost as an end in itself. Second, such textual dissection in the Torah was driven by modern theologies which have little to do with many likely original meanings of the document. Thus, on these two grounds, although the precise analysis of source-critical scholars achieved many rich results, it did not ultimately serve the wider interests of interpreting the full narrative before us. Third, the general approach of 19th century scholars excluded by definition some important backgrounds through which the Torah should be read. Most important among these, as Oden has recently pointed out through elegant examples, is the background of comparative myth studies, which is naturally linked to a broad anthropological and cross-cultural orientation including kinship studies.[10] Thus, overall, while critical and religious goals of the late 19th and early 20th centuries took the biblical text in their own directions, the most reductionist methods of religious scholars came to serve holistic interpretive interests less and less.

I share orientation and interests with numerous contemporary commentators and analysts of the Torah, most of whom have made some sort of break with traditional assumptions about the nature of the text. These include structuralist, literary, and semiotic readers who are working toward understandings of connections between seemingly senseless juxtapositions of such elements as genealogy, myth, folklore, legal pronouncements, poetry, and other elements of code or narrative. Some of these scholars, though they remain attached to traditional views on Torah authorship, have attempted to put biblical studies back on the track of interpreting biblical documents as unified compositions. Others have sought more radical revisions of assumptions. Several deserve special mention here. A recently-published first resource for anyone who would read Genesis in depth is George Coats' discussion of literary forms and genres.[11] The work is as important for Genesis as Gunkel's source-critical commentary, more so since it signals how much is to be done in developing conceptions of literary unity for Genesis. On a broader front, Northrop Frye has shown the capacity of literary critics to offer rich insight into biblical texts as part of a global critical process.[12] Calum Carmichael, working on a much more detailed literary front, has offered several thoughtful analyses of textual links serving holistic understanding of the Torah and the development of Jewish law.[13] Martin Buss, Daniel Patte, and numerous other structuralist and semiotic readers have also provided innovative and informative readings of Genesis and related texts.[14] Finally, building on the excellent base provided by Robert Wilson, Robert Oden has made major steps toward the full integration of anthropological concepts, including kinship studies, into the analysis of biblical genealogy and narrative.

We must not expect, of course, that new methods of cultural analysis will totally eliminate or invalidate older methods. Each approach should have some level of efficacy in representing the "reality" of the text. The semiotic orientation taken in this book implies the complementary nature of sign systems pertinent to a common phenomenon, for no single representation replicates the objective whole. Thus, we must be prepared for our work to become a part of the tradition we engage, which as a whole, representing a community of readers, approaches the meaning potentials of the text under scrutiny. Such a view is not inconsistent with the view of the Torah taken within Judaism since the 1st century A.D., which in many respects has been as flexible as Christian scholarship, if not more flexible, in achieving derivations from the books of law. We should also expect, as recent work by Calum Carmichael seeks to document for legal connections of code and narrative in the Torah, that interpretations and derivations of meaning were not totally rigid in earlier times, and that they operated on numerous levels of literary construction.[15] My approach to genealogy in Genesis is guided by a few basic questions about the connections and organization of the whole series of reports. I presume that most of the genealogical references were included as contributions to a large, unifying pattern. It will become quite clear, also, as I proceed, that I see this pattern as serving social-political interests rather than strictly theological concerns. Indeed, theology seems to be used in the cultural validation of arguments about hegemony, and so is secondary to the kinship concerns of the whole text. My primary question, in any event, is: What general political pattern is indicated by the combined genealogical materials? This question involves the premise that names in the genealogies should be read as signs of groups, and that narratives about events within families signal political and social relationships of groups. In this sense, the plot development of narrative is read as a kind of idealized political history. I use the word "history" in this context with some reservation, since the constructions we will observe stand more properly in the realm of ideology. Since the literary organization forms its own historical progression, however, the word is not inappropriate. My readers should keep in mind, still, that when I speak of the *historical sense* of the text, I am not referring to a sequence of lives or events we may presume to have actually occurred. "History" means a constructed view of some past posited by the text.

Once the social construction of Genesis is better understood it will be appropriate to ask additional questions: To whom was the fixed text significant politically? What actual historical period, if any, is suggested by the social viewpoint? How do the Genesis genealogies relate to other lineage accounts in the Torah? I suggest some beginning solutions to these problems in subsequent chapters. These areas of inquiry move the discussion beyond the realm of kinship into truly historical and literary problems. As a consequence, I develop some of the source backgrounds of the genealogical segments in this chapter, even though they are not always immediately pertinent to the task at hand.

Genealogical Patterns in Genesis 1–11

The most prominent genealogical materials in Genesis are lineal kin lists. That is, they trace lines of kinsmen through several generations, often naming only one individual per generation. The most regular of these lists are found in chapters 5 and 11. These lists are referred to as the "Priestly" genealogies, because they are attributed to the "Priestly" or "P" source of Genesis materials.[16] The first Priestly genealogy (Genesis 5) presents the descendants of Adam and the second (Genesis 11) gives the descendants of Shem. The lists share several stylistic features, the most important of which are age reports for each individual. Several authorities have speculated upon the potential significance of the numbers in these lists, but it is generally agreed that some of the esoteric meanings of the numbers are impossible to determine.[17] From the point of view of the questions guiding this analysis the numbers do not appear to have significance.

Brief consideration of the two genealogies in question shows that they contain different numbers of generations. Genesis 5 includes thirteen individuals from Adam to the three brothers Shem, Ham, and Japeth; Genesis 11:10–26 includes twelve names from Shem to the three brothers, Abram, Nahor, and Haran:

Genesis 5	*Genesis 11*
Adam	Shem
Seth	Arphaxad
Enosh	Shelah
Kenan	Eber
Mahalalel	Peleg
Jared	Reu
Enoch	Serug
Methuselah	Nahor
Lamech	Terah
Noah	Abram, Nahor, Haran
Shem, Ham, Japeth	

When these lists are linked through their shared naming of Shem, they cover 20 generations from Adam to Abram. Critical information from Genesis 4 allows us to generate the following genealogical table incorporating Adam's other sons, Cain and Abel:

Adam	Noah	Terah
Cain, Abel, Seth	Shem, Ham, Japeth	Abram, Nahor, Haran
Enosh	Arphaxad	
Kenan	Shelah	
Mahalalel	Eber	
Jared	Peleg	
Enoch	Reu	
Methuselah	Serug	
Lamech	Nahor	

This reorganization of the two lists produces interesting parallels between Adam, Noah, and Terah. Each had three sons, all of whom figure more or less prominently in the narrative texts of Genesis. Cain's opposition to his brother Abel is similar to the opposition of Ham, the "father of Canaan," to his brothers Shem and Japeth. Similarly, Abram and his brother Nahor establish lines connected in marriage, while Haran dies, and his line, continued through the character of Lot, becomes differentiated and separated.

Note also that this reorganization requires use of an additional source, the "Yahwist" or "J" source, illustrating in the first instance the utility of genealogical reading without reference to the primary assumptions of the documentary hypothesis. The sources are different, to be sure, but the pattern is a derivative of their conflation. In other instances we shall see similar relationships between genealogy and narrative which does not include kinship reports.

The genealogical pattern of these early patriarchs divides the ancestors into recognizable cyclic repetitions. The people from Adam to Noah represent the generations born before the flood. Noah begins a series of ten generations to Terah who completes a second cycle. By implication, Terah should begin yet another cycle. He accomplishes this new beginning by instigating the "travel" or "wandering" to the west which is continued by his son Abram, later by Jacob, and ultimately by the whole of Israel. Hence, we may identify in the only reported "action" of Terah the central Torah theme of patriarchal wandering, seen earlier as well in the story of Cain, and in Noah's aimless drifting on the sea of the deluge.[18] Since we have very little other information about Terah, we usually think of Abram as the starting figure of the supposed historical section of Genesis (chapters 12–50). Abram, of course, is the key ancestor in the ensuing story, but he occupies a position logically parallel to Shem or Seth, not to Adam or Noah. The Terahite genealogy (Genesis 11:27–32), moreover, breaks the pattern of lineal kin reports to recite a list of brothers, their children, and marriages which obtain between these kin. Thus, the new era is not matched with a complete parallel of lineal kinship structure, moving instead to additional elaborations on the line of Abram-Abraham, Isaac, and Jacob-Israel.

The lineal kin lists of Genesis 4 and 10 must be considered before moving to a full treatment of Terahite genealogy. These alternative or supplemental genealogies are distinguished by source critics as belonging to the Yahwist source. The two lists of Genesis 4 are particularly interesting to many commentators, since together they form a variant of the genealogy given in chapter 5.[19] In their narrative order within the chapter, the lists relate first to Cain and then to Adam (after the death of Abel). Thus, nearly identical lists of names are attached to separate lineages. Robert Wilson's detailed analysis of the backgrounds of these genealogies stresses the differences in function carried by each version. The Canaanite genealogy expands upon the story of Cain and Abel, transmitting the curse of Cain to subsequent generations and offering brief explanations of the origins of particular cultural traits, while the Adam genealogy connects Noah to the creation through Seth.[20] The short, segmented reference to Adam and Seth in Genesis 4 supports the differentiation of two lines. The genealogical distinction, citing one blessed line and another beset with curse or difficulty, is comparable to other accounts of parallel "fortunes," including accounts and lists relating to the sons of Noah, Ishmael and Isaac, Esau and Jacob, and the northern and southern kingdoms in Kings I and II. Whether this is the only intent of including parallel lists in close juxtaposition is certainly a subject for consideration, but I want to stress the point that we should not interpret the parallels, no matter how striking, as mere repetition. It is clear that the framers of Genesis intended for the genealogies to be taken as independent lineages.

Genesis 10 offers an even more complex list of kin which contains certain parallels with Genesis 11. The genealogy includes reference to diverse peoples and descendants from Japeth, Ham, and Shem, in that order, with strong attention to the Canaanites—descended from Ham—and competitive lines descended from Shem. The Shemite list comprises the following names:

Shem*	Aarphahxad* Lud	Aram
Elam, Asshur,	Shelah*	Uz, Hul, Gether, Mash
	Eber*	
	Peleg,* Joktan (13 sons)	

Here we see the same basic progression through Peleg (indicated by asterisks) as that of the Priestly genealogy of Shem, without the additional links (Reu, Serug, Nahor) running to Terah and Abram. Thus, in narrative context, the genealogy of Genesis 10 is consistent with that of Genesis 11 but elaborates on lateral relationships in order to contrast the lineage of Shem through Abram with other groups of the region.

The story line of Genesis clarifies the relationships between genealogies of chapters 4, 5, 10, and 11. We begin with stories about Adam and Eve and their sons, proceed to the selection of Noah and the destruction in the flood, and then move to the exploits of "historical" people, especially the descendants of Abram. Genesis 4 and 10 provide political background for the chosen line, but are insufficient to accomplish the critical links between the people of all these stories. The Priestly genealogies offer the only directly stated ties between creation, the flood, and the later patriarchal traditions.

The symmetry of genealogical placement within the narrative is striking and demonstrates the sense in which the lists are to be seen as central to the narrative:

Chapter 4   ...... Cain and Abel, Cain and Adam genealogies
Chapter 5   ...... Priestly genealogy of Adam
Chapters 6–9 ...... Noah and the Flood
Chapter 10   ...... Descendants of Noah's sons
Chapter 11   ...... Tower of Babel, Priestly genealogy of Shem

Note, however, that the Priestly materials are not in literary opposition to each other. The parallel of the Priestly lineage for Shem is found in chapter 4, since both are linked with narrative material. We will consider the narrative ties of chapters 4 and 11 in a subsequent chapter. For the moment, note that the content of the two narratives is similar—Cain becomes a marked outcast roaming the earth, and the builders of the tower of Babel are scattered over the earth, their languages having been confused by the deity.

These associations provide the theological significance of genealogies of the early patriarchs. The people of chapter 4 are the prominent "evil" men against whom the flood is directed, just as those of the next chapter are intended to be the blessed line from Adam to Noah. Similarly, much of the content of chapter 10 concerns people regarded as against Yahweh, while the lists following the Babel narrative resume enumeration of the line of the blessed. These are not mere ancillary concerns. Much of the central meaning of Genesis is tied, in fact, to the content and connections provided by these distinctive kin lists. They are the foundation of the political context of the central patriarchs which also prestate and socially validate the notion of selection driving the stories of Abraham, Isaac and Jacob.

We have already noted the Terahite genealogy, the last few verses of Genesis 11 introducing the kin framework which is elaborated throughout the rest of the book and the Torah as a whole. The structure includes females as well as males, initiating a practice of attending to women as a crucial part of the background of individuals. It is worthwhile to review the complete scripture (Genesis 11:27–32):

> These are Terah's descendants;
> Terah became the father of Abram, Nahor and Haran. Haran became the father of Lot. Haran died in the presence of his father Terah in his native land, Ur of the Chaldeans. (Abram and Nahor both married: Abram's wife was called Sarai, Nahor's wife was called Milcah, the daughter of Haran, father of Milcah and Iscah. Sarai was barren, having no child.)
> Terah took his son Abram, his grandson Lot the son of Haran, and his daughter-in-law the wife of Abram, and made them leave Ur of the Chaldeans to go to the land of Canaan. But on arrival in Haran they settled there.
> Terah's life lasted two hundred and five years; then he died at Haran.

The segment in parentheses is attributed to the Yahwist source, while the remaining verses are generally attributed to the Priestly authors. Note that the Yahwist does not directly connect Lot to Haran, offering instead three children including Milcah. The name Haran, moreover, is given double meaning as a place and person. The full sense of the text creates a brother-sister tie for Lot and Milcah. The specificity of Lot's parentage is important, since in Genesis 12 the Yahwist refers to Lot as Abram's nephew without indicating through whom they àre linked (Genesis 12:5). The precise relationship is fundamental to the kinship pattern underlying the stories about Lot and Abram, as well as to the interpretation of Sarai's place in the Terahite lineage when we discover (in Genesis 20:12) that she is also Terah's daughter. Thus, this relatively brief genealogical segment becomes the crucial passage through which the social-structural interpretation of Genesis 12–50 may proceed.[21]

Social Patterns in Genesis 12–50

It is difficult to achieve a single, satisfying social analysis of Genesis 12–50, principally because several levels of social implications are to be found in the text. At the core of any interpretation there should be, at least, the essential genealogical facts of the text. Most of these facts, the full extension of the Terahite genealogy in Genesis 11, can be reported in a single chart (Figure 1). But a chart alone is not an analysis. If we are to understand why certain people were included (or excluded), why certain relationships were clearly asserted (or only implied), or why particular lineages were given emphasis, then we must rely upon the sentiments expressed in the connected narrative.

My emphasis in assessing the narrative for information pertinent to social connection is upon place associations of patriarchs, patterns of mobility, and metaphorical usages which contrast sons, wives, competing lines, or allies. Raw genealogical structure, given these additional elements from the text, becomes charged with potent social meanings. Thus, the stylized patriarchal life histories and associated genealogical grid offer very formal statements of political relationship.

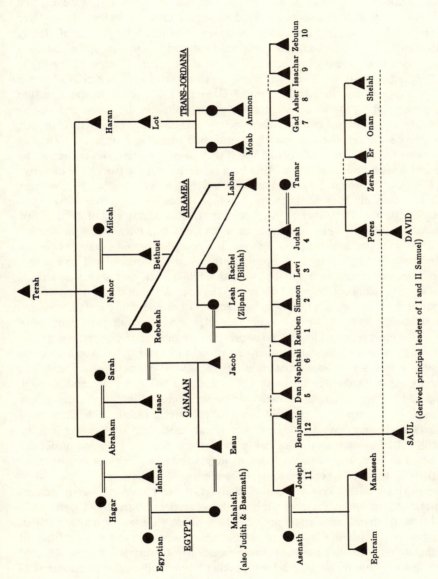

Figure 1. The extended Terahite families of Genesis, with geographic notes and connections to later kingships.

My reading of Genesis 12–50 stresses the final editorial stages of Genesis, probably a relatively late circle of priestly redaction and authorship associated with the construction of the Torah as a whole. We should keep in mind, however, that the kinds of textual relationships observed as surface elements in the full narrative were created, in some cases embedded, in the text through a long process of literary construction. Observation of whole and partial patterns tied to kinship content may provide clues to the order of redaction of major stories, even though timing of the redaction sequence is not indicated through such analysis. Specifically, kinship evidence suggests that the Abraham cycle (Genesis 12–25) is a compilation of old sources essentially "fit" to a pattern already established in the Jacob and Joseph stories. My argument, the evidence for which will be discussed later in this chapter, is based upon the premise that loosely coordinated stories and fragments, such as those found from Genesis 12 through 25, if they display pattern similarities to the Jacob and Joseph cycles, are most likely built on the plan of the latter. The narrative from Genesis 25 through 50 represents such a tightly woven conflation of sources that it is essentially impossible to recover individual "strands" which may confidently be identified as either Yahwist or Elohist. This complexity of composition seems very unlikely to be a construction fit to some generalized and uncohesive textual block. Stated in more general terms, it is more likely that a complex pattern will be replicated by a simple composition than that the reverse will be true.

Such concerns are important to the extent that biblical scholars have often treated genealogy as disconnected and inconsistent. Because of the oral and literary backgrounds of the text, I expect to find some elements of discontinuity and uncertainty. On a structural level, however, some very clear and arguably late patterns of composition emerge, providing a kind of prevailing order out of the apparent chaos.

Pursuing this line of thought further, the process of making the Abraham cycle consistent with other materials also indicates the mythic character of the text. The patriarchs are stylized characters with similarities and differences dictated through kinship and literary-structural necessity. In the structures of mobility, then, places and religious observance are central features of patriarchal identity. The creation of such a Genesis may have theological purpose at one level, but the text is more political and religious than theological in the construction and meaning of details. Because of the diversity of the included materials and complexity of construction, Genesis may become a book of several theologies.

When I speak of theology as a part of analysis, the emphasis is upon the critical interpretations people make about relationships, responsibilities, and rights possessed from or shared with a god or gods. To the extent Genesis joins the body of Torah law in Jewish life, an aspect of the developing cultural communities of Judaism, it forms a basis for critical interpretations of everyday actions. Offered against this ongoing theological activity, taking the probable cultural meanings of the text as ultimately constructed, the actual political ties, contrasts, principles, and historical associations of Genesis yield one of many potential theologically justified social viewpoints.

A search for unified structures in Genesis, interrupted though they may be by elements of the underlying narrative fragments, imposed additions, and artifacts of intermediate readings such as the chapter divisions established in the medieval period, becomes a search for a very particular social community and a very special set of theological premises. In this literary Pandora's box, the kinship reports provide one of the most useful and significant lines of evidence about authorship. Reading Genesis through the background of kinship theory presents its own problems, however, most notably that our own social world—the categories, corporate entities, and sentiments through which we organize daily life—often seems to us as though it is based in nature. Kinship analysis requires the suppression of these categories and ideas, and the adoption of new principles founded in careful comparative study of a wide range of different systems of relationship. Thus, the kinship specialist is likely to cite familistic notions of native Australians in making a point about patriarchal connections. Such a path to solutions is often worse than the perplexity created by the text itself. For this reason, I keep such references to a minimum, even if they form the groundwork on which the reading is pursued.

My groundwork also includes studies of the Bible by anthropologists, notably E. R. Leach, though I do not begin with his essays that are most widely known to biblical scholars. Rather, I prefer to start with some of his earlier structuralist writings, especially those which incorporate commentary on myth. In a pair of essays included in Leach's *Rethinking Anthropology,* Leach offers especially pertinent discussion of the reckoning of "time" and patterns of alternation in social symbolism.[22] He cites in these essays the simple alternating pattern:

A.1
     B.1
A.2
     B.2

The social relationship potentially represented by the As and Bs in this pattern are the generations of a single lineage. The pattern makes sense as a "generational moiety"—a division of the society into halves which receive membership from alternating generations. For example, in Genesis we find:

Terah (mobility confined to Mesopotamia)
     Abram (mobile between Aramea and Egypt)
Isaac (mobility confined to Canaan)
     Jacob (mobile between Aramea and Egypt)

On close scrutiny of stories about Abram and Jacob, we find them sharing common experiences of theophany, regional association, and alliance interests, as well as possessing other detailed identifying factors.[23] Terah and Isaac, on the other hand, share the characteristic of being relatively confined within well-defined regions. In the narratives dealing with their mobility, furthermore, neither establishes lengthy relationships with surrounding groups or leaders.

These commonalities point to a refined narrative pattern in which Abram and Jacob are logical opposites—or perhaps more accurately, logical "duals"—of each other.[24] Wherever Abram moves, Jacob moves opposite. Whatever Abram does, Jacob does the opposite. Both encounter similar problems, however, such as strife with kinsmen and neighbors, and both occupy similar social contexts within and outside Canaan.

Figure 2 shows the basic elements of the logical pattern linking Abram to Jacob. It is important to observe that Abram's movements in the region all occur before the circumcision covenant (Genesis 17), in the first half of the total Abraham cycle when he is still called "Abram." He travels by way of Shechem and Bethel through the Negev to Egypt, where he obtains wealth, and back to Bethel. In Bethel he resolves strife with his kinsman Lot in an honorable separation. This is followed by his move to Hebron and the eventual establishment of the covenant. Jacob, on the other hand, moves from Beersheba to Haran where he obtains wealth, and then returns to Succoth/Peniel where he resolves strife with his brother Esau through deception. From Succoth/Peniel he moves on to Shechem, and ultimately south to the territory of his father.

Other points of detailed comparison yield an even more refined pattern of opposition. While in Egypt, Abram's wife Sarai is given a handmaiden who is destined to become the mother of Ishmael. Because of her inability to have children,

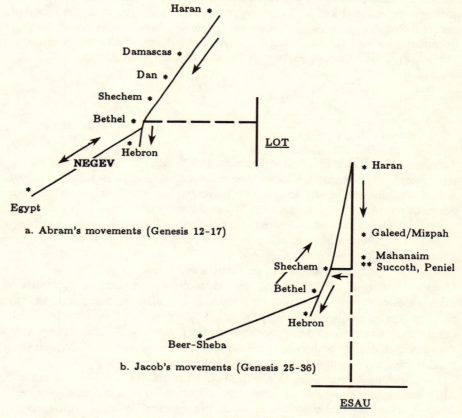

Figure 2.   Comparison of mobility patterns of Abram and Jacob.

Sarai gives Hagar to Abram for the purpose of producing a child. Ishmael, the offspring, should technically have been considered Sarai's child, but because of a behavioral breach on the part of Hagar, Sarai never actually accepts Ishmael as her own. The text suggests that Abram is also culpable for the conflict between the two women (Genesis 16:5). Although Abram affirms Sarai's control over Hagar, she becomes like a competing wife, her son standing in opposition to Isaac.[25] This is substantiated by the eventual expulsion of Hagar and Ishmael, reluctantly by Abram, and the marriage of Ishmael to a woman of his "mother's kinsmen." The suggestion of this sequence is that Abram has formed a weak matrimonial connection to Egypt. The direction of the alliance places Abram in the position of "wife-taker," as opposed to the original connection represented by Abram's attempts to "give" Sarai to Pharaoh in Genesis 12.

We should note that Sarai represents a similar alliance to the north, with Abram being wife-taker from some Terahite lineage. Considering the structural pattern in which the line of Haran gives wives to the line of Nahor, and the line of Nahor gives wives to Isaac and Jacob, the implication is that Sarai comes to Abram as the sister of Bethuel. This is also suggested by the meanings of the names Milcah ("Queen") and Sarai ("Princess").

Observe now the matrimonial relationships of Isaac and Jacob to Aramea. First, the relationships are parallel to the implied connection between Abram and Sarai—a marriage we may not characterize per se as representing either a strong or weak alliance. Second, the marriages of Isaac and Jacob are opposite to Abram's Egyptian link, and they are strong if for no other reason than being reconfirmed through all three generations of the Abraham-Isaac-Jacob lineage. But there is other textual justification for considering these matrimonial ties strong. Each of these marriages, and the offspring they produce, form part of the divine promises to Abraham, Isaac, and Jacob. Jacob's separation from Laban, moreover, ends with the oath of mutual non-aggression, a somewhat more positive result than the forced exit of Abram and Sarai in Egypt. Perhaps most important, several instances of theophany involving the patriarchs reaffirm the selection of the Aramean women and their sons. In contrast, the theophany associated with Ishmael's blessing by God is directed to Hagar (Genesis 16:7–14, Genesis 21:17–20; consider also the indirectness of God's statements to Abraham about Ishmael (Genesis 21:12–13).

Strong and weak kinship ties also characterize the links between Abram and Lot as compared to Jacob and Esau. These links are both subject to alliance dissolution or "separation" of kinsmen, but the relationships obtaining between the kin after separation are quite different. We have already noted that Abram's separation from Lot is honorable. But a strength in the continuing tie between them is shown by Abram's reaction to Lot's capture in Genesis 14. Just the opposite situation emerges between Jacob and Esau. Not only does Jacob fear Esau, he deceives him by saying that he will follow him south when he intends to move west toward Canaan. Thus, Jacob and Esau share no further action in the text except the burial of Isaac (Genesis 35:28–29), a formula parallel of Abraham's burial by Isaac and Ishmael (Genesis 25:7–9).

The marriages and segmentations pertaining to Abram and Jacob form a general pattern which is depicted in Figure 3. For each patriarch there is a zone of travel marked at opposite ends by points of "matrimonial alliance" and "alliance dissolution." Either of these points may be a "strong" or "weak" relationship. For Abram, the matrimonial alliance in Egypt, the destination after he leaves his father's house, is weak, while the tie to his kinsman Lot is strong. For Jacob, the matrimonial alliance in Aramea is strong, while the relationship with his brother Esau remains consistently weak. We will consider later the possibility that the relationship between Abram and Lot is an implied matrimonial alliance similar to the one between Jacob and Laban. If this implication is valid, it shows the sense in which a point of opposition may also be construed as a parallel—Abram and Jacob undergo different narrative transformations of the common underlying pattern.

This idea is given further weight when we consider the points of movement within the zone of travel covered by each of the men. I have labeled these points (1) the point of segmentation, (2) the point of regional strife, and (3) the point of transformation. We have already seen the points of segmentation, where Abram and Jacob become differentiated from their kinsmen Lot and Esau. In each case they move on to a stopping point where they become involved in regional strife. Abram intervenes in the war of the kings (Genesis 14) to save Lot, with the outcome that he is blessed by Melchizedek. This is paralleled by the episode in which Jacob's daughter Dinah is "humbled," and his sons Simeon and Levi take revenge on the Shechemites causing Jacob to fear general reprisals from the Canaanites (Genesis 34). Note that at the end of Abram's strife he refuses any part in the spoils of the

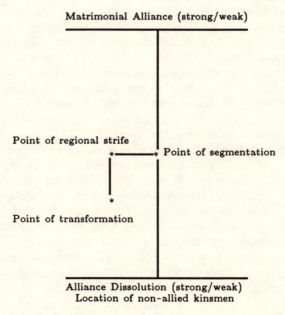

Figure 3.   Ideal pattern of mobility for Abram and Jacob.

conflict, though he has rescued both people and property. The sons of Jacob, however, take property and women after killing all of the men. The texts are parallel inasmuch as Abram allows his retainers to accept their share of the spoils, but the honor accorded the patriarch in the cases is quite opposite.

The points of separation deal with strife within a kin group with close genealogical connections, while the points of regional strife deal with conflicts between the patriarchs and foreigners. The point of transformation involves a validation of promises from God to each of the characters. Abram is transformed to Abraham through the covenant of circumcision (Genesis 17), and Jacob is renamed Israel. The social transformations within the broader narrative may be viewed as historically related: "Abraham" represents the apical member of an ambiguous marriage circle, the circumcision covenant which includes Ishmael and Esau, while Jacob is brought from the ambiguous circumcision association to a new, well-defined marriage circle, Israel.

From the point of view of narrative construction, the ideal pattern outlined for Abram and Jacob links Genesis 12–17 directly to Genesis 25–36. The Abram part of the Abraham cycle rests upon a very different kind of source manipulation, however, than that of the Jacob story. Several key points of the Abram sequence, especially the rescue of Lot (Genesis 14) and the transformation of Abraham (Genesis 17), result from insertions of Priestly writing or highly divergent source material. Note also that there are two reports of Jacob's transformation to Israel, only one of which fits the pattern proposed here. The materials indicate, nonetheless, that oppositional similarities between Jacob and Abram are imposed by textual manipulation, including relatively free reorganization of the original stories brought together to create the Abraham cycle.

Before moving to other evidence of this process, I want to offer a final expansion on the idea of alternating generations forming generational moieties. Since Abram and Jacob are each given two names, their transformations constitute a kind of ritual death and rebirth. This is not an unusual sense for the rite of passage involving circumcision, but it is less commonly associated with Jacob's transformation. Yet in the renaming story which does not fit into the ideal mobility pattern, Jacob wrestles with a man (Genesis 32:22–32). Thus, we account for two renamings in the need for literary parallel in the movement sequence *and* ritual parallel involving "ordeal" and physical change, functions which are combined in Abraham's circumcision. Isaac has his ordeal in Genesis 22, but is not renamed. Thus, it is noteworthy that the transformed persona of Abraham and Israel are, like Isaac, much more confined in their movements than their former selves, and thoroughly linked to the south Canaan area. The genealogical effect of these transformations is to force a modification of the generational alternation with which we began. It now becomes:

Abram (a mobile figure associated with the north)
    Abraham/Isaac (stationary figures in the south)
Jacob (a mobile figure associated with the north)
    Israel (a stationary figure in the south)

This implies a narrative link between Abraham and Isaac involving more than mere juxtaposition, yet the textual parallels in the Abraham/Isaac sections (Genesis

17–27) are somewhat less convincing than those linking Abram and Jacob. The prominent exceptions are the dual accounts of deception at Gerar (Genesis 20 and 26) with material associated to each describing establishment of wells in the region and residence at Beer-Sheba. We will consider some of these parallels as part of other pattern analyses. Other lines of evidence for patterning of Genesis 12–25 after the Jacob and Joseph stories must be considered now.

Birth, Death, and Rite of Passage

Returning to Edmund Leach's original arguments about representations of time, we find an emphasis upon the basic events of human existence—birth, death, and rites of passage.[26] These events punctuate the generations and in this case also structure the narrative of Genesis. There are many genealogical reports of this sort prior to the Abraham cycle, but beginning with the last verses of Genesis 11 they occur mainly as isolated bits of genealogical information. Three features signal the importance of these reports. First, people are traced by both male and female connections, especially the central patriarchs. Second, individual reports become part of a narrative flow, so a birth or death cited in a single obscure verse may receive considerable elaboration, as in the case of the death of Sarah (Genesis 23). Third, and most important, the reports of births and deaths form a clear pattern linking *all* of the Abraham cycle (Genesis 12–25) to the combined stories of Jacob and Israel (Genesis 25–50).

Birth and death details in Genesis 11 through 50 mainly cover the key individuals of the central Shemite genealogy:

Terah
•
•
Abram/   Abraham
•   •
•   •
Ishmael   Isaac
               •   •
               •   •
             Esau Jacob
               •   •
               •   •
         Elder Sons   Benjamin

Among the "elder" sons of Jacob we may distinguish between the Leah and Rachel offspring, with Reuben, Judah, and Joseph figuring prominently in the narrative action.[27] Surrounding the central characters of the narrative are other kinsmen—Lot and his children, highborn women, and numerous others listed in stories or mentioned in passing. The longest genealogical lists are associated with Ishmael's descendants, the groups of Edom descended from Esau, the children of Milcah (reported with the birth of Rebekah in Genesis 22), and the children of Abraham and Keturah. Most of these people provide evidence for the ambiguity of the circumcision covenant and, like the Yahwist genealogies of Genesis 4 and 10, serve as contrasts to the central line of inheritance from Abram through Israel. When the long lists are taken out of consideration, individual birth and death reports remain.

My analysis of these "life-cycle" reports considers narrative order and parallels or contrasts of content. The pattern of correspondences (Figure 4) shows a structural inversion of elements relating to either the birth and death of key individuals or the comparison of sets of brothers in succeeding generations. The structure also in

A. Terah d. (11:32)

    B. Ishmael b. (16:15)
        ....Abram and Ishmael Circumcised (17:23-27)

          C. Lot's Wife d. (19:26)
              Moab b. (19:37)
              Ammon b. (19:38)

              D. Isaac b. (21:2)

                  E. Ram (replacing Isaac) d. (22:13)
                      Rebekah b. (22:23--list of Nahorites)
                      Sarah d. (23:1)

                      F. Abraham d. (25:8)

                          G. Ishmael d. (25:17-18)
                              (list of Ishmaelites)

                          G. Esau and Jacob b. (25:25-26)

                      B. Reuben to Joseph b. (29:32-30:24)

                  E. Deborah (Rebekah's nurse) d. (35:8)
                    Benjamin b. (35:17)
                    Rachel d. (35:19)

                D. Isaac d. (35:29--also list of Edomites in 36)

          C. Judah's wife d. (38:12) (Er and Onan killed by Yahweh)
             Perez b. (38:29)
              Zerah b. (38:30)

    ....C2. Manasseh b. (41:51) ....alternative to Genesis 38 or
               Ephraim b. (41:52)   a possible opposition to 17:23-27

    F. Jacob d. (49:33)

A. Joseph d. (50:26)

Figure 4. Primary birth, death, and rite of passage reports in Genesis beginning with the death of Terah and ending with the death of Joseph.

cludes four "groups" of reports derived from narratives concentrated on matriarchal fortunes. The first of these involves the death of Lot's wife and the subsequent births of Ammon and Moab through Lot's unions with his daughters. This corresponds in the structure to the death of Judah's wife and the birth of Perez and Zerah through Judah's inappropriate union with Tamar. The story of Judah and Tamar also relates the deaths of Er and Onan, story elements necessary to establishment of the plot which brings Tamar and Judah together. Thus, I have excluded Er and Onan from the formal set of correspondences.

The other two grouped reports derive from materials which are juxtaposed by redaction of originally unrelated source narratives. The first of these links the story of the sacrifice of Isaac, the genealogy in which the birth of Rebekah is announced, and the death of Sarah. In the accepted view of these texts, the sequence links Elohist, Priestly, and Yahwist documents. The death of the ram involves the symbolic replacement of Isaac (hence his death and rebirth). The overall effect of the sequence is worthy of special attention, since it establishes a structural parallel involving the ram, Isaac, Rebekah, and Sarah. First, the ram dies, replacing Isaac who is allowed to live. The juxtaposed genealogy followed by the death of Sarah produces the logical sequence: Rebekah is born (lives), replacing Sarah who dies as the matriarch of the chosen line. By implication, just as God has "provided" a suitable replacement for Isaac in the ordeal of passage, a suitable replacement for Sarah is provided at the passage of a generation.

The parallel series of reports occurs in the story of Jacob's travel from Bethel to the south. In this sequence we are informed of the death of Deborah, *Rebekah's* nurse, an unusual person for Jacob's entourage who is not mentioned elsewhere. Note that this occurs just prior to the second renaming of Jacob, recalling again the rite of passage which he has already undergone in Genesis 32:23–32 and providing a precise connection to the story of the sacrifice of Isaac. Jacob's renaming and his subsequent sacrifice to El Shaddai are followed by the birth of Benjamin and the death of Rachel. In a very short series of reports we thus encounter the end of Rebekah's matriarchal tenure (note that Isaac's death also soon follows), a striking parallel between Benjamin and Isaac who are born to men of transformed status (Israel and Abraham), and a parallel of Rachel with Sarah. Rachel and Sarah, we should note, both have difficulty with competing wives who bear offspring senior to their sons. The sons, furthermore, become linked to the ultimate fortunes of Israel in significant ways throughout the Genesis narratives. Ishmael is set against his brothers but shares a boundary point at Beer-Lahai Roi with Isaac. Joseph, Rachel's firstborn, is sold to Ishmaelites by his brothers. Without pushing these details too far, suffice it to say that the structural relationship of Genesis 22:13–23:1 with Genesis 35:8–19 presses some very critical points about the argument over succession among Jacob's offspring. Specifically, these passages seem to argue the case for the succession of Benjamin, and hence form part of the evidence asserting the later rights of Saul. Indeed, given the broader symmetry incorporating the grouped reports concerning Lot and Judah, a contrast is suggested in which Judah's incest with Tamar is elevated in severity, and so David's ancestry is brought into a pejorative light.

My organization of the birth and death reports in Genesis includes other elements in close proximity, such as the deaths of Abraham and Ishmael and the birth of Esau and Jacob. These elements are generally separated from each other by short bodies of narrative or formula textual markers (such as the toledoth divisions of Genesis 25:12 and 25:19). Thus, I view all of the other reports between Genesis 11 and 50 as independent elements in my proposed structure.

The correspondence of Ishmael's birth and the births of Jacob's first eleven sons (the "B" elements in the sequence) relates "elder sons" of the generation of Isaac and the generation of Isaac's grandchildren.[28] The parallel is clearly shown, as we have seen, in the announcement of Benjamin's birth, though not through direct opposition of Isaac and Benjamin. The counterpart association in the pattern links the two "F" elements, the deaths of Abraham and Israel. These patriarchs are the oppositional "duals" who remain stationary after their rites of passage, and again represent grandfather and grandson generations. The "A" elements of the structure cite the deaths of Terah and Joseph and serve to bracket the whole sequence beginning in Aramea and ending in Egypt. The "G" elements are more difficult to construe as similar, except that these events are the turning point of the whole pattern. They also share the toledoth formula, and thus its inclusion in the relatively short account of Ishmael's descendants is given a broad rhetorical justification. Two other points of association deserve attention. First, since the "G" elements form the center of the whole sequence, they might well be related to the deaths of Terah and Joseph. That works well if we suggest that Ishmael's association with Terah is one of a "blessed" descendant off the line of God's chosen inheritance. Following such a pattern, the association of Joseph back to Jacob makes him "blessed," but contrasts him to his younger brother by implication. Again, the legitimation of Benjamin's claim seems to be at stake but is argued through implication.

The second avenue of approach to the interpretation of the "G" and "A" elements is more direct, but less satisfying. Jacob's birth can be seen as representing the emphasis of Isaac's offspring over the descendants of the deceased Ishmael. This is made less obvious by the inclusion of Esau, though his parallel to Ishmael is clear enough. Note, however, that Esau's death, an event which would disrupt the sequence somewhere after Isaac's death if it were reported, is not mentioned in the text. At any rate, the connection to the "A" reports might suggest the opposition of a Terah-Jacob-Joseph lineage to the segmented lineages of Ishmael and Esau. Such an argument for Joseph's primacy would be more compelling if Terah were replaced by Abram. I note this alternative because of the tendency of readers to consider Joseph the most legitimate heir within Israel. The Joseph narrative, however, recounts his transformation from a "sacred" figure involved in dreams and blessings from God to a "secular" figure who enslaves the people of Egypt, including Israel by association (and in spite of the narrative explanation offered in Genesis 50 and Exodus 1:8–11). Indeed, after Genesis 45, where he reveals his true identity to his brothers, Joseph's secular position is established and dominates the text. Israel, underscoring Joseph's status, accepts him back only through the adoption of his sons, the younger of whom receives the fuller blessing. It is noteworthy that Israel specifically excludes any other offspring Joseph might produce (Genesis 48:6). As we shall see in a later discussion, the elder of Joseph's sons is in a sense "reduced" by falling into divided responsibilities and alliances in Canaan (see also the assignment of cities to the Levites, Numbers 3).

My interpretations of the birth and death cycles between the last verse of Genesis 11 and Genesis 50 suggest reorganization into a crossing or "chi" diagram, as in Figure 5.[29] This "chiastic" rendering yields a better visual image of the textual parallels, with the reports linking to form a series of nested boxes. My preference for the interpretation of the "A" and "G" units as implying the primacy of Benjamin over Joseph is reflected in lines forming the complete outer box. Inside the box the "B" and "F" units are linked, forming a tier of associations among major persons in the political succession, except Isaac and Benjamin. Inside these reports, the grouped "C" and "E" elements form a third tier, dealing with the ranking of women and other refinements in the determination of political succession, notably association of the line of Benjamin with Isaac. Finally, the whole sequence is centered on the birth and death of Isaac. Such treatment of the life-cycle information is quite consistent with the alternating generational links of genealogy, and Isaac, in this pattern as elsewhere, is given the central position.

The structural parallels of this pattern provide clues about the redaction process of the Abraham, Jacob, and Joseph cycles. Symmetry in the birth-death sequences, in particular, seems to account for the placement of the Ammon/Moab birth account, which disrupts what appears to have been an originally unified Ishmael story.[30] The pattern also accounts for the placement of the genealogy introducing Rebekah and the story about the acquisition of the patriarchal tomb in Canaan. While it is possible that some elements of the Joseph and Jacob stories might have been placed to conform to events in the Abraham story, the bulk of evidence suggests that this was not the case. Other than Genesis 38, Genesis 49, and a few obvious Priestly insertions, documentary critics cite few elements of Genesis 25–50 which are not part of the Yahwist-Elohist conflation, a well-formed narrative, the underlying documents of which have become increasingly suspect to many specialists. Indeed, even Genesis 38 and 49 have been recently argued to be integral to the Joseph narrative on stylistic and linguistic grounds.[31] The cohesiveness of Genesis 25–50, however, is in stark contrast to the materials underlying Genesis 12–25.

To summarize the redactional conclusions developed from structural analyses of Genesis 12–50, we have observed two kinds of organizational links which support the idea that the Abraham stories were "fit" to an established narrative pattern in the Jacob/Joseph stories. The meanings of the two patterns are generally tied to the political characterization of the competing patriarchal lines. While in some cases the meanings of particular associations may appear to be trivial, most of the parallels between characters in the birth-death cycles have political and theological significance. The mobility structure common to Abram and Joseph is given political nuance because of its concern with proper and improper matrimonial alliances, processes of kin segmentation, and transformations of patriarchal status.

One final imperfection in the pattern of births and deaths suggested here remains. The difficulty is with the births of Manasseh and Ephraim in Genesis 41:50–57. The

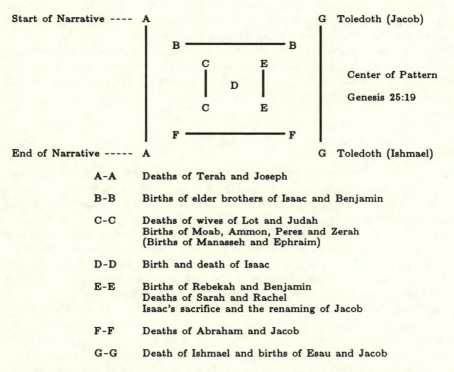

Figure 5. Chiastic organization of birth and death reports in Genesis 12-50.

position of these reports in the Joseph narrative suggests a possible opposition with the births of Moab and Ammon. Such treatment of Joseph's sons makes as much sense as the opposition between Lot's incestuous offspring and the children of Judah and Tamar, and for similar reasons. The parallel is enhanced when we consider that Joseph avoids a form of incest with the wife of Potiphar (Genesis 39:1). As the ranking servant of his master, Joseph stands in a similar position to that of Eliezer in Genesis 15:2. His ultimate marriage to the "daughter of Potiphar" carries the implication of generational correctness. In contrasting Joseph to Lot, then, we find the common subject of "incest" and the problem of how one cut off from one's people is to generate offspring. Such a juxtaposition puts Joseph's potential claims of ascendancy in Israel on a stronger footing than Judah's, but if Genesis 38 were not included in the text the broader argument for Benjamin would probably still be compelling. That is, assuming the opposition of Lot and Joseph merely states Joseph's case; it does not establish a perfect argument. Asenath, like Lot's daughters, Ishmael's Egyptian wife, and Ishmael's daughter Mahalath who marries Esau, is still the wrong kind of woman. This is probably the strongest evidence of the present analysis that Genesis 38 is an intrusion into the Joseph narrative. One must consider, however, that a group of redactors with kinship problems in mind would probably have found little difficulty in linking the children of both Judah and Joseph back to Lot's case. Thus, the presence of two alternative stories fitting the "C" element in the pattern does no real damage to the overall sense of the structure. Whoever ordered the text appears to opt for expansion on an idea and complication of nuance rather than for slavish attention to structural symmetry. I find the imperfections in the overall pattern comforting, since it reminds us that the full narrative is not, after all, pure formula.

Time and Place

The political claims created in Genesis, in addition to informing us about redactional communities, offer a view of general social concepts in the Near East during the first millennium B.C.E. and earlier. Most of the work on problems with Genesis genealogies has concentrated on the historicity of the textual reports, comparison with other written traditions of the region, and the operation of specific political regimes—not always through models appropriate to the subject matter. Only recent work by Robert Wilson and Robert Oden, among others, has begun to sort through the vast literature on kinship for appropriate models, allowing direct interpretations of kinship structure in Genesis.[32] We may attribute this activity in part to the reactions of biblical scholarship to Edmund Leach's direct efforts with Genesis and other biblical literature.[33] Oddly enough, given the arguments of the preceding section, kinship concerns have often been seen as divorced from the documentary issues of narrative construction. Thus, biblical scholars tend to see kinship reports as somewhat ancillary, connecting material subordinated to the primary narrative interests.

Anthropological scholarship sees the narrative as supporting the primary, genealogical structure of Genesis. One kind of support for genealogy in the narrative is the attribution of territorial associations to the patriarchs. Place references serve the emerging kinship structure in a very special way, not only creating a map of geographic divisions, but an ideological-historical model of social relationships.[34]

For the main line flowing from Abraham there exist three stages of ideological development which represent the "historical" progression through the generations of Abraham, Isaac, and Israel. These are (a) an early marriage circle involving Terah's sons, (b) the Covenant of Circumcision, and (c) the association of Israel. The three divisions also possess overlapping geographic associations (Figure 6). Through the patriarchal narratives a subtle but sophisticated set of historical fictions is created to justify social principles underlying the political associations between actual historical groups in the region covered by the text. The narrative thrust of Genesis, then, is to produce a well-ordered language map and political construction. Genesis is a manifestation of political consciousness benefiting from a complex of closely related genealogical and folkloric traditions in the region where Israel was formed. Indeed, the fictional "stages" of marriage association offer a sociological and legal debate of particular practices, with justifications of certain marriage situations as garnering claims to considerable power and authority in the region for Israel, and within it.[35]

Figure 6 is a map of the kernel framework of social associations, rooted in the logic of myth and folkloric symbols, for the whole Torah. It is a direct reflection of a specific priesthood and a partial reflection of several antecedent priesthoods. The "theory" behind this map of Israel, in its more developed form, represents perhaps the clearest set of meanings in the whole of Genesis. In order to see the full system, we must become somewhat more technical in our appreciation of social categories in traditional societies.

All societies possess—mainly through kinship categories—unique cultural viewpoints governing rules for marriage and descent, means of legitimizing offspring, conventions for the inheritance of property, and recognition of some relationships as constituting incest. The formation of Israel historically involved the construction of one such unique set of rules, based in common patterns of thought about society spanning the whole region of the ancient Near East. Thus, the formation of Israel as a social process represented some form of cultural transformation. On one level, the transformation engaged practical situations of lineage succession, alliance, and competition. On another level, the resultant cultural structure became a process of symbolic definition and identification. To a great extent, the practical solutions to

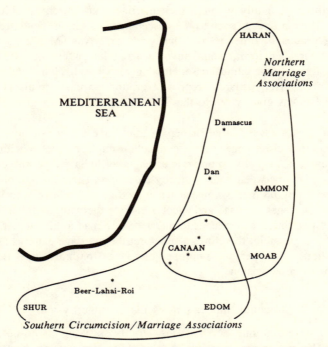

Figure 6. Map of social associations depicted through genealogical materials in Genesis (Points in Canaan, North to South: Shechem, Bethel/Ai, Hebron/Mamre, Beer-Sheba).

problems and the ideal understanding of these practical results have become intertwined in Genesis.[36]

From this perspective we may view the individual transformations of patriarchs in Genesis as ideological constructions representing social transformations presumed to have been necessary for the formation of Israel. As to the specific transformations leading to Israel, the Genesis text cites two. The first is the Covenant of Circumcision, and the second is the differentiation of Israel from the other circumcised groups. Thus, the "historical" stages posited by the text are plainly represented in the personal rites of passage of Abram and Jacob. If the Covenant of Circumcision is a transformation, then before circumcision there must have been some expressed social order, some rules for marriage and legitimation of offspring to which Abram was subject. We have already observed the core of this system in the genealogy of Terah (Genesis 11:27–32).

What is most interesting about this genealogy is the marriage of Milcah and Nahor. By itself such a union would be of little interest, but in its broader genealogical context the marriage establishes the precedent for the marriages of Isaac and Jacob. Such systematic marriages of cousins are quite familiar to students of kinship. The specific relationships of Genesis imply what anthropologists call an "indirect exchange" of women, or a "circulating connubium."[37] In its most basic form an indirect exchange system requires at least three groups of people. Each group constitutes a family within which marriages are strictly prohibited by an incest rule. Thus, a lineage such as the descendants of Abram would require other comparable groups in order to find husbands or wives. Marriages among the groups, in their ideal form, would involve a regular pattern of wife-giving and wife-taking. Thus, in the biblical case, Haran gives wives to Nahor and Nahor gives wives to Abram. The patriarchs represent groups, so the formula is rather like saying "the Browns give wives to the Smiths, and the Smiths give wives to the Johnsons."

When families are very large, a person may have many potential spouses to choose from, so a close genealogical connection might not occur with each marriage. However, it is equally common in actual cases to have a permissible, or even preferred marriage between genealogically close kin. The marriage of Nahor and Milcah, then, is by no means unusual when read as a case involving individuals. Further, the marriages of Isaac and Jacob illustrate the way in which a continued "alliance" of two lines of men leads to marriage of a man to his mother's brother's daughter.[38] It is possible, therefore, to interpret the marriage patterns as providing ideal definitions of proper and improper marriages for individuals in the social system prior to circumcision.

Structural Implications of the Terahite System

The alliance system among Terah's sons, strictly speaking, is an open series of marriages. Abram's group does not provide wives for anyone, and the line of Haran, represented by Lot, includes a woman with a nonspecified heritage.[39] These details place emphasis on Abram's lineage—his status as elder is preserved in every genealogical report. However, if we were to make the Terahite genealogy the basis of a minimal circulation of women among all the groups, then we would expect Abram's line to give wives to the men in the line of Haran. Such a system would have the effect of equalizing the status of the three patrilineages. Let us now observe, then, several aspects of the text which suggest just such an indirect exchange relating the lines of Abram, Nahor, and Haran.

First, there is the relationship between Abram and Lot. When Abram leaves northwest Mesopotamia and travels to Canaan and Egypt, Lot travels with him. Later, when the herdsmen of the two men quarrel, Abram and Lot separate honorably. These events parallel the relationship between Jacob and his father-in-law Laban. Jacob spends twenty years with Laban performing brideservice—work toward the legitimation of his marriages. When his wives have both borne children, however, Jacob begins his move toward independence. Although there is friction and deception between Jacob and Laban over herds and other possessions, the ultimate separation is with honor and mutual respect. Thus, Jacob seems to stand in relation to Laban as Lot does to Abram. Even given the limited scope of the Lot story and other parallels we might derive, is there other evidence in the narratives which might support the hypothesis that Lot's wife is from the household of Abram?

As it turns out, there are several lines of evidence. First, the story of Genesis 15 tells us that Abram is childless. At the same time, however, Abram's servant is clearly stated to be in line to inherit from his master, signaling the inclusion of retainers in the corporate body of Abram's house.[40] Further, in Genesis 14 Abram brings together a force of "three hundred and eighteen of his retainers, born in his house. . . ." (Genesis 14:14). Under the notions of corporate organization in most traditional kinship systems, such retainers constitute part of the corporate body or "family." We might also note that a corporate sense of family leadership is maintained in later Jewish law, extending specifically to slaves or servants (see Exodus 21:1–5; cf. Deuteronomy 15:12–15). The number of retainers under Abram's control implies a substantial source of women through which Lot might have formed a marriage alliance with his uncle. The lengths to which Abram went to rescue his kinsman would also seem to support the idea of a matrimonial alliance with Lot. Note the continued wording of Genesis 14:14–16:

> When Abram heard that his nephew had been captured, he mustered three hundred and eighteen of his retainers, born in his house, and went in pursuit as far as Dan. He and his party deployed against them at night, defeated them, and pursued them as far as Hobah, which is north of Damascus. He recovered all of the possessions, besides bringing back his kinsman Lot and his possessions, *along with the women and the other captives.* (Emphasis added)

Recall that when Laban, in a very different situation, pursues Jacob, he compares the situation of his daughters to that of women taken in war (Genesis 31:26). Of course, the women and other captives of Genesis 14 could simply be the women of Sodom, Gomorrah, Admah, Zeboiim, and Zoar. But we must also wonder if Abram did not have a greater interest than the rescue of Lot, especially when he chooses not to take a portion of the spoils.

A second support for the idea of a matrimonial alliance between Abram and Lot comes from the comparison of Abram's and Jacob's life cycles. As we have already observed, these patriarchs each underwent transformations of character at the end of their periods of mobility. The story of the rescue of Lot and the conflict between Jacob's group and the Shechemites (Genesis 34) immediately precede these transformations. The Shechemite affair also involved a proposition of matrimonial alliance and the capture of women. The structural analogy suggests that Abram's regional strife is tied to matrimony, clearly as an "honorable" defense, in contrast to the dishonorable contract and strife into which Jacob is drawn by his sons.

A third support for the alliance of Abram and Lot rests in the fate of Lot's line. When Sodom and Gomorrah are destroyed (Genesis 19) Lot's wife dies, and the incestuous events leading to the births of Moab and Ammon soon follow. A standard interpretation of Lot's wife "looking back" is that she is concerned for her kinsmen in the cities. This does not totally fit with the notion of Lot's *righteousness,* however, the theme which allows him to be rescued in the first place. Is he really supposed to have married into the families of Sodom and Gomorrah? If we compare Lot's situation once again to Judah in Genesis 38, using the parallel posited in the chiasmus of life-death reports, we find that Judah's first wife is stated to be a Canaanite. The origin of Tamar, however, is not stated. I suggest that when the origin of a woman is not specified in the text, her appropriateness as a spouse is not in question. Thus, Lot's wife, whoever she is, is not significant in the text because of her background. She is significant precisely because she is removed from the scene. The question we must ask, then, is what kind of kinship justification is operative in the removal of the woman, setting up the opportunity for Lot's incest?

If we postulate an implied connubium on the basis of evidence from Genesis 12–17, then at some point the relationship must be broken to accommodate the unfolding social transformation of Abram to Abraham. Since a connubium equalizes the status of the three Terahite lineages, we would expect to see continual marriages in the pattern expressed in the marriages of Milcah, Rebekah, Leah, and Rachel. These women all marry up one generation. Thus, if we looked in Abram's line for the woman who should be given to Lot, we would look for a daughter of Isaac. Similarly, one generation up, the wife of Haran would be a daughter of Abram, and one generation down the women given to Moab and Ammon would be the daughters of Jacob—the women of Israel!

I suggest that the genealogical material implies a connubium specifically so it can be rejected through the Lot narratives. The message is simple: Israel will not give its women in marriage to the other groups of the region; it stands as an endogamous group. The narrative rejection comes in three points. First, the circumcision symbol of Genesis 17 identifies the lineage in close association with God. Lot, having separated from Abram in Genesis 13, is not party to the Covenant of Circumcision. If we accept the arguments of Simeon and Levi about circumcision (Genesis 34:14–16), then the covenant prohibits Isaac from forming (continuing) a marriage alliance to the descendants of Lot. Second, Lot's wife is killed, thus negating any implied structural connections between Abram and Lot. Finally, the origin of the Moabites and Ammonites (Genesis 19:30–38) provides a cultural justification against association with the descendants of Lot.

A final argument supporting an implied connubium connecting Abram, Nahor, and Haran (Lot) is territorial. Terah brought his entire household to northwest Mesopotamia where Nahor becomes associated with the placenames Haran, Paddan-Aram, and Aram Naharaim. Abram moves south and becomes associated with Canaan, specifically the highlands around Bethel. Lot separates from Abram and becomes associated with the Transjordanian area. These positions establish a triangular pattern conducive to a "closed" circulation of women (Figure 7).

These diverse forms of evidence suggest that Genesis makes Abram initially subject to a northern circle of marriage alliances. The form of the alliance permits the taking of wives from the region of northwest Mesopotamia, specifically among the descendants of Nahor, but does not clearly link Sarai to Nahor's line.[41] Further, the text implies that Lot's wife should originate in Abram's group, but does not specify her origin. The change of status of Abram under the Covenant of Circumcision calls forth a new social association. Thus, the text presents a set of images consistent with a connubium, but *emphasizes* the social identification intended to replace it. In this sense, the first half of the Abraham cycle posits a period of history and a social organization prior to the covenant promises.[42]

The Covenant of Circumcision

With the Covenant of Circumcision an important new principle of alliance is established for the line of Abraham. The men of the line may take wives from other groups, but after the covenant they do not give their sisters as wives outside the circumcised alliance. The "circumcised" constitutes the group within which men exchange sisters to create tribal definition. As we shall see, the transformation of Jacob to Israel further delimits the application of the principle. This means that the "circumcised" group is an imperfect entity. The flaw, likely an intentional irony, is a creation of the compilers of the text who generated the contrasts of Esau and Jacob, and later Ishmael and Isaac. Both sets of brothers are brought into conflict. A division in the interests of the parents in each case identifies the source of trouble. Both situations result in the blessing and political legitimation of the younger son over the elder. These instances fit with theological affirmations of the providential character of the deity supporting the patriarchs. Sociologically, the cases define the origins of powerful groups to the south of Israel. Let us examine the characters individually.

Ishmael is brought into Genesis through a very clear segmentation of an originally independent story cycle. Several commentators express this view, including Bruce Vawter, Gerhardt von Rad, and Hermann Gunkel.[43] Vawter notes the discontinuity of Ishmael's age, supplied by the priestly source, with the imagery of Genesis 21, and cites the topical continuity of this Elohist segment about the expulsion of Hagar with the Yahwist material in Genesis 16. Von Rad offers a

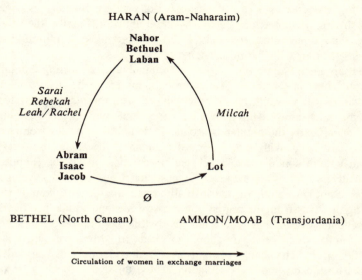

Figure 7.   Map showing the Terahite association as a territorial system.

similar argument, which is consistent also to the source treatment in the standard work of Gunkel. The fragments of the Ishmael story are manipulated to supply dramatic contrast between Ishmael and Isaac. We might question why particular pieces of the narrative were placed in their present context without more efficient modification, but the effect of the redaction for kinship purposes is clear. Ishmael is born prior to the Covenant of Circumcision, so he shares in its foundation with Abram. Indeed, Ishmael and Abram go together and become the first circumcised representatives of Abram's house (Genesis 17:13–27). But Ishmael becomes the sign of conflict between Hagar and Sarai, a dispute in which Abram seems tortured with conflicts of his own (cf. Genesis 16:6 and 17:18–20; 21:9–11). For the most part the potential direct conflict between Ishmael and Isaac is only weakly suggested (Genesis 21:9 has Ishmael "playing with" or "making fun of" Isaac), or simply declared in general terms (Genesis 16:12 and 25:18). Sociologically, Ishmael is a clear threat to Isaac.

The problem of Ishmael's presence may be interpreted on two different levels. First, there is the question of individual succession in the line of Abraham. Second, there is the question of alternatives of group alliance through marriage, represented both in the origins of Hagar and Sarah and the ties of Abram to Egypt and Haran reinforced by the marriages of the two sons. The act of circumcising Ishmael suggests Abraham's closure of the debate over the legitimacy of the boy. Ishmael was never accepted by Sarah, but Abraham clearly held him in favor. Thus, although Ishmael's mother is considered a slave, he stands as a legitimate successor of Abraham as long as he is part of Abraham's household.

The case of Ishmael is interesting in comparison to several rules listed in the Mishpatim (see Exodus 21:7–10). These rules state first that a female slave taken as a concubine may not be sold to foreigners, but is instead to be sold back to her original household. If her food, clothing, or conjugal rights are violated, however, the woman may leave freely, according to the next two provisions in the sequence. These rules suggest that if Abraham intended to keep Hagar and Ishmael in the group, he would be required to maintain her in a manner which, if we are to believe Sarah's actions in the text, would be totally unacceptable to Sarah. On the other hand, if Sarah's wishes were to be followed by Abraham without treating Hagar unfairly, he would have been required to sell her back. The conflict hinges on the complication created by Sarah's transformation of status from barren to fruitful. The sense of the text is that the two women are threats to each other's conjugal rights and status as wives (which might well include markers of food and clothing).[44] That Abraham ultimately sends Hagar away rather than selling her back to Egypt suggests that her rights were, in the end, abrogated. In this context, Ishmael's legitimacy is rejected by *his* expulsion, but is affirmed by the manner in which his mother is sent away.

The conditions of Isaac's birth complicate matters by providing an offspring for the foremost, clearly highborn woman within Abraham's house. Isaac is the first son born to Abraham, the most prominent man of circumcised status. Isaac is a pure symbolic expression of the covenant, a gift provided by divine intervention (see Genesis 17:17–21 and 18:13–14). The narrative suggests that the divine plan will supersede all human intervention. Thus, Abraham's desires and Sarah's fears express the covenant clearly, giving it precision in human terms. Isaac becomes the first son of a patriarch circumcised in accordance with God's direction, on the eighth day of life (Genesis 17:12; 21:4).

Ishmael is territorially placed on the southwest in the Paran wilderness, the district of Shur east of Egypt. He takes a wife from his mother's kinsmen (Genesis 21:21), confirming an alliance to Egypt, and he shares association to the boundary point Beer-Lahai-Roi; when Rebekah joins Isaac to become his wife he is encamped at Lahai Roi, the well named by Hagar immediately prior to Ishmael's birth (Genesis 16:13–15; 24:62).

Isaac not only succeeds Abraham, but he remains in the same geographic area as his father. After the establishment of the Covenant of Circumcision, Abraham traveled toward the south and became essentially fixed in the hinterlands of Gerar where he established several wells (Genesis 20:15 and 21:22–32). The trip to Moriah for the sacrifice of Isaac (Genesis 22) is the only major movement of either Abraham or Isaac out of the axis running between Beer-Sheba and Hebron/Mamre. Both Abraham and Isaac deceived Abimelech in Gerar (Genesis 20 and 26), and Isaac reestablished the wells of his father (Genesis 26:16–25). The crucial point is that Isaac is never directly placed in any of the northern localities, nor is Abraham, and they never travel outside southern Canaan.

The distinction of brothers in the Abrahamic succession is continued with Esau and Jacob. For twins there can be no resolution of status by differentiating between mothers. Esau has every right to expect a prominent blessing according to strict rules of succession. But in this case the mother becomes involved on behalf of the younger son, and the father favors succession through the elder. So far, the parallel with Ishmael and Isaac is clear enough. It is Jacob, however, even with his father's blessing, who is sent away from his father's house. This is first justified by reference to Esau's anger at losing his birthright (Genesis 27:42–45). A second justification is more informative from a social perspective. Rebekah complains about Esau's wives, Canaanite women, and Isaac sends Jacob to Laban for the purpose of obtaining a wife (Genesis 27:46–28:2). If we recall that Abraham expressly prohibited his servant from taking Isaac to Haran (Genesis 24:5–6), we may wonder about Isaac's intention in so freely allowing his own heir to make the trip. Such a question is bolstered by our knowledge of what is about to happen in Jacob's relationship to Laban. In any event, the wish of Rebekah is consistent with the effect of alliance systems to keep related women in the household. For his part, Esau adds insult to injury in the situation by taking Mahalath, the daughter of Ishmael, as his third wife. His action is intended to please his parents (Genesis 28:8–9), but the result is a formal matrimonial alliance between the circumcised lines of Ishmael and Isaac. The unwitting insult by Esau in recognizing the lineage of Ishmael is consistent with his character. Like Briar Bear, he plods through the text being duped or merely acting simple at every turn. Esau's third marriage, however, formalized his distinction from Jacob, and helps set the stage for his territorial placement upon Jacob's return. That is, Esau's identification with Edom and his location in the Seir district provide the territorial complement of the social ties implied by his marriage to Mahalath.

The posited second stage in the formation of Israel, spanning the narrative reports from the establishment of the Covenant of Circumcision through the transformation of Israel, is essentially identical with the lifetime of Isaac (Genesis 21–36). Let us recall that the birth of Isaac (Genesis 21) is supposed to be within a year of the establishment of the covenant, and that the intervening story deals with Lot. But the "stage" is more appropriately a territorial construct (Figure 8). From the point of view of the text, time and place are one coextensive system. The final territorial associations of the brothers on the two generations are real associations undoubtedly born in some actual political competition of real groups, and provide in Genesis a formal sociological justification of relatedness among the diverse "southern" Canaan groups. Circumcision serves as a weak, imperfect, identification of southern alliances, clearly juxtaposed against the Aramean connections posed for Abram, Isaac, and Jacob. For their part, Ishmael and Esau are comparable to Ammon-Moab in becoming "peripheral" to the core political fabric of the text.

This leaves for us the concern of the last alliance marriage between Jacob and northwest Mesopotamia. By analogy, the northern region is the counterpart of Egypt—it is distant and a source of wealth (Genesis 12 and 30:25–43). The final separation of Jacob and Laban, accomplished through an oath and sacrifice (Genesis 31:43–55), puts Jacob on his own en route to Canaan and the final confrontation with his brother. Jacob's transformation to Israel is thus associated in the narrative with his separation from Laban (independence and wealth), his final differentiation from Esau (legitimacy through blessing), and the death of Isaac (ascendancy to his inheritance). These events announce the creation of a new social order. After final genealogical embellishments pertaining to Israel are noted, the reader of Genesis is fully prepared for the Joseph cycle.

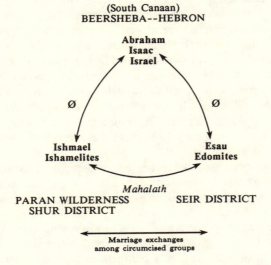

Figure 8. Map showing the Covenant of Circumcision association as a territorial system.

The Definition of Israel

In his recent work *The Bible Without Theology,* Robert Oden posed two questions, one of which the preceding analyses have partially considered, and the other upon which we are about to proceed:[45] "Why is it that the patriarchs enter into the kinds of kinship relations they do? How do the resulting kinship alliances shape both the narratives before us and the issue of who is included and who is excluded from Israel?" Oden develops his answers to these questions through analysis of the Jacob story, Genesis 12–36. This is in part because he regards the transformation of Jacob to Israel as the essential social process recounted in Genesis, and to a great extent in the Torah. Even though I press the notion of "social system" into earlier sections of Genesis than Oden, his stress of the symbolic centrality of the "Israel" label is both appropriate and correct in detail. Oden makes two other points which bear repeating. First, he warns against the conclusion "that the kinship tensions within the Jacob narratives offer proof that these narratives were composed against the background of changing residence and settlement patterns."[46] This is an absolutely essential point to recognize, for even with the precision of the kinship relationships posited in the text, it is unlikely that we can differentiate actual historical process from practical political assertions which are mainly fictional. Oden's other point considers whether kinship studies will ever provide a foundation for any historical conclusions. He suggests that such conclusions might be possible in the future. If by "historical conclusions" we refer to a process of establishing historicity of Genesis narratives, I doubt we shall ever engage in such a process. On the other hand, if "historical conclusions" refer to assessment of the communities responsible for the narrative composition, I am more optimistic. Much of the preceding analysis has engaged broad redactional questions. In developing kinship models pertinent to the definition of Israel, I expect the results to point to relatively refined periods in the later history of Judaism. Effective results will emerge, however, not from the pure political intentions of the text, but from consideration of the kinship connections against a background of Judaic law and refined literary assessment of the patriarchal characterizations. This is because the placement of a patriarch in a structure suggesting his downfall, as for example through incest, can represent an illustration of his honor. In the end, patriarchal narratives do not so much represent "case law" as they do examples from legend. Their use in calling forth later codes and pronouncements succeeded precisely because they presented ideal, or sometimes even impossible situations.

With these thoughts in mind, let us begin consideration of the social meaning of "Israel" by observing that Jacob's sons form a large scale marriage circle which is independent and politically antagonistic to outsiders. When we continue to read the relationships within Israel as those between groups, we recognize that Genesis speaks in an ideal way about the organization of a constellation of tribes which had their existence in Canaan long after the supposed patriarchal period. A fictive, preterritorial notion of Israel is highly pertinent to the interpretation of territorial events presented in much later historical or quasi-historical scriptures. But a pre-territorial Israel is part of the ideological assessment of social change. Thus, if the Terahite connubium creates an historical fiction and territorial association to express the principle of exogamy, and the Covenant of Circumcision similarly founded offers the principle of endogamy, then *Israel* integrates the two principles. The name identifies a collection of kinsmen who practice endogamy, at least as regards the giving of women, and also creates divisions that *could* practice exogamy. We must say "could" with emphasis because nowhere in any of the traditions is exogamy mandated. Indeed, later we see endogamy within the tribal units. Nonetheless, Israel is a fundamental social identification which informs us about the tension between "alliance" and "segmentation" as continuing social processes.[47] There is much evidence that a preterritorial Israel is simply a fiction constructed to justify an historical alliance system.[48] Genesis is not bad sociology and not bad social history, as long as we do not press for the historicity of the narrative.

As sociology, Genesis looks very much like an effort to differentiate one sort of alliance system from others that might be possible. The fictions about the Abraham-ic line construct several kinds of descent distinctions. One potentially important opposition is between "matrilineal" and "patrilineal" descent. Some analyses even suggest that Abraham represents the adoption of patriarchal rules after separating from "settled" or "matriarchal" kin.[49] It is interesting to note that the name *Bethuel* (Laban's father) can be read as a feminine name glossing as "maiden of God."[50] It is possible that the text presents a female from an oral tradition as a male. In the story of Rebekah's marriage she identifies herself as the daughter of Bethuel "son of Nahor and Milcah," yet in the negotiations it is Laban and his mother who receive gifts finalizing the marriage settlement (Genesis 24:53).

It seems likely that the subtle undercurrents of potential matriarchy are merely the artifacts of cross-cutting clan distinctions, female associations significant in marriage, similar to those of many patrilineal systems in the world, especially those of the Near East. Perhaps all that is at stake in Rebekah's marriage is an identification of the kinds of people who normally would be involved in matrimonial negotiations; the prominence of the brother is certainly not unusual.

Openly stated or implied rules of lineage association in Genesis offer technical issues, establishing legal principles for the actual system being justified. This is rather like the kind of talk people in the United States use to differentiate the working of government during the period of the Articles of Confederation and after, or before and after the Supreme Court's decision in the case of Marbury vs. Madison. A small change of principles, or even the emphasis of one principle over others, can make a tremendous difference in kinship practice.

Conflicts between co-wives or between wife and spouse, prefigured in the relationships of Hagar and Sarai, Sarai and Abram, or Rebekah and Isaac, come to full force in the competition between the sisters Leah and Rachel and in their respective marriages to Jacob. The situations involving "cast out" sons, in all cases the favorite of the father, and the subsequent rise of that son to blessings, position, and wealth, serve to illustrate diverse operative principles in the regulation of intra-family conflict. Ishmael, Esau, Jacob, and Joseph provide, from the point of view of their respective separation from brothers, different kinds of links to historical situations in Canaan.

Thus, preterritorial Israel only prefigures its territorial counterpart in social and cultural terms. Every story, every genealogical report, every tidbit of good or bad information is germane to the interpretation of the social array. But the traditions of Genesis are accurate and meaningful only for some "present" very far removed in time from the era it purports to represent. This realization does not demean the historical or theological significance of the scripture. In fact, for many of the faithful it adds to that significance. For those of us with literary, anthropological, and historical interests, the mythic sense of Genesis is an exciting realization, and a compelling impetus to reasoned interpretation of the conditions that have brought the text to its traditional written forms.

A full analysis of Genesis genealogies, including assessment of the tribes of Israel, must reach far beyond points of genealogy or social articulation. What are the structures through which layers of literary meaning are produced in the text? What is the articulation of kinship content with Judaic law? What can we say about who puts the meaning into our readings? Can we know the full intent of the text on a political level, or do we to some extent only create meanings for today, hopelessly far from the resonance of the original recitations? Do we *draw* structure and meaning from the foundation tradition, consciously or unconsciously making the text synonymous with our lives? Some content, no doubt, we read into the text, but much of even contemporary reading is consistent with notions we know must have been intrinsic to the scripture. Everywhere, there are notable regularities of pattern which stand out for our scrutiny.

II

POLITY AND HISTORY

Historicity

The presentation of time and place in history is always complex, always formally controlled and constrained in narrative, and therefore always artificial. In oral traditions, and, as we have seen in chapter 1, in the written narratives of Genesis, the metaphors of life-cycle occur as vehicles representing supposed historical stages styled through vignettes about real or adopted culture heroes. This can be true whether the actual events behind history are remote in time or part of ongoing cultural action. Cultures, traditional or complex, create plausible history in order to explain the present in the most direct and convincing ways, the historian's culture serving as a means of bending past events into a "present" perspective. In our literate, critical, and technically sophisticated era we may be less apt to accept a clearly make-believe formulation of current or recent events. On the other hand, media experts are quick to point out that the first and most prominent public expression of a falsehood is much more powerful than its retraction.

As we become removed from events in time, we become much less discriminating about authenticity in historical interpretation. Thus, we must distinguish between the idea of historicity as an expression of "accurate representation of the past" and historicity in the sense of "culturally acceptable understanding of the past." If we had the luxury of writing our history and ignoring the criticisms of our enemies, perhaps we could construct it with fewer contradictions. Our images would resonate only with current events, justify them, or even take the Orwellian form of embellished fact. Of course, we would then be creating myths about our history, but at the same time very accurate portrayals of our current values and motivations.

Modern history is always somewhere between that "mythic" kind of construction and the dry, experiential, unique progression of taken-for-granted images we live. It is involved enough with the mundane that it is accurate and meaningful, but historical narrative can never fit von Ranke's formula of being "wie es eigentlich gewesen ist." Our discussions of biblical history and historicity become myths about myths. We become, at one level, a part of the very same constructive and interpretive tradition engaging us.

In this intellectual context, it is important to specify what cultural object we hope to construct through our interpretive efforts. Do we seek in Genesis clues to the historical context or contexts it purports to represent? Do we seek an understanding of the community which created the representation? And in either case, do we seek mainly an expression of our own place in the broader tradition connecting us to the text? My answer to the third question is that I work from my interests in comparative culture toward a modern conception of traditional polity, embracing Genesis alongside other ancient sources and the array of ethnographic studies produced over the past century. I embrace the second question. That is, I believe Genesis yields very useful "data" about a particular view of a world far removed from the time it represents. As to the first question, I reject the idea that Genesis is appropriate material for reconstructing events or actual systems operative at the time during which the patriarchs are supposed to have lived.

Robert Oden's emphasis on the sons of Jacob as the social core of Genesis—the idea that the creation of "Israel" is the book's essential point—forces us to see the social constructs of Genesis as part of the larger biblical tradition.[1] His stress on the full narrative cycle from Genesis 12 through 36 also captures most of the genealogical and narrative information pertinent to the mythical account of Israel's foundation. On the other hand, though his argument recognizes the "narrowing" process through which Israel is created, Oden fails to fully investigate the symbolic features through which the definition of "Jacob's sons" is given social meaning.[2] This symbolic system relies more upon place references, women's social statuses, and the mythic stages of social formation (the Terahites and Circumcision), than it does upon the narrative material dealing with Jacob's sons directly. Thus, before we discuss the political order within Israel, we must better understand how "Israel" is wielded in the mythic structure of Genesis.

Mythscapes

We have already viewed an ideal structure of mobility for Abram and Jacob. The points in the structure represent only a small part of the total list of places noted throughout Genesis, but they are among the most significant. When we consider a total list of place references, six broad groups may be distinguished (Table 1). First, and to an extent most important, are places named by the central patriarchs. In this group are also included the well named by Hagar (Beer-lahai-roi) and Laban's alternative name for Galeed/Mizpah (Jegar-sahadutha). The places include locations of altars, theophany, and conflict described in narrative. Second, the text cites numerous places which become important as travel stops for the patriarchs, as camp locations, or as additional points of conflict or deception. Several of these locations are also associated with theophany, altars, or sites of burial. Three of the references locate trees at Shechem, Bethel, and Mamre. Two of these places, Shechem and Machpelah (at Hebron) are linked to purchases of land by Abraham and Jacob/Israel. Together, these first two categories of place references form the core points associated with the patriarchs.

The third kind of place reference in Genesis involves regional names or points used to generally locate another named place in the narrative. Most of the names on

Places Named by Characters:

Beer-Lahai-Roi (16:14)
Beer-Sheba (21:30-31; 26:33)
Esek (26:30)
Sitnah (26:21)
Rehoboth (26:22)
Bethel/Luz (28:19; 35:7, 15)
Galeed/Mizpah (31:48-49)
Jegar-Sahadutha/Galeed (31:47)
Mahanaim (32:3)
Peniel (32:31-32)
Succoth (33:17)
Bethlehem (35:19)

Places Associated with Travel:

Haran (11--35)
Shechem/Terebinth of Moreh (12)
Sodom (13--19)
Gomorrah (13--19)
Terebinth of Mamre (13--50)
Hebron/Kiriatharba (13--50)
Dan (14)
Hobah (N. of Damascus) (14)
Gerar (20:26)
Cave at Machpelah (Hebron) (23--50)
Wadi-Gerar (outside Gerar) (26)
Oak of Tears (Allonbacuth) (35:8)
Tower of Eder (35:20)

Regions and Reference Points:

Egypt (Abram, Joseph)
Negev (Abram)
Jordan Plain (Lot)
Aram-Naharaim (Laban)
Paddan-Aram (Laban)
Land of Kedem (Keturah's Sons)
Havilah-by-Shur to Asshur (Ishmael)
Wilderness of Paran (Ishmael)
Seir (Esau)
Edom (Esau)
Goshen (Israel in Egypt)
Damascus (locates Hobah, Abram)
Road to Ephraith (locates Bethlehem, Jacob)

Other Places:

Ellasar (14)
Elam (14)
Goiim (14)
Zeboiim (14)
Bela (Zoar) (14)
Valley of Siddim (Salt Sea) (14)
Ashteroth-karnaim (14)
Ham (14)
Shavehkiriathaim (14)
Enmishpat (Kadesh) (14)
Admah (14)
Valley of Shaveh (14)
Salem (14)
Gilead (37:25)
Chezib (38:5)
Timnah (38:12)
Enaim (38:14, 21)
Dothan (37:17)

Places Listed in Genealogy:

Dinhaba, city of Bela (36:32)
Bozrah (36:33)
Land of the Temanites (36:34)
Avith, city of Husham (36:34)
Masrekah (36:36)
Rehoboth on the River (36:37)
Pau, city of Hadar (36:39)

Holy Places -- Unlocated

Land of Moriah (22)
Yahweh-yireh (22:14)
Goren-ha-atad (50:10-11)
Abel-mizraim (50:11)

Table 1.   Classification of place references in Genesis 12-50.

the list can be linked to specific patriarchs, and several are clearly intended to be territorial designations.

The last three groups of place references can be differentiated by their literary associations. The short list of "Holy Places" includes designations linked to mortuary rites for Israel and the sacrifice of Isaac. None of these points can be placed on a map, though the location of Moriah has been a subject of intense speculation by biblical scholars. Since, like points in the other two lists, these places are noted only once in the text, they do not represent a part of the dominating mobility structure of the combined narratives. To the "Holy Place" list we might have added Salem, the city of Melchizedek in Genesis 14. I have left Salem in the "Other Place" category, however, because the whole name series of Genesis 14 presents a common problem of place reference. The names in the chapter are tied to people off the line of the patriarchs and, with the exceptions of Sodom, Gomorrah, Zoar, and Kadesh, do not occur elsewhere as references for patriarchal travel. Finally, seven places are mentioned in the Edomite genealogical segment of Genesis 36:31–39.[3] Three of these are introduced by the formula "the name of his city was . . ." and thus locate seats of Edomite authority in Seir. The three cities fit in a broad pattern created by the major place references in the narratives and hence are of greater interest than most of the other minor designations in Genesis.

The major point references and several of the regional designations, together with some of the minor points just mentioned, appear with lines of travel by patriarchs in Figure 9. Except for the more distant points, the position of each place is approximately scaled on the map. Places located by region are encircled on the chart, and points without relatively firm placements are indicated by circles.[4]

Several of the lines of movement on Figure 9 depict travel in single stories, while some of the lines indicate travel replicated by more than one patriarch. The line crossing the regional designation "Negev" from Bethel to Egypt is the route of Abram in Genesis 12, for example. Other movement into and out of the southwest Canaan region and adjacent places is much more specified and is tied to Abraham, Isaac, Hagar, and Ishmael. Thus, Abraham moves to Gerar from Mamre, while Isaac moves there from the well at Lahai-Roi (Genesis 24:62 and 25:11). After each deceives Abimelech (Genesis 20 and 26), he removes to the surrounding countryside and eventually settles in Beer-sheba. During this movement, Isaac names Abraham's wells in the hinterland of Gerar (most likely along the break between the hill country and the coastal plain). The dashed line running between Mamre, Beer-sheba, and Lahai-Roi represents Hagar's wandering in the region; the extension of the line depicts the final movement of Hagar and Ishmael after their expulsion from Abraham's group.

On the southeast, Lot's relocation from Bethel to the Jordan plain links him to the cities of Sodom and Gomorrah, as well as to Zoar. These points are placed only tentatively in most Bible atlases. Inclusion of Sodom, Gomorrah, and Zoar on the map is based on their prominence in narratives about Lot. Finally, the cave in which Lot's daughters seduce him is on the east, toward the Transjordanian zone associated with Ammon and Moab. Keturah's sons, Abraham's descendants from his concubine, are placed further east, representing their position after their departure from around Hebron.

Jacob's travel to Haran is not shown on Figure 9, though it involved links from Beersheba to Bethel, and from there to Paddan-Aram and the city of Laban. Jacob's return trip is shown by the lines on the northeast part of the map. His stages took him from Haran to Galeed/Mizpha, and then to the three closely associated points

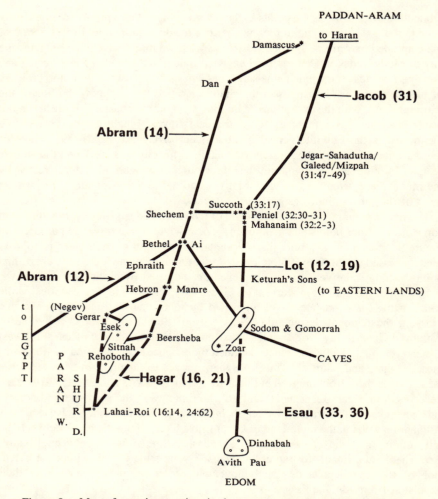

Figure 9.   Map of prominent points in the movements of patriarchs and related family lines.

Mahanaim, Peniel, and Succoth. The three places function in the narrative to help develop Jacob's confrontation with Esau. Esau's travel to Mahanaim and back to Edom is shown by the dashed line traversing the length of the Salt Sea valley. In Edom, the three cities named in Genesis 36 are given emphasis, since they represent the seat of Edomite kings. The last link in the travel of Jacob involves his move across the Jordan into the highlands at Shechem. From that point on his travel south recapitulates the movements of Abram, with the elaboration of a stop between Bethel and Mamre to bury Rachel.

The core points on Figure 9 are those where most of the narrative pertaining to Abram/Abraham, Isaac, and Jacob/Israel takes place. Thus, emphasis upon

Shechem, Bethel/Ai, Hebron/Mamre, and Beer-sheba rests upon their central literary importance, including symbolic features of each spot. Abram built altars at Shechem, Bethel, and Hebron, and also planted a Tamarask tree at Beer-sheba in association with his worship. This tree is a counterpart to the trees used in constant reference to Hebron and Mamre, the Oak of Tears where Deborah was buried at Bethel, and the Terebinth of Moreh at Shechem (Genesis 12). Jacob also built an altar at Bethel, and offered sacrifices at Beer-sheba on his way to Egypt (Genesis 46:2). Last among the central group of points is Bethlehem, the place "on the road to Ephraith" where Rachel was buried after the birth of Benjamin. Although technically not a "place named by a patriarch," I have included Bethlehem in that list because Jacob marks the place with a stone. It is included on Figure 9 because it is the only point figuring in the prominent lines of travel, which is associated with a son of Jacob. The significance of this inclusion rests upon a more idealized treatment of the structure of mobility. In that context, we shall see that the place may be one of the most significant references in the total narrative.

Although it is not immediately evident from the scaled map of Figure 9, the places describing the key movements of the patriarchs form a symmetrical array. The representation of this symmetrical structure (Figure 10) still constitutes a map of the region with branches running north, southwest, and southeast. In the center of the array is a triangular zone formed by the names used in "paired" references throughout the narratives: Bethel/Ai (sometimes Bethel/Luz), Hebron/Mamre, and Sodom and Gomorrah. Connecting to each of these paired places is a more distant place: Shechem, Beer-sheba, and Zoar.

The disassociation of Zoar from Sodom and Gomorrah is based upon its use in the narratives, together with the fact that Sodom and Gomorrah are usually mentioned together. Note also, that Zoar is described as the limit of the green zone in Genesis 13, giving it the sense of "terminating" the territory Lot finds appealing. This is the same sense given to Shechem and Beer-sheba within Canaan, for these points serve as places of "departure" from the district of primary interest to the patriarchs. The more-distant places all involve either contested territory, boundary points, or places linked in part to people off the main line of inheritance from Abraham. Thus, on the north, Abram's war takes him to Dan and Hobah (north of Damascus), while Jacob's return from Haran brings him to Galeed, Succoth/Peniel/Mahanaim, and back to Shechem. On the southwest, Hagar's travel takes her to Lahai-Roi and beyond to the Shur District, while the movements of Abraham and Isaac bring them from Gerar to wells outside Gerar, to Beersheba. Lot's final move links Zoar with Transjordania, while Esau's location places him south of Zoar and the Salt Sea valley he uses in his move to and from Mahanaim.

The structural symmetry of the points in Figure 10 is completed by the inclusion of the three seats of Edomite power listed in Genesis 36:31–39. These points reinforce the idea that Figure 10 is an analog of both geographic and narrative structure, though in the narrative it is clear that the most important lines of connection are those on the north and southwest. Still, the symmetry of the three points named by Jacob during his confrontation with Esau, the three cities named in association with Edomite Kings, and the three wells named by Isaac between

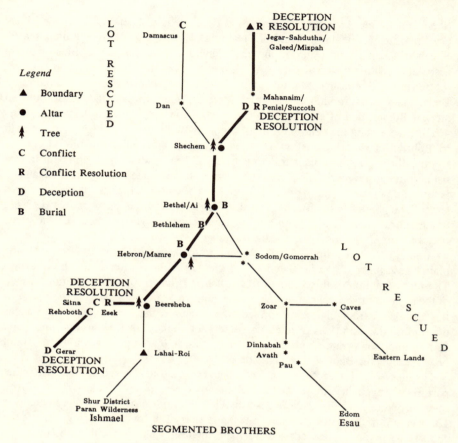

Figure 10. Symmetrical place associations in Genesis.

Gerar and Beer-sheba, suggests careful control of narrative content. These structural parallels may explain why Genesis 36:31–39 is included with the purely genealogical material for Esau.

The regular geometric form of Figure 10 is similar to structural models anthropologists use in kinship studies.[5] Given the content of Genesis in general, we should not be too surprised if such a geometric figure would have kinship implications. We shall turn to those implications shortly. But a more important question concerns whether the ideal geographic array and its implications can be considered indigenous to the text. It seems doubtful to me that anyone would have thought of the text in precisely the geometrical sense of the figure, except perhaps some late Jewish mystics.[6] On the other hand, because the points form a logical symmetry related to territorial associations of peoples, it also seems doubtful to me that the symbolic sense of Figure 10 would have been missed by those most familiar with the text, including especially its creators. I argue, then, that spatial descriptions in Genesis yielded symbolic expectations to those experiencing the narrative. Action can to a great extent be deduced from location. Thus, when Abram talks with God in Bethel he has encountered "men," but when the "men" arrive at Sodom and Gomorrah they are called "angels." Variations in the manifestations of God or God's messengers are patterned according to place. Moreover, births, deaths, property acquisitions, conflict resolutions, burials, trees, and the building of altars, all occur most often in symmetrical associations. In this sense, the word map offered in Genesis 12–50 yields an extraordinary mythological space, or "mythscape."

The social implications of the geographic array are also based in symmetry derived from Figure 10 and constitute a definition of "Israel" as an historical and political unit. Consider the outer circle of Figure 11. Using the point framework as a series of boundary points, our reading of the map turns to the spaces occupied by the eponymous ancestors on the lines descended from Terah. In the core of the map on the northwest we find the lines of Abram/Jacob in north Canaan, and Abraham/Isaac in south Canaan. The division of the two zones is accomplished by the dashed line extending from Bethlehem toward the northwest in line with the connection between Sodom/Gomorrah and Zoar. Similar extensions of the branches of the graph differentiate the regions of Paddan-Aram and Transjordania to the north and east, and the regions of Shur and Edom on the south. The reported marriages between Milcah and Nahor and between Mahalath and Esau suggest that all of these divisions indicate boundaries within marriage circles. The zone of Abram/Jacob and Abraham/Isaac is linked, then, through potential marriages. From this reading of the map, the birth of Benjamin signals the final transformation of Jacob to Israel, becoming the critical symbolic unification of Israel as a marriage circle.

The narrative declares Israel a marriage circle by direct statement as well as by structural implication. But the direct statement (Genesis 34) provides the wrong metaphor (circumcision) for the Israel association. The symbolic definition of Israel, though only implicit, is much more precise. It is based on several aspects of genealogical and territorial connection: (a) the other groups on the map (Laban, Ammon/Moab, Esau, Ishmael) are seen as removed to a wider geographic sphere, and separated by zones where no marriage should occur; (b) the closest places outside the zone intended by God for the line of Abraham are destroyed; (c) no marriages are posited between south Canaan and Seir or Edom and Transjordania; (d) direct appearances of God or the voice of God occur at the four altar sites; (e) the counterpart zones to Canaan on the map have expressed marriages between groups. All of these features suggest that Israel is to be a social association over the whole of Canaan engaged in marriage alliances which preclude any further matrimonial connections to Paddan-Aram.

Finally, observe how the territorial logic plays out the "stages" of social construction developed by the compilers of Genesis in chapters 12–17 and 17–35. The northern two-thirds of the map represents the oldest association, the Terahite connubium (see above pp. 24–27), which when read as a social model stresses the principle of exogamy. The southwestern two-thirds represents the Covenant of Circumcision group (see pp. 27–31), stressing the principle of endogamy. And the

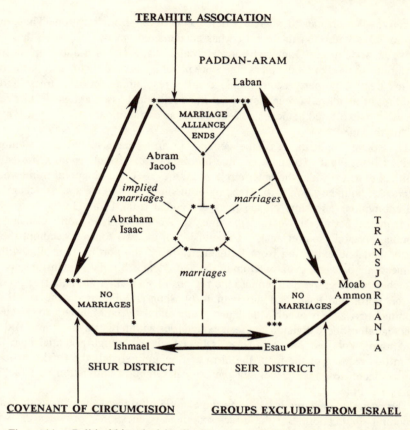

Figure 11.   Political/historical implications of symbolic structures in Genesis.

southeastern two-thirds indicates the groups excluded from Israel. On a theological level these people are excluded from the followership of Yahweh, leaving Israel as the beneficiary of God's promises to Abraham, Isaac, and Jacob. The "Israel" designation implies a righteous marriage association employing the principle of endogamy for the whole, and exogamy for the tribes. Since we know tribal exogamy was not required at later times (and I presume also that the construction is a late one), let me point out that the exogamous principle can be intended only for the immediate lineage level. In this case, the "tribes" linked to the sons of Jacob can be seen as "false-exogamous" units. This is precisely the language Claude Lévi-Strauss used in developing a similar resolution of exogamy and endogamy in his essay "Do Dual Organizations Exist," basing his arguments on three unrelated ethnographic cases.[7]

Figures 10 and 11 express the sense in which narrative precision in a myth of origin yields powerful social images. Yet it is still difficult to identify these images with a particular historical priesthood or political organization. The two hypotheses for association which readily present themselves are that the construction works toward legitimation of either Benjamin (therefore Saul) or Judah (therefore David or someone in the Davidic line). Another possibility is that the text recounts several claims, in which case other clues from the text (or even other historical evidence) is required to resolve questions of authorship. Such evidence rests partially in our interpretation of the twelve tribe system within the Torah and other biblical literature, especially as seen in conjunction with the evidence for Jacob's son's ranking provided by Genesis.

Tribal Ranking and Monarchic Succession

Tribal ranking and monarchic succession present related but very different aims in the social analysis of the Bible. The study of tribal ranking derives from several direct lines of textual evidence, most notably the birth accounts of Genesis 29 and 30, the blessings of Israel's sons in Genesis 49, and character attributions which may be gleaned from the Jacob and Joseph narratives. Character assessments for these purposes should proceed mainly from narrative context, since the mythic story forms include their own evaluations of action which are often apparently contrary to later Jewish law. The topic draws us into a consideration of legal questions, nonetheless, and so we shall have occasion to contrast ideas presented by the writers of law in Exodus, and to an extent in Deuteronomy. This form of analysis will be considered mainly for the characters of Reuben, Judah, Joseph, and Benjamin.

Assessment of tribal ranking is also informed by other genealogical or tribal presentations of the Torah. The most useful and connected materials are the description of Israel's camp in the wilderness (Numbers 2–3), assignment of the Levite cities in Canaan (Joshua 21), and tribal attributions found in Deuteronomy 27:9–14 and in the book of Joshua. The major goal of the expanded analysis is to understand why the tribal order changes in different lists, and to determine especially if the logic of birth-order ranking can resolve questions about tribal ranking. Another goal is to describe any alliance structures which are posited either directly or indirectly by the genealogies or narratives.

Questions about monarchic succession flow from tribal assessments, but at times they may be historically resolved on very different terms. Indeed, earlier arguments in this book suggest that tribal structures in Genesis likely flow from some particular political situation, and thus constitute justifying traditions rather than a body of "first principles" for political organization. In this context the tension between law and narrative is again important. The codes and other statements of Torah law are, after all, intended to be read as pertaining to a later Israel than the "mythical" or very early historical Israel of Genesis. To the extent Genesis may represent a document contemporary with other parts of the Torah, we are presented with two lines of thought about family organization and responsibility, one built in mythic structural contrasts and the other based on statements of normative interests in Judaism. These may be read against the larger corporate context of kingship as an institution introduced in the books of Samuel, as well as against a more convincingly historical treatment of Israel from David through the period of the exile. In sum, our task is to link mythic notions of tribal identity with legal ideas about corporate responsibility, and to link these in turn to the historical contexts of the Davidic and post-Davidic era.

Birth Order and Maternal Heritage

The combined genealogy and narrative from Genesis 29–50 offer several useful lines of commentary on Jacob's sons. First, we are given an order of birth, a direct expression of age-ranking which is cross-cut by two other kinds of features that modify rank distinctions. Maternal status influences the rank of the sons most prominently, since the mothers comprise two "high-born" women and two "hand-maidens" who serve as surrogate mothers for their mistresses. The ranks of Jacob's wives are confused by the fact that Leah, the elder and first wife, is less favored than Rachel. The ranks of the handmaidens are similarly confused by the fact that Jacob is given Bilhah, Rachel's woman, before he is given Zilpah. The sons of these unions are named by Leah and Rachel—signs of their legal acceptance—but their rank in Israel is determined in part by their actual maternal heritage. Territorial association of birth also modifies birth-order rank. Benjamin's birth in Canaan stands in contrast to the first eleven births in Paddan-Aram. Recall that Benjamin is linked to Isaac in the broader narrative and genealogical contexts (see above, pp. 18–20). Thus, territorial treatment prestates the interests of the whole text in the ultimate placement of Jacob's sons in Canaan.

The second line of commentary on Jacob's sons involves their naming. Indeed, the naming of each son constitutes much of the narrative. The names initiate a kind of treatment of the tribes which is continued in the blessings of Genesis 49 and in the development of familial strife between Jacob, Leah, and Rachel. As we shall see, the names of the sons often not only fit their actions in the Genesis narrative, but figure as well in the representations of the tribes in other biblical documents. Another line of naming, found in Jacob's blessings, is the association of the sons with animal metaphors.[8] Thus, we have two lines of attribution associated with rank, one stemming from the perceptions of mothers, and the other from Jacob.

Table 2 presents three consecutive views of rank for Jacob's sons, based mainly on material from Genesis 29–30, 34–35, and 48–49. The first sequence indicates rank according to strict birth order. The sequence draws our attention to the importance of contrasts between elder and younger sons, a distinction often related to the idea of "ultimogeniture" (passage of inheritance to youngest sons). When we consider the parallels of preceding patriarchal narratives, we recall that Isaac and Jacob each inherited over their elder brothers. The same feature is implied by the departure of Abram from Haran, leaving continuity of the Terahite line to his younger brother Nahor. Further examples occur with the sons of Judah (Genesis 38) and Joseph (Genesis 48). Thus, the birth order of the first eleven sons draws our attention to the contrasts between Reuben and Judah, Reuben and Joseph, Judah and Joseph, and in general between pairs of sons born in the middle of the sequence to Bilhah, Zilpah, and Leah. The addition of Benjamin to the birth order offers up

LEAH	BILHAH	ZILPAH	RACHEL
Reuben (1)			
Simeon (2)			
Levi (3)			
Judah (4)			
	Dan (5)		
	Naphtali (6)		
		Gad (7)	
		Asher (8)	
Issachar (9)			
Zebulun (10)			
			Joseph (11)
			Benjamin (12)

a.   Direct birth order of Genesis 29-30 and 35:16-20.

LEAH 1-1	RACHEL 1-2	ZILPAH 2-1	BILHAH 2-2
Reuben (1)	Joseph (1)		
Simeon (2)	Benjamin (2)		
Levi (3)			
Judah (4)			
Issachar (5)			
Zebulun (6)			
		Gad (1)	Dan (1)
		Asher (2)	Naphtali (2)

b.   Relative rank of sons determined by rank order of mother.

LEAH 1-1	RACHEL 1-2	ZILPAH 2-1	BILHAH 2-2
Judah (1)			
Zebulun (2)			
Issachar (3)			
Reuben (4)	JOSEPH:		
Simeon (5)	Ephraim (1)		
Levi (6)	Manasseh (2)		Dan (1)
	Benjamin (3)	Gad (1)	
		Asher (2)	Naphtali (2)

c. Modifications of rank through Jacob's blessings of Genesis 48-49.

Table 2.   Interpretations of rank within Israel based upon the texts of
Genesis 29-30, 34-35, and 48-49.

additional contrasts between Benjamin and all his brothers, Benjamin and Judah,
and finally Benjamin and Joseph.

We must note several reasons why Issachar and Zebulun do not figure more
prominently in the debate over succession, for in fact they provide the most direct
evidence for the rules of succession. Though Issachar and Zebulun are sons of Leah,
their appearance far down in the birth order places them in a quite ambiguous
position. If they applied a strict rule of ultimogeniture as a claim for succession
rights, their claim would be negated by Joseph and Benjamin. On the other hand, if
Issachar or Zebulun claimed rights only within the Leahite group, their case might
be stronger. These brothers, however, do not figure prominently in narrative action,

as do Reuben, Simeon, Levi, and Judah; they also receive short blessings from Jacob, an indication of their relative lack of importance. It seems reasonable, then, to connect the lists of Leah's sons in Table 2-a to create the list of Table 2-b. Their status is determined by birth order among Leah's true sons.

Considering Table 2-b further, one will note that Gad and Asher are placed below Issachar and Zebulun in the rank structure. This is because, regardless of actual birth order, a "true son" of Leah is of higher rank than a son born under a surrogate arrangement. This leads us to a significant principle regarding the status of wives. The rank of Jacob's "wives" including Leah, Rachel, and the concubines, is based upon the elder-younger distinction made for Leah and Rachel. The rank order of the wives, then, is Leah (eldest), Rachel (youngest), Zilpah (handmaiden of the eldest), and Bilhah (handmaiden of the youngest). Under this system, Reuben and Joseph are nearly equal in status, because they represent the firstborn sons of their mothers. Gad and Dan are in a similar juxtaposition, but neither can be considered of higher rank than any of the true sons of highborn women, even the sixth son of Leah. Finally, the second sons in each birth order reflect the same relationships of rank as those obtaining for first sons.

All of the cases of elder-younger distinction in Genesis form contrasts between pairs of sons, with the exception of the list of Leah's offspring in Table 2-b. As is so often the case, the exception informs us of the rule: Inheritance passes to the oldest "fit" son of the ranking wife. This rule accounts for the inheritance of Isaac, a case clearly stating maternal rank, as well as to the succession of Jacob over Esau. The problem with Esau as presented in the text is that he marries improperly. He is also depicted as a dullard. Jacob marries correctly, is smart, and *has the favor of his mother*. The rule, moreover, will explain why Judah comes into the inheritance of political prominence and "kingship" (Genesis 49:8–12).

We should recall that Abraham and Isaac each fully intended to see their elder sons receive inheritance, as did also Joseph when his sons were adopted by Jacob. It comes as a surprise to us, then, that Jacob should favor Joseph and Benjamin. This comes as an expression of Jacob's favor of Rachel over Leah, presents the same contradiction of later biblical law we have already observed in the case of Sarah versus Hagar (see above, pp. 27–28). But Jacob's blessing for Judah is consistent with later law, just as is the apparent solution of Abraham's domestic problem. Jacob also places Rachel's elder son over the younger, again following the sense of Abraham's feeling for Ishmael and Isaac's feeling for Esau. Indeed, Benjamin is dropped in the blessings with a one-liner. We shall view the curious logic through which Benjamin loses out to still younger "sons" in the course of this discussion. For the moment, let us note that if the "second son of the second wife" could claim superiority to the "fourth son of the first wife"—given the status changes of Reuben, Simeon, Levi, and Joseph—we would expect prominence to be heaped on Benjamin. But Jacob's blessings clearly adjust the ranks of his sons to a form approximating that of Table 2-c.

Jacob's blessings include Levi and Joseph to complete the twelve-tribe scheme. The presence of Manasseh and Ephraim is also signaled by two bits of literary information. First, the structure of the blessings has a clear center marker (Genesis

49:18). The order of blessings before the marker is: Reuben, Simeon and Levi, Judah, Zebulun, Issachar, Dan. After the center mark come Gad, Asher, Naphtali, Joseph, Benjamin. The order suggests a rhetorical inversion, though not a convincing one, of the form:

```
Reuben                        Benjamin
    Simeon/Levi                   *
        Judah              Joseph
            Zebulun    Naphtali
                Issachar  Asher
                    Dan  Gad
```

By placing Benjamin opposite Reuben we draw emphasis to the possibility of inserting Ephraim and Manasseh as implied sons opposite Simeon and Levi. Such an arrangement is also suggested by the alternative readings of the blessing of Joseph, beginning in most translations: Joseph is a fruitful bough by a well (creeper near a spring), whose branches run over the wall (whose tendrils climb over the wall). The alternative readings are: Joseph is a wild colt (wild donkey by a spring), a wild ass (wild colt) on a hillside.[9] The implications of such animal references parallel the usual reading in Judah's blessing for verse 11: He tethers his donkey (foal) to the vine, his purebred ass (ass's colt, foal of his she-ass) to the choicest vine. Judah's *and* Joseph's sons are incorporated into the blessings, and even the plant images of the standard reading of Joseph's blessing perform the reference to Ephraim and Manasseh well enough. But Joseph will be excluded from later enumerations of the tribes, unlike Judah, so the implied inclusion of his offspring in Genesis 49 is more critical.

If the rhetorical arguments for the inclusion of Ephraim and Manasseh in Jacob's blessings are insufficient, then the juxtaposition of their own blessing account in Genesis 48 offers other significant information. The blessing of the two boys involves three important elements. First, Jacob tells Joseph that he will make Ephraim and Manasseh his *own* sons "as much as Reuben and Simeon." Why not "as much as" Joseph? I call your attention to the fact that the narrative, by this time, has already excluded Joseph from the association of Israel—he is the secular leader of Egypt, second only to Pharaoh. The comparison to Reuben and Simeon suggests that Ephraim and Manasseh will replace Joseph in a more exact sense, as firstborn and second son in the rank order, displacing Benjamin. Joseph's blessing in Genesis 49 confirms the promise, bringing Benjamin into an alignment somewhere between Simeon and Gad on Table 2-c. My justification of this claim is based again on the proposed rhetorical alignment of Genesis 49:

```
Reuben                        Benjamin
    Simeon                (Ephraim/Manasseh)
        Judah              Joseph
            Zebulun    Naphtali
                Issachar  Asher
                    Dan  Gad
```

If Judah and Joseph are central elements in the structure, a reasonable assumption given the nature of their blessings, then a more perfect symmetry is achieved by aligning Zebulun and Issachar, as opposed to Asher and Naphtali. Such a change links the pairs Simeon/Levi, Ephraim/Manasseh, Judah/Joseph, Zebulun/Issachar, Asher/Naphtali. To whom, then, do Reuben, Dan, Gad, and Benjamin connect? The most natural reading of the blessings will link the pairs Reuben/Dan and Benjamin/Gad. This is because the thrust of Reuben's blessing is a *judgment;* he is reduced from his position as firstborn for violating his father's concubine. Dan is made a *judge* over his people, elevating him from his relatively low status to a position at least above that of Gad, who should by rank-of-mother be of higher status. Now compare the blessings of Gad and Benjamin:

> Gad, raiders will raid him
> and he will raid them in pursuit.
>
> Benjamin is a ravening wolf,
> in the morning he devours his prey,
> in the evening he divides the spoils.

The approximate parallels of conflict, raiding, and spoils bracket the second half of the blessings. The implication is one of uncontrolled behavior, like that of Reuben *except* that it seems less subject to judgment. Further, Joseph's sons are suggested by wild images, and Naphtali's short reference is to a "swift hind, dropping beautiful fawns." These are in contrast to the tethered asses of Judah, the restrained presence of Judah's own animal image, who "crouches like a lion, recumbent," and Simeon and Levi, who are ultimately controlled by being scattered (and "attached" as implied by Levi's name) in Israel.

The second element of the blessing of Ephraim and Manasseh is the justification given by Israel to Joseph: "I do this because, when I was returning from Paddan, your mother Rachel died, to my sorrow, during the journey in Canaan, while we were still a short distance from Ephrath; and I buried her there on the way to Ephrath" (that is, Bethlehem). Let us recall that Rachel died giving birth to Benjamin, who was then named by the nurse "Benoni" or "child of sorrow." Let us also recall that Joseph was favored over *all* of his brothers before being sold into slavery. The other derivation for Benjamin's name is "child of the right hand." This could mean the child *intended to be blessed* with the right hand. The notion is picked up again in Genesis 48:12–14:

> Joseph removed them (Manasseh and Ephraim) from his father's knees and bowed down before him with his face to the ground. Then Joseph took the two, Ephraim with his right hand, to Israel's left, and Manasseh with his left hand, to Israel's right, and led them to him. But Israel, crossing his hands, put out his right hand and laid it on the head of Ephraim, although he was the younger, and his left hand on the head of Manasseh, although he was the firstborn.

Benjamin's name, then, can be thought of as opening a breach between Benjamin and Joseph ("he may add") which is resolved in the blessings of Ephraim and

Manasseh. Ephraim and Manasseh are younger still than Benjamin. Israel's cross-ing his hands, as he might have once thought of doing for Joseph and Benjamin (thus conferring the blessing on Benjamin) has not been undone by Joseph's ultimate performance. After all, even Jacob was upset about Joseph's early dreams (Genesis 37:10). But the crossing of the hands, the third element of significance in the blessing, reaffirms the order Joseph/Benjamin by declaring a reversal of bless-ing for descendants from the Jacob-Rachel union. As we shall see, later lists confirm the order Ephraim-Manasseh-Benjamin.

The rank order list of Table 2-c reflects all of these changes, plus the elevation of Judah, Zebulun, and Issachar above all the other sons. Judah, Zebulun, and Issachar are to be seen as the ranking lineages descended from Leah, against whom no serious claim may be made by any other brother. Consider also that Zebulun and Issachar are reversed by the blessings, and through their blessings they can con-stitute no serious threat to Judah.

Names, Blessings, Rank, and Social Structure

The final rank order of Jacob's sons in Genesis defines three rough groupings. These are expressed in Figure 12a as a slight modification of Table 2-c. In the figure the distinction between Benjamin, Dan, and Gad is less blurred, reflecting the blessing order rather than blessing content. The groups, then, involve the true sons of Leah (without Levi), the true sons of Rachel (replacing Joseph with Ephraim and Manasseh), and the base grouping of the concubines' sons. The two major groups display structural parallels, in that the older sons are placed below younger sons. In the upper tier of each of these reversals is a secondary reversal which parallels Ephraim and Manasseh with Zebulun and Issachar. The reversal of Dan and Gad from their original status placements (based on their mothers' respective statuses) merely reaffirms the actual birth order of the men.

Four individuals on Figure 12a are marked with asterisks. These are the leaders of the camp groups of Israel described in Numbers 2, the structure of which is described in Figure 12b. Note that the tribal camp listings reflect the status assessments we have observed so far, as might well be expected of such an arrangement. The camp organization maintains the Leah/Rachel distinction except for the case of Asher, and the composition of each group runs in status order suggested by Genesis, except that Issachar and Zebulun appear again in the birth order of Genesis 30.[10]

The animal references imposed on the camp organization are from Genesis 49. The particular readings of Ephraim and Manasseh, though strained, were chosen to emphasize their relative blessings and to offer a parallel to the juxtaposition of Lion and Ass for Judah and Issachar. The meaning of Issachar's name, moreover, is related to the idea that Leah "hired" Jacob's favors by giving Rachel the mandrakes collected for Leah by Reuben. The literal meaning "I have hired you" (or "I have paid for you") is also a play on the obligations of conjugal rights owed to Leah by Jacob. In the legal language of the Mishpatim, such rights are stated in terms of concubinage, or female slavery. Indeed, the contractual basis of marriage and

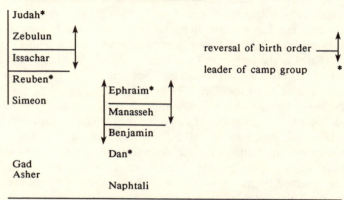

a. Genesis rank order showing reversals of inheritance and camp
   leaders of the Numbers 2 tribal organization.

East Group Judah's Camp	South Group Reuben's Camp	West Group Ephraim's Camp	North Group Dan's Camp
Judah (Lion) Issachar (Ass) Zebulun			
	Reuben Simeon		
	Gad	Ephraim (Colt) Manasseh (Ass) Benjamin (Wolf)	
	(Asher)		Dan (Serpent) Asher Naphtali (Hind)
LEAHITE ALLIANCES		RACHELITE ALLIANCES	

b. Numbers camp organization considered against Genesis rank
   order, also showing moieties based on maternal origin.

Figure 12.   The Genesis rank system compared to the organization of the camp of
Israel described in Numbers 2.

slavery are textually linked (see the laws from Exodus 21:1–11). Calum Carmichael
has read these laws in relation to the full narrative of Jacob's marriages, linking him
as a "slave" to Laban during the period of his brideservice.[11] This kind of reading,
together with the blessing of Issachar (Genesis 49:14–15) which makes him a
"slave," open the possibility that the camp groups and status groups of Figure 12
represent connubial circles. If the divisions are marriage circles, then they are also
consistent with the social-structural meanings of "Israel" developed earlier in this
chapter and represented in the model shown in Figure 11.

The meanings of names in each group of Figure 12b also develop themes
associated with the notion of justice. The issues involved in Leah's conflict with
Jacob and Rachel centered on conjugal rights, with each side claiming kinds of
justice or vindication. A full list, organized along the lines of the Numbers 2
material, is as follows:[12]

Ia.	Judah	I will give grateful praise (to the Lord)
Ib.	Issachar	I have hired you (also "my reward")
Ic.	Zebulun	a bridegroom's gift ("he will offer me presents")
IIa.	Reuben	he saw my misery
IIb.	Simeon	he heard (that I was unloved)
IIc.	Gad	what good luck
IIIa.	Ephraim	he has made me fruitful (in the land of my affliction)
IIIb.	Manasseh	he has made me forget (the sufferings I endured at the hands of my family)
IIIc.	Benjamin	son of the right hand ("son of sorrow")
IVa.	Dan	he has vindicated me (*dannanni*)
IVb.	Asher	what good fortune
IVc.	Naphtali	in a divine struggle I have struggled (*naptule elohim niptalti*)

The first group stems from Leah's feelings when she receives sons beyond the bounds of expectation. These are in a slight contrast to the second group, since Reuben and Simeon refer to God's answer to her unloved status while Judah, Issachar, and Zebulun all involve notions of "giving" or "rewarding." The first group, then, concentrates on Jacob's contractual fulfillments, while the second group stresses a more providential sense of solution for Leah's plight.

The names Gad and Asher are closely related in meaning and imply the capriciousness created by Jacob's lack of apparent intent to treat Leah fairly. This implication is given further force in the division of Zilpah's offspring between the two minor groups of the Leah and Rachel enclaves. In many societies a handmaiden, often a lesser kinswoman, would only be provided as a surrogate mother if a wife were barren. This is certainly the sense of Genesis in the instances of both Leah and Rachel, as earlier with Sarai who waited years before giving Hagar to Abram. The positioning of the names divides the notion of luck influencing the situation, adding to each woman's claim of vindication. The idea here is that the individual claims of Leah and Rachel come under scrutiny by God because of some unstated broader purpose, and so divine intervention mitigates apparent unfairness in Jacob's human relationships with his wives.

The third group of names presents the major Rachelite theme of struggle, contest, and affliction in terms of fraternal conflict. Unlike the first group, where stress is on Leah's relationship with Jacob, the meanings of the names Ephraim, Manasseh, and Benjamin refer directly to the relationships of Joseph to his brothers. The idea of "fruitfulness" as a sign of God's blessing, a common element throughout the naming process, is applied to emphasize the continuation of sororal strife in the later political relations among competing sons. The clear sense of Ephraim (fruitfulness) and Manasseh (forgetting) is one of political and social segmentation. This carries over into the naming of Dan and Naphtali, offering a central insight into the claims of vindication stated by Rachel and Leah. We see that Rachel's claim is posited through Bilhah's children, not through her *own sons* or their offspring. This is in stark contrast to Leah, who uses her own children as the strongest signs of vindication by God. Zilpah's children are explained as "good fortune" and spread between the halves of the society; Issachar and Zebulun are cited as just compensation and elevated to the foremost group of Israel.

What we encounter in Numbers 2 is a social formation in close keeping with the social sense of Genesis, including a moiety structure based upon maternal status, and submoieties based upon paternal blessing. The maternal associations are reinforced by names, while the paternal associations are developed through animal references and other features of blessings. The submoieties of the Rachelite divisions comprise sons of four women: Asenath, Rachel, Bilhah, and Zilpah. They thus rely on the differentiation of maternal statuses and perhaps suggest marriage circles deemed appropriate by virtue of the highborn statuses of Asenath and Rachel versus the lower status of Bilhah and Zilpah. The submoieties of the Leahite division differentiate her blessed offspring from those of less merit. The placement of Reuben and Simeon with a son of Zilpah signals their loss of status, and forms an understandable marriage division from the main group.

Intersecting Alliances of the Levites

Levi's removal from the social organization is not complete. The Levites remain one of the most important groups designated in narrative, and are the central subject of Numbers 3. On first inspection of the Levite lists, they appear to have the most elementary connection to the camp organization of Numbers 2: Gershon on the West, Merari on the North, and Kohath divided between the sons of Aaron on the East and the remainder on the South. These placements link the ranking Kohathite lineages with the camp of Judah, the lesser Kohathites with the camp of Reuben (again affirming the status of Leah), the next ranking lineage with the camp of Ephraim, and the least ranking lineage with the camp of Dan.

One will also note that the assignment of Levite cities in Joshua 21 does not appear to reinforce this pattern. These associations are as follows:

Kohath (Aaron)	Simeon		
		9 towns	Hebron
	Judah		
	Benjamin	4 towns	
Kohath (remainder)	Ephraim	4 towns	Shechem
	Dan	4 towns	
	Manasseh	2 towns	
Gershon	Manasseh	2 towns	Golan in Bashan
	Issachar	4 towns	
	Asher	4 towns	
	Naphtali	3 towns	Kedesh
Merari	Zebulun	4 towns	
	Reuben	4 towns	Bezer
	Gad	4 towns	Ramoth-gilead

On closer inspection, however, the town associations of Joshua 21 show an interesting relationship with the camp associations of Numbers 2–3. Each triad of tribes from the north, west, and south camps in Numbers shows a correspondence of at least two names with the groups providing cities for the Gershonites, the lesser Kohathites, and the sons of Merari; Judah, then, falls into association with Benjamin and Simeon in providing cities for Aaron's branch of the Kohathites, and with Issachar and Zebulun on the east side of the camp. Manasseh complicates the structure because its contribution of cities includes two groups (Ephraim-Manasseh-Benjamin and Manasseh-Issachar-Asher-Naphtali). The simple chains of names from the two sources can be organized into the regular geometric graph of Figure 13. The double lines running between Simeon, Judah/Reuben, and Zebulun indicate that the Judah and Reuben tribes are not associated directly in either list, while Manasseh is linked at the other central position to the west camp (Gershon), the Kohath cities, and the Gershon cities. Naphtali is associated only with the right side of the figure, the North (Merari) group and the Gershon cities.

The significance of the associations of Figure 13 is that the symmetries of Levite associations from Numbers 2–3 and Joshua 21 support a single system which is again consistent with birth-order and rank considerations from Genesis. The graph offers one possible image of cross-cutting Levite sodalities suggested strongly by Norman Gottwald's analysis of Israelite social structure.[13] There are several lines of evidence for this interpretation, as well as for the general adequacy of model as a demonstration of parallel social conceptions running between Numbers, Judges, and Genesis. The most direct evidence of the parallels lies in the absolute preservation of the Leahite and Rachelite moieties, groups which naturally emerge from the Genesis rank system (see again Table 2-c and Figure 12a). The crucial point is that the integration of Joshua's levitical cities does not disrupt the coordination of Numbers 2–3 tribal lists and the Genesis rank system, but provides instead an elaboration of the connections.

Second, the Levite model preserves the birth-order and rank treatments within the two groups. Thus, within Leah we may trace the sequence Judah-Issachar-Zebulun-Reuben-Simeon-Gad, a listing consistent with the rank-order assessment of sons representing Leah. The Rachelite groups, however, do not present a single maternal association, nor is such an association traceable on the graph. One must trace Ephraim-Manasseh-Benjamin (or Benjamin-Manasseh-Ephraim) and Dan-Asher-Naphtali (or Dan-Naphtali-Asher) in separate sequences, because of the absolute separation of Benjamin and Dan. The centrality and superiority of Judah is firm, since his juxtaposition to Reuben without actual connection signals the fact that he occupies the place of the first-born. This is in stark contrast to Manasseh's division across three groups, and his juxtaposition to the least ranking tribe, Naphtali.

Third, the connections of the two moieties are achieved by one tribe from each group. It is noteworthy that Benjamin and Issachar are both victims of blessing reversals by Israel. Benjamin, the "child of the right hand," was placed below Joseph (or, if one prefers, Ephraim and Manasseh) while Issachar was blessed after Zebulun. But their juxtapositions make sense in a more positive reading too. Benjamin and Issachar become central to the whole structure, and are connected to

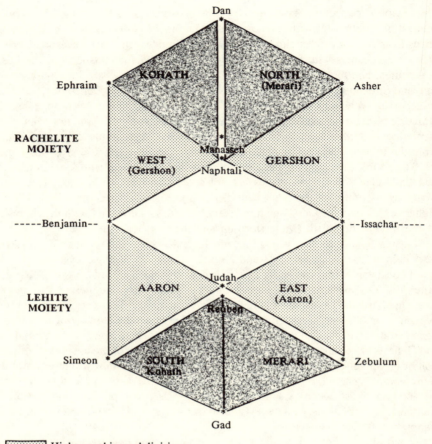

Figure 13.   Cross-cutting Levite subdivisions from Numbers 2-3 and Joshua 21 as a single system.

the two apparently most central Levite groups. Thus, their placements might be read as a reaffirmation of their birth-order positions over their younger kinsmen. Taken individually, Benjamin's associations to high-ranking Levites and to Judah suggest his possible birth-right claims as the only remaining true son of Rachel. Issachar's placement, aligning him with the "inferior" moiety, seems quite consistent with his blessing attributions as "Ass" and "slave."

Finally, the Levite rankings of Figure 13 show their own symmetry. The placement of the lesser Kohathites implies that they are of lower rank than Gershon, since it mirrors the placement of the Merari associations. The links of Kohath to the higher division of the Rachelite moiety are only partial in any event. The alternative interpretation is that the ranks derive from the listing orders of Numbers 4 and Joshua 21, but as we have seen in the case of the tribes, genealogical order of presentation is usually modified by other ranking features. We must note that the order of sons reported in Numbers 3:17 is Gershon-Kohath-Merari. Gershon was assigned responsibility for maintaining the tabernacle, the Tent, screens, hangings, and cords used in construction of the Tent (Numbers 3:21–26). Kohath was assigned care of the ark and other sacred equipment (Numbers 3:27–31). Merari was in charge of the structural frame of the tabernacle and other fittings (Numbers 3:32–37). This listing is consistent with the lineage rank order Gershon-Kohath-Merari, although one might argue that Kohath was assigned a more significant responsibility. The matter seems to be resolved in that the camp of Moses and Aaron, the group responsible for actual ritual performance, was listed last (Numbers 3:38). Thus, the order of treatment in Numbers 3 posits a birth-order justification of lineage rank, then draws the descendants of Aaron out of Kohath to give them ritual functions. The Numbers 4 and Joshua 21 lists elevate Aaron to the first position, and include the lesser Kohathites because they are not fully segmented from Aaron genealogically. They remained laymen, nonetheless, distinct in status from the descendants of Aaron and inferior to those of Gershon, at least in the context of Numbers 3:38.[14] From the point of view of Joshua 21, as we shall see, the distinction between Aaron and Kohath is territorial. The Levites clearly tie "Israel" together into a formal political system. Like so many other elements of Genesis, the event which appears initially to be a curse ends up being critical to achieving the final social association. In this case, the "scattering" of Levi through his blessing, and the meaning of his name ("attached"), are as significant to the fortunes of Israel as are the selling of Joseph into slavery in Egypt and the reversals of blessings which leave Judah virtually uncontested politically. It is no accident that these two brothers disappear from the original twelve tribe list, nor that Joseph's fortunes and Levite leadership dominate Genesis and Exodus.

Territory, Kingship, and Social Structure

We began this chapter by developing abstract models from relatively simple maps of places mentioned in Genesis. We shall now move from social models to maps, using the birth-order lists and ranking features of Figures 12 and 13 to present an interpretation of territorial alliances within the Israel defined in Joshua 13–21. Also, in order to better understand the forms of relationship created in territorial alliances, it will be helpful to consider some of the basic categories of social organization reviewed by Norman Gottwald in his comprehensive treatment of Israel's political system (Figure 14).[15]

The basic unit proposed by Gottwald within "Israel" (and potentially other larger constructs) is the *shēvet,* a term which from biblical usage glosses essentially as "tribe." Because of many common and unfortunate notions associated with the term "tribe," we are better served by using the term *shēvet.* This organization comprised a number of smaller divisions, *mishpāhāh,* which were made up of territorially linked families which Gottwald considers "protective associations." Relationships

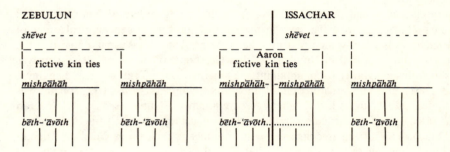

| *shēvet* -- | "tribal" associations of territorially linked *mishpāhāh* organized around fictive kinship assertions which rank leaders of the groups (hence the groups) according to similar logic to that used with known relationships. |

| *mishpāhāh* -- | protective associations of families, usually territorially linked, which probably also serve as local marriage circles stressing group endogamy, lineage exogamy, and especially the practice of distant parallel-cousin marriage. |

| *bēth-'āvōth* -- | extended family networks and lineages organized around known kinship ties and possessing strong alliance ties to other families of the *mishpāhāh*. |

Figure 14. Proposed social arrangement of Levite lineages in tribal organization of Israel (based on Gottwald).

between *mishpāhāh* constitute alliances which could have been asserted by fictive kinship ties, but among ranking families likely were also grounded in actual marriages. The primary marriage group was probably the *mishpāhāh*, with regular marriages occurring between the distantly related agnatic associations of the families, the *bēth-'āvōth*. Thus, from the perspective of the family association, marriages were exogamous, but from the perspective of territorial groupings, village or the *mishpāhāh* alliances, marriages were apparently statistically endogamous.[16] The degree of agnatic connection between the extended families of the *mishpāhāh* need not have been great, and would likely have been at considerable genealogical distance. The political significance of a particular family, then, would have been determined through variable genealogical reckoning in family traditions. This context is the likely source for the kind of narrative used in establishing higher-order fictive ties among the different *mishpāhāh* to justify inclusion in a particular *shēvet*. Hence, the traditions creating the organization at the level of the *shēvet* would have been mainly fictive, while those justifying the *mishpāhāh* asserted many real relationships in telescoped versions. Everyday political alliances, in this context, were created by taking a distant real or fictive *agnate* group as the source of a marriage, creating close affinal association.[17]

The position of Levites within a *shēvet* was based upon territorial association. If we presume a similar organization of Levite families to that for the divisions tracing to a particular eponymous ancestor, then a situation such as that shown in Figure 14 emerges. Ordinary *mishpāhāh* within the *shēvet* employ a fictive tradition to justify their current alliance composition, which includes several "attached" groups of Levite lineages similarly organized in *mishpāhāh*. The Levite traditions, however, tie themselves back to one of the sons of Levi, thus giving them a basis for claiming close relationships to lineages allied with other *sheᵛvatim*. The connections of these groups to the host *shēvet* could involve intermarriage, and their performance of religious duties for the united *shēvet* or subdivisions comprised of several *mishpāh-āh* groups would further reinforce their attachment and the collective identity of the largest scale alliances. On the other hand, the fictive ties of ancestry from either Aaron, Gershon, Kohath, or Mirari, would open the possibility of forming close marriage alliances across *shēvet* boundaries. We cannot say if a Levite association in adjacent *sheᵛvatim* did act as though they constituted a single *mishpāhāh,* as Figure 14 suggests, but classificatory equation through fictive ancestry of this type occurs in many societies. Given the specialized religious functions of Levite groups, we can expect that they felt strong affinity which could be turned into real political action.

The historical background for the formation of such groups is difficult to assess, for they could have formed through two different processes. First, it is possible that "Levites" represent what Gottwald calls a "bottom-up" process of social formation. In this case the Levite *mishpāhāh* would have originated as a typical group in a territorial alliance, but would secondarily have taken on religious functions. The original justification for religious specialization would be based on any criteria, and could have involved diverse cosmologies, gods, or kinship justifications within the *shēvet*. Given similarly based groups in different large-scale territorial associations, a leader or group seeking means of unification on a higher level could have instituted fictive kinship justifications for the religious *mishpāhāh* of a region. The second, or "top-down" process would involve creation of diverse *sheᵛvatim* from a very large collection of previously unallied territorial groups, and the installation of a priestly class oriented toward particular religious and political goals. The cross-cutting political organization created by the priests, along with the other features of state organization, could then be justified in a unified tradition of origins citing largely fictive kinship ties.

Each of these models has some merit, though the bottom-up model seems more likely given the occurrence of so many similar cross-cutting alliance organizations in human societies, including those of the Near East. If we interpret the religion of Yahweh as an ideological system which was adopted by extant groups, perhaps at the instigation of a powerful territorial association within the region, then a combination of the two models is possible. Such a process would merely involve extension of the principles of *shēvet* formation in group religious association to a larger scale of social identification. The consistency of links between God and patriarch or God and king is a striking feature of biblical literature. For example, the *Mishpatim* includes a rule which states "You shall not revile God, nor curse a prince of your people" (Exodus 22:27), while Jezebel instigates the false charge that "Naboth has cursed God and king" (I Kings 21:13). Thus, the Levites represent, either as an autochthonous development or a political movement, one of the best means of linking what would otherwise be independent, fluid, and potentially hostile enclaves of territorial polity in the Canaanite region.

When we viewed the organization of the Israel camp we observed that the triads of tribes, in addition to forming groups based upon rank, look like potential marriage groups. We may refine this statement by saying that the description looks like a *justification* of marriage groups. The Joshua 21 groups, though clearly intended to be territorial, also suggest marriage groups. Given our observations about the organization of the *shēvet*, we might well now ask: Marriages of whom? The answer to this question, I believe, is marriages of Levites working through the structure suggested in Figure 14. When we produce a list of the Levite associations posited for each tribe in the descriptions of Numbers and Joshua, we find that each tribe except Judah possesses two associations:

TRIBE	Joshua 21	Numbers 2–3
Judah	Aaron	Aaron
Issachar	Gershon	Aaron
Zebulun	Merari	Aaron
Reuben	Merari	Kohath
Simeon	Aaron	Kohath
Gad	Merari	Kohath
Ephraim	Kohath	Gershon
Manasseh	Kohath	Gershon
Benjamin	Aaron	Gershon
Dan	Kohath	Merari
Asher	Gershon	Merari
Naphtali	Gershon	Merari

Only three pairs of tribes have identical associations, Reuben-Gad, Ephraim-Manasseh, and Asher-Naphtali. Additionally, Dan-Gad (Reuben) and Issachar-Benjamin have reversed associations of the same two Levite groups. On the maps locating the tribes in Canaan we find Reuben-Gad, Ephraim-Manasseh, and Asher-Naphtali closely co-located, while Dan is separated from Gad (Reuben) and Issachar is separated from Benjamin.

Maps showing the individual territorial placements of the twelve tribes and Levites, according to the two lists of associations, are presented in Figure 15. The territorial nature of the Joshua 21 material (Figure 15a) is clear enough. The only unusual feature is the inclusion of Zebulun in the Merari group with Gad and Reuben. The territorial plot of Numbers 2–3 is less convincing on first glance, since both the Aaron group and the Kohath group are separated by territory for Gershon. Combined, the territories form a mosaic in which Aaron dominates from Zebulun south on the west side of the Jordan, Kohath covers the area surrounding Judah and Benjamin to the south of Ramoth-Gilead, Gershon covers all of the north except the territory of Zebulun, and Merari presents an association north of Zebulun and east of the Jordan. Only the Merari territory is completely broken by the intervening territory of Gershon, assigned in both lists to the northeast extension of the territory of Manasseh.

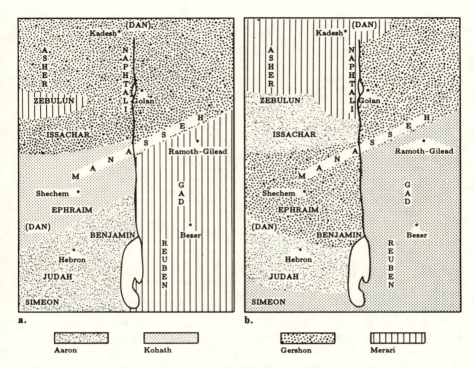

Figure 15. Distribution of Levites by tribal territories of Joshua 13-21: (a) Levite associations listed in Joshua 21, (b) Levite associations in camp lists of Numbers 2-3.

The associations of the cities of refuge are asymmetrical. Hebron is the only city of refuge tied to Aaron; note also that Judah is exclusively associated with the Aaronite priesthood. Golan in Basha is linked to Gershon exclusively, and Gershon shares associations with the minor groups in Shechem and Kadesh. Kohath and Merari also share association with Bezer and Ramoth-Gilead, completing a pattern of three cities each for Gershon, Kohath, and Merari. The division of the Levites into four groups is produced by bifurcation of the Kohath group, but the placement of the Aaronites suggests that the division is more political than religious. This could mean that the territorial conception of Aaron was intended to reinforce the primacy of a particular group, not only Aaron but Judah. It could also mean that the depiction of the Levites in Numbers and Joshua was intended in the tradition to impose the moiety structure on the twelve tribe scheme. The genealogical treatment of the tribes producing a rank structure, then, would come after the formation of the priesthood as a separate justification, drawing from pertinent shared regional narratives. These social-organizational data suggest that Genesis, as a part of the Hexateuch and perhaps other biblical material, was compiled very late.

Indeed, the underlying Levite structure of the Genesis genealogies for Jacob/Israel is suggested by the territorial images they produce (see Figure 16a). Using the birth-order as a basis for plotting connections of groups which are placed according

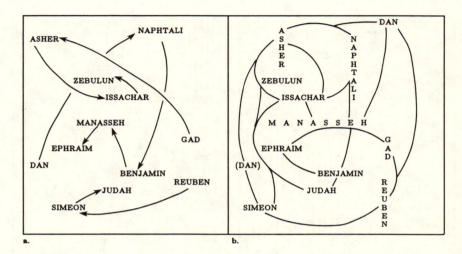

Figure 16. Territorial alliance circles implied by (a) birth-order reported in Genesis, and (b) Levite correspondences of Numbers 2-3 and Joshua 21.

to Joshua's territorial association, we find three key groups. On the south, the Reuben-Simeon-(Levi)-Judah birth order yields the Kohath division. The remaining Leahite sons, Gad-Asher-Issachar-Zebulun, form a similar back-and-forth pattern tied to all four Levite groups. Finally, the Rachelite birth order Dan-Naphtali-Benjamin-Manasseh-Ephraim produces a crossing pattern which also includes all four Levite groups. Through this diagram we view only a segmented alliance system, but the parts are consistent with the moiety reversals of Dan from Gad and Reuben, the Levite social-territorial identity of Asher and Naphtali, and the identity of priestly associations for Manasseh and Ephraim. Further, Gad and Reuben are the firstborn sons of the two Leahite mothers, share adjacent space, and have identical moiety divisions. If we presume the Levite links of Numbers and Joshua, all of the maternally-based "tribal" connections on Figure 16a represent *possible* Levite alliances, and only the Gad-Asher tie posits a link not directly stated in Numbers or Joshua.

The alliance structure of the Levites suggested by Numbers 2–3 and Joshua 21 (Figure 16b) is more complete than the series of Genesis connections but does not change the essential alliance picture greatly. Moreover, as we have already observed, the inclusion of Levi in Genesis, only to have him dropped from the twelve tribe list, seems as noteworthy as the inclusion of Joseph, especially in view of the prominence of Levites in the remainder of the Torah. To the extent the Genesis narratives and genealogies present an "Israel" structured by Levite principles, Genesis offers a justification for state-level, not tribal, political organization.

A natural organization for a state-level system built from a tribal base involves the symbolic segmentation of one major group from the general pattern of association, creating a hierarchic organization through which tributes, military cooperation, and the settlement of disputes may flow. Such an organization can be cemented by strategic marriages down to the ordinary tribes, as well as through forms of institutionalized power including, among other things, religious organizations and warrior societies. Such an organization is suggested for "Israel" by the definition of Judah as unparalleled in rank, the exclusive association of Judah with the Aaronite priesthood, and the total control of the Aaronites over Hebron, one of the four principal loci of the Abraham-Isaac-Israel narratives.

Given the primacy of Judah in the political assessments of Genesis, the centrality of Judah in the Joseph narrative (a feature we will observe in a later chapter), and the apparent state-level justification Genesis forms in its larger biblical context, a political placement of the text after the time of David seems likely. How far after is uncertain, but the broad design of the Torah, including Leviticus and Deuteronomy, suggests that Genesis could easily be exilic or postexilic. The focus of the constructions, however, is squarely on the political legitimation of Judah, hence the line of David. The Davidic period is certainly a time when a priesthood such as that suggested by the texts *could* have operated, but we must keep in mind that our picture of the actual situation, even in the "historical" books, is somewhat idealized. As far as a mechanism for the social formation of Levite priesthoods in Israel is concerned, the text must relate to some actual historical process. To review my view of the process, I see the potential for political unification of Israel as a state taking advantage of the extant religious structures within fluid confederacies at the organizational level of the *shēvet*. But there is strong textual evidence for the occurrence of an essentially "top-down" process which either co-opted or replaced local religious leadership. The result of this essentially political reorganization, which undoubtedly would have required some tribal redefinition, is a unified biblical compilation involving, at the least, Genesis, Exodus, Numbers, and Joshua, but potentially also incorporating the books of Samuel and Kings.

A unified biblical tradition working to justify Judean hegemony could come from many periods and represent many kinds of historical or political documents. Genesis could simply be a fictional, kinship justification of Judean kingship produced during the time from David to Solomon. But we must ask why such a document would have been created? If David's kingship was institutionally and militarily secure, why justify the unifying structure in a written document? Such an instrument would seem of relatively little utility at the beginning of a social reformation, and superfluous after the fact. Considered against such documents as the Magna Charta or the Declaration of Independence, the thrust of the writing seems aimed in the wrong direction. If the broad composition is intended to assert the balancing authority of a priesthood, however, then we might better understand Genesis as coming from a Davidic context.

Genesis and related traditions could also intend to justify a kind of kingship, using the Davidic period as a prime model and example. In this case the "history" presented by the documents may never have occurred except in the most superficial sense. Such a series of documents would be quite natural at the end of a period of hegemony, or more likely after the dissolution of a state-level confederation. We would also expect them to display high degrees of coordination, so that the "history" presented would prefigure and, in this case, theologically justify the intended ideal social organization. The uncanny prefigurement of Davidic problems in Genesis narrative—not to mention the social-organizational connections we have just viewed—suggest that Genesis is part of such a tradition. If this is true, then biblical representation of myth and history are one system, and we may never be able to tell if the suggested "top-down" organization of Levite priesthoods was historical reality or mere ideological desire.

III

STRUCTURAL HERMENEUTICS

The people of every culture have characteristic ways of expressing meanings. A century of anthropological scholarship has refined this point. Crossing a cultural boundary, we argue, is like crossing into a different world, because the significant things, classifications, perceptions of events, flows of behavior, and expressive forms are changed. It is easy to underestimate the difficulty of moving across cultural boundaries. This is especially true when we encounter the artifacts of past cultures, including literary compositions such as Genesis. The signs concatenated by other minds, created in the poetic forms of an ancient language from everyday experiences, come to us as a cultural fragment. To add to the difficulty, unlike the stone tools and ceramic vessels unearthed by archaeologists, historically intermediate or modern views of the original Genesis are imbedded in the organization and language through which most of us usually experience the "artifact."

Indeed, the "original" Genesis was not the book we know at all. Form critics tell us that Genesis was brought together from a wide range of documents, originally representing different times and peoples.[1] The documentary pieces which found their way into the tradition include many stories and genealogical segments that were drawn from oral traditions, while some appear to be "literature" in the strict sense of the term. Sometimes we see the tantalizing evidence of several "strands" of tradition in single stories, together with editorial "stitching" that holds the narrative tapestry together. Sometimes the apparent "voices," "authors" and "editors" vanish into the page, yielding a sense of scriptures etched by one hand. What we mean by the "original" Genesis, then, can be several different things. It could mean the broad tradition and values underlying the actual pieces of text that found their way into the document. It could mean the manuscripts comprising parts of the "original" complete form we know as Genesis, or the full Hebrew text we suspect they represent. It might even mean the Hebrew book in its Torah context, or the established translations of Genesis in our modern world.

Of course, our modern texts offer a medieval systematization of Genesis, the artifacts of which we see in chapter and verse numberings, Hebrew section marks, and paragraphing. As translations, moreover, they recast the original documents into terms which are not only intelligible to us, but are conveniently fit to our cultural and religious predispositions. Because of the theologies behind our reading, "original" meanings in Genesis are often irrelevant, or come into play as assertions unjustified by any consideration of ancient cultural background. Over the centuries, as the understandings of each era have brought forth doctrine, new translations have offered inspired reinterpretations of the words of biblical narrative. Today, then, we must contend with biblical justifications for beliefs quite foreign to Genesis, but read into its verses by the translator's cultural heart. All these things fragment our appreciation of the artifact before us.

In a very real sense, like archaeologists approaching the excavation of an archaeological site, we must consider how we will destroy Genesis in order to encounter it. Will we take it apart in the method of the form critics, attending to cultural strata and the structures of narrative disconformity, intrusion, and mixing? Will we treat Genesis as a unified order, attempting to rectify the blurred images produced in our translations, by mapping its general narrative topography? Will we seek historical process or synchronized pattern? And how will we resolve the archaeological ties between pattern and process?

The outcome of biblical interpretation changes radically when we take the established text of Genesis as a very specific cultural product, unrelated to its historical transformations. If we drop religious claims and theological readings, seeking instead something like a "general cultural intention" behind the composition, then we must immediately become concerned with the literary structures binding the whole collection of scriptures together. But our treatment of structure radically changes when we take the premise that the "original" composition served a narrow circle of readers in a narrow historical timespan.

My readings of Genesis structure do not give priority to the interpretive backgrounds of genre, style, or "form." I seek instead the textual features which provide consistency or continuity of story, rhetorical completeness, and structural precision. This approach is similar to the kind of reading which brought about medieval divisions of the text, divisions which served a holistic conception of narrative flow. I will not totally disregard the useful information gained in the dissections of documentary theorists and form critics. If we took away Stephen Langton's parsing of Genesis and started renumbering from scratch, we would probably agree to end Genesis 1 a few verses after its present terminus, just as many other divisions of the text would be changed on literary grounds.[2] But in my conception of chapter organization, we would not take away Langton's assumption of unity in the way Gunkel's reorganization of sources did, or in the way many of our arguments about myths, fables, genealogies, sagas, and poems do today. Too often, we forget to ask the critical question: Why are whatever units we see found in the particular order in which they occur?

Rhetorical Structures and Cultural Themes

In the preceding chapters I took advantage of particular kinds of kinship and place reports to show formal relationships between narrative, historical construction, and kinship organization. The analysis relied upon a notion of "structure" which was only partly dependent on the text of Genesis. That is, I did not always tap the narrative system of Genesis in forming my broader arguments. Now I want to ask the questions: Does Genesis reflect an overall rhetorical structure? And if so, what is its form and what rules apply to the interpretation of narrative parts in the system? I contend that the answer to the first question is yes, and offer the redactional arguments of my first chapter as part of the evidence. But my more radical thesis is that the formal structure of Genesis is more well-ordered than most form critics would admit, and that it has been appreciated in part by various readers through the ages. Had such a structure not existed sufficiently to be seen, then Genesis would not have maintained its position in the Torah or maintained its power for non-Jewish readers. Hence, this chapter stresses my particular reading of the overall structure of Genesis, and the identification of rhetorical rules which seem to have inspired the narrative order we encounter.

I should now point out that an "ideal" structure for Genesis is consistent with the results of documentary theory, but that we are confronted with other signs of its presence every time we read and cite the text. The medieval divisions of the text, Christian and Jewish, mark the common sense of narrative organization in the book, providing us with a head start toward formal tracing of a broad systematic organization. As we have already observed, our "more-perfect" literary judgment might put us at variance with the details of Stephen Langton's view of the text, but we would also be hard pressed to radically revise his scheme. As we shall see, Langton's divisions make sense and are consistent with the marks of rabbinic reading when organized into an ideal pattern. My structural reading of Genesis is "new" only in that it assumes medieval readers saw something pertinent to an overall system and that it attempts to outline some of what they saw.

Once given a general structure, my interpretive direction is quite different from that of most criticism. I have tried to go beyond the task of outlining, or the historically interesting scrutiny of Stephen Langton's mind, to link an ideal structure to the social and political conceptions already developed in earlier analyses. In this aspect of my reading, then, I remain convinced that Genesis is a very political book—a unified genealogy supported by carefully selected narrative. Since my stress stays with political themes, it remains for me to introduce some orienting points of methodology for cultural analysis, specifically Morris Opler's "theory of themes."

Several anthropologists have constructed theories of culture based in linguistic analogies. The structuralist circles inspired by the work of Claude Lévi-Strauss are notable mainly for a quasi-linguistic method. In his approach to myth analysis, Lévi-Strauss argues that *only* linguistics has developed a scientific method for analysis of cultural performance, and that the method should be extended to discourse to achieve similar precision in the study of cultural meanings. This form of structural analysis, however, has been soundly critiqued for its lack of operational connection between structure and meaning. The analyst, it seems, is left too free to give conjectures the aura of scientific precision. The late work of Clyde Kluckholn developed a similar formal linguistic metaphor, like Lévi-Strauss's work inspired by the mathematical orientation to phonology of the Prague linguistic circle.[3] Kluckholn, together with Ruth Benedict and Morris Opler, is generally associated with the analytic orientation in anthropology called "configurationalism." This approach asserts that each society possesses a limited set of popularly shared orientations which are stated informally through behavior, or formally in anthropological descriptions as an array of premises, postulates, or, to use Opler's term, "themes." Though similar to structuralism in many ways, the configurationalist circle expresses a much stronger sense that cultural description bridges scientific explanation with humanistic understanding.

I draw from Opler's conception of "themes" because he recognizes, more than any of the others, the distinction between elucidation of structure and interpretation of meanings.[4] Structural elucidation in language studies is performed to show *how* meanings are produced rather than *what* meanings are possible. Linguists stress that the interpretation of meaning from structure rests almost entirely with the individual speaker/hearer. This essential semiotic point undermines the claims of some anthropologists that meaning can be derived directly from structure. In my view of themal analysis, one begins with structural study to determine how to read features of behavior, physical organization, or narrative, and then one proceeds to interpretations from other cultural backgrounds using structure to contain or guide the kinds of logical associations generating meanings. As applied to Genesis, I seek first to describe the rules of composition, then to read against each other the passages that are brought into systemic juxtaposition. In such analysis, meaning is derived from structure only in the sense that the broad pattern of the narrative suggests themal domains which deserve attention. I may share orientation with other readers from different times, places, and cultures, but any justification of how my meanings fit with theirs is a separate issue from the basic literary analysis.

My method may create uneasiness among many readers, since it joins the tasks of delimiting structural principles and circumscribing expressive domains appropriate to meanings. For this reason, I apply the term "reading" rather than "interpretation" to the result of the work. The idea of "reading" reminds us that no matter what elements of structure we formally recognize, even if they are blatantly intentional, they operate on a subconscious level in everyday encounters with the text. Normally, then, meanings of a scripture on successive readings can be different because of selections of scriptural context, the durations of each reading event, the nature of surrounding activities, or the effects of meanings derived from prior readings. And so the text is always the same, and never the same.[5] But the method, far from dropping us into an abyss of uncertainty, invites us to consider the means we possess to formally trace the elements of our textual experience.

If we can trace the experience, then we have better hope of controlling it. We tend to be conditioned to think in linear ways, for example, moving from point to point and expecting cues of causality, connectedness in time, or explicit centrality of purpose. Other cultures often have quite different conceptions of how to structure an effective argument. Among many Native American groups, an argument designed to convince may not include any direct reference to the subject or specific logical connectors between points. The structure of such argument is said to be like a wheel with spokes—each spoke consists of an argument pertinent to the whole, the "hub" or central point remaining unstated, a matter for the hearer to fill into the formula. Similarly, arguments intended to persuade often include disclaimers of expertise as a means of authenticating individual authority. There are examples of similar practices in biblical literature, such as the introduction to the speeches of Elihu in Job 32:6–22. Such devices work because they are an expected part of the system of argumentation, understood tacitly by all the participants in the communicative setting.

Other signs of different rhetorical or literary practices in biblical literature include the apparent composition of legal proverbs, such as occur in Deuteronomy, under the inspiration of readings of Genesis narratives or other biblical writings.[6] The resulting "laws" then replicate the interests of the narratives and hence jump from topic to topic without a clear topical order. We also encounter various "inversion" principles in the composition of prose and poetic material at several levels of narrative organization, the inversion patterns being cued by sound, word repetitions, reversal of phrasing or topic order, and even occasionally by nonfunctional "marker verses" or abrupt shifts in linguistic form. When a text includes such nonlinear cues, the "whole" organizational sense becomes very much more important to our understanding than the immediate linear order of units.[7] Thus, when we formally approach Genesis, our "analysis" and "reading" are often fundamentally one activity.[8] I must clearly concur in the view that the experience of reading the text should be a natural and active process—an activity in which the logical structure is not consciously overemphasized. On the other hand, it is nonsensical to say that any "analysis" of the text is destined to produce false meanings. An awareness of conventions of narrative structure is simply more likely to produce links between "scriptural events" which were intended logically to go together. The analytical process, then, is one of demystification, recognizing that mystical experience is the cultural realization of profound meanings without awareness of their conventional sources. Through a heavy application of common sense, in the end, we can turn mystery into a formal grasp of what was once perhaps quite obvious.

Structural Patterns in Genesis 1–14

We have observed already the ways genealogical material in Genesis is structured to create a life-cycle "punctuation" for the text, and how the substance of narrative contributes to the formation of ideal characterizations of social organization. On a larger scale, some of the same pattern-forming devices create parallels among story sections, contribute to theological meanings, generate a sense of anticipation and fulfillment, and develop irony. It would be absurd, of course, to argue that any one organizing principle is central to meanings in these scriptures; but it is fair for us to ask what structures account for basic meanings in long scriptural sequences. Should there not be some relatively simple, large-scale patterns running through the text?

Conventional treatment of the structure of Genesis posits four major units. First, the materials from Genesis 1–11 are recognized as quite distinct from the remainder of the book, comprising the "mythic" section as opposed to the supposedly "historical" sections commencing with the travels of Abraham. The second section is the Abraham story, beginning in Genesis 12 and continuing through Genesis 25. Third, the Jacob story includes chapters 25 through 36. Finally, the Joseph story completes the book in chapters 37 through 50. These textual divisions are supported, though imperfectly, by the *toledoth* formulae—the linguistic pattern usually glossed "these are the generations of" or "this is the story of"—as well as by kinship reports we observed in detail in the first two chapters of this book.[9]

I want to argue now that these divisions are by no means so crisp as our usual treatment of narrative structure suggests, and that they form part of a larger, more regular narrative rhythm which unites all of Genesis. My discussion is divided into two parts. First, we will consider the structure of Genesis 1–14, a rather unconventional "unit" within the traditional view of the book. Second, we will move to a full treatment of Genesis, based on implications from the analysis of the first 14 chapters. Throughout, I shall use the Langton chapter divisions of Genesis, not because they offer a perfect system, but because they are convenient and commonly understood points of reference. Stephen Langton's reading of the text, if the chapter divisions he introduced stand as its signs, seems to have tapped into many of the narrative unit breaks pertinent to essential story transformations of Genesis as a unity.

Several form critics have recently presented large-scale narrative structures for sections of Genesis, giving special attention to the literary device known as *chiasmus*.[10] Chiasmus introduces a series of conditions and events as a linear sequence without necessarily bringing each element to an immediate logical conclusion. The series is formally "concluded" in inverted order. There are several ways to show such relationships graphically. For example, the sequence A, B, C, D . . . D', C', B', A' may be graphed in these two ways:

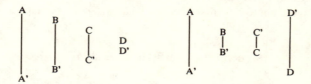

The lines show relationships among the nested story units.

The crossing pattern of the second graph is reminiscent of the Greek letter "chi"—hence the term "chiasmus" is applied. Such a graph helps us see the nonlinear connections of units in a long narrative sequence. The units of a story developed on such principles might be spoken of as a constellation. The meaning of any segment in the constellation, then, is more dependent upon the broad structural syntax than upon immediate juxtaposition with other segments in a linear sequence. Ideally, a chiastic reading of a text would seek to account for all of the material in a connected linear sequence. An alternative approach would account for relationships through reference to particular domains of representation, such as the organization of kinship reports presented in Figures 4 and 5. Since other kinds of linguistic structure cross-cut this kind of text construction, I have attempted to build arguments for chiastic organization on as consistent an application of stylistic, themal, or linguistic evidence as possible, offering a weight of evidence for the whole constellation.

When I began this work, there was no immediate textual reason for selecting Genesis 1 through 14 for analysis, although elements of inversion are clearly visible in the Noah story. The Hebrew text includes a major section mark at the end of chapter 11, as well as numerous minor division marks in chapters 1, 3, 5, 8, 10, 11, and 12. There are also minor marks separating chapters 13–14 and 14–15, but the terminal mark of Genesis 14 is unexceptional. The next major Hebrew division comes after the Covenant of Circumcision in chapter 17.

Source critical considerations originally directed my attention to the Genesis 1–14 unit. The creation story and the story of Abram's rescue of Lot are both attributed to the Priestly authors, although they individually represent quite different literary styles. But these stories offer opposing ideas, creation and upheaval, which parallel the themes of destruction and replenishment of the Noah story. Thus, what we encounter in the text—and what Stephen Langton apparently saw—are two groups of stories and genealogies beginning with fundamental events of creation/replenishment, and ending with events of destruction/upheaval. Using the narrative junctures and topical connections of the pieces as a guide, these blocks became Genesis 1–7 and Genesis 8–14. The outer brackets of the structure punctuate the constellation, forming a pair of "order" to "chaos" oppositions:[11]

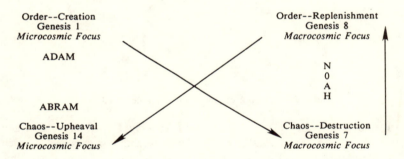

The other elements in the two narrative blocks are brought into chiastic alignment centering on Genesis 4 and 11, the elements occupying the central point of the constellation. This contrasts three narrative segments: (a) the Adam sequence dealing with the creation and life in Eden, (b) the Noah story, (c) the stories of Abram's travels outside Canaan from his central camp positions at Bethel/Ai and Hebron/Mamre. Precise elements of direct relationship between the two narrative blocks, viewed here as simple chapter oppositions, are graphically outlined in Figure 17. The figure stresses the vertical associations of the two texts, but note that the four punctuating units also operate independently by paralleling chapters 1 and 8, as opposed to 7 and 14. The first narrative block deals with a "macrocosmic" world, the locations within which are not firmly fixed, while the second block more carefully locates the patriarchs in a new, "microcosmic" terrain. The idea of cycles

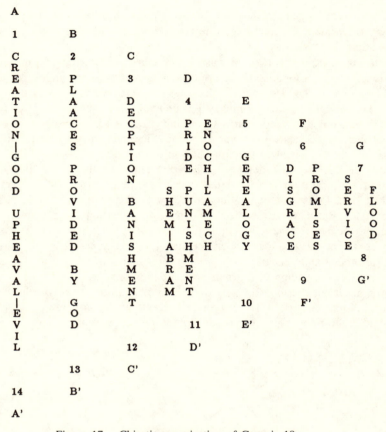

Figure 17.   Chiastic organization of Genesis 19.

of birth and death, then, is introduced with striking forcefulness as a general principle in creation. The narrative moves from the chthonic existence of Genesis 1:1–2 to the world beyond history destroyed by the watery forces from which it emerged, to a world we can "know" in a very direct sense. The vertical links of the chiastic formula form a bridge between what is intended to be myth and history, showing how the character and situation of humanity is ultimately tied to the forces unleashed by the gods. Let us view these links in more detail.

Genesis 1 and 14

The story of the creation and the story in which Abram rescues his kinsman Lot possess no stylistic parallels. Indeed, Genesis 14 is one of the most distinctive stories in all of the patriarchal narratives, as we have observed with regard to its place references (see again Table 1). On a themal level, however, the stories can be related to each other. The creation represents an ordered process, and is clearly associated with a notion of *good*. The disorganization of warfare is not an absolute opposite of creation, as is the absolute destruction of Genesis 7; but the features of armies routed, captives taken, bloodshed, and tension between even those not at war, all serve as a contrast to the images of creation. Genesis 14 also introduces the idea of *evil* through the appearance of the king of Sodom and his treatment by Abram (Genesis 14:21–24):

> Then the king of Sodom said to Abram, "Give me the people, and take the possessions for yourself." But Abram said to the king of Sodom, "I swear to the Lord, God Most High, Creator of heaven and earth, that I will not take so much as a thread or a sandal strap, or anything that is yours, lest you say, "It is I who made Abram rich." For me, nothing but what my servants have used up; as for the share of the men who went with me—Aner, Eshkol, and Mamre—let them take their share.

In addition to the mention of creation, we find also an appearance by Melchizedek (a theophoric name, "my king" [i.e., the diety] is *sedeq*) who blesses Abram in the name of God Most High (El Elyon). We may also note that the *order/good* and *upheaval/evil* opposition further implies a subtle interplay of themes in the broader narrative context: with the creation of man a potential "evil" is inserted into the primal world, while amid the chaos of Abram's world there is potential righteousness. These ideas are strengthened in Abram's intercession for Lot (Genesis 18), the promise of God after the flood which cites inherent human evil (Genesis 8:21), the curse of men before the flood (Genesis 6:5).

Genesis 2 and 13

The story of the garden in Eden is juxtaposed against the separation of Abram and Lot and the promise of the land to Abram and his descendants. The stories clearly possess parallel themes of "a place being provided" for the selected ones of God, a key element in the continuing territorial interests of Genesis. There are also some specific topical parallels between the two texts. The river in Eden is divided into four principal streams, and the "well watered" plain of Jordan is described as "like the garden of the Lord." There is also mention of the four directions in the description of the land given to Abram. The streams span the length and breadth of the region, while Abram is told to travel throughout the whole region of Canaan. The creator forms Adam from the dust of the ground, and God tells Abram his seed will be as "the dust of the earth." The Hebrew constructions in these references are different, but both carry out the association of earth and fertility. God blows the breath of life into Adam's image of dust, a process alluding to impregnation commonly seen in myths, while the earth is used to cite Abram's own fertility. There are also oppositions in the treatment of land and people, which continue the contrast of good and evil. The well-watered place is blessed and pure in Genesis 2, but is a place where wicked men live in Genesis 13. Finally, Abram's separation from Lot implies the "giving" of a woman (see pp. 24–27), while Adam "receives" a woman by literally "giving" part of his body, providing a final emphasis to the fertility interests of the segments.

Genesis 3 and 12

The story of the deception of Pharaoh by Abram and Sarai in Egypt is set against the story of the fall of Adam and Eve. Parallels in these stories include the deception of a superior person (God and Pharaoh; also Adam by Eve and Eve by the Serpent) by a man and woman, the punishment for the deception by banishment, and material "reversals" of the banished pairs before they are sent away.[12] Adam and Eve are "clothed" and placed in poverty, while Abram and Sarai take away the valuable gifts they have received in Egypt. It is important to note the difference between Abram's attitude in Egypt and his attitude when offered property by the King of Sodom. In this story he gives something which should not be given, namely Sarai as a wife to Pharaoh, and takes away goods which rightfully belonged to the Egyptian. Adam and Eve take something which should not be taken, namely the fruit of the tree of knowledge, and are given "clothes" symbolizing their change of status. The status is one of self-consciousness, something rightfully belonging to God. It is fair to say that the deception theme is most clearly played out in the actions of the serpent toward Eve. The intent of Adam and Eve toward God to hide their nakedness, however, is deception no less explicit than the implied revealing of Sarai's nakedness to Pharaoh in Genesis 12. The fall story, then, beginning in a garden and ending in desolation, is in clear opposition to the Egyptian venture beginning in famine and ending in wealth. The common interpretation of Genesis 3 as representing the discovery of sexuality is nicely paralleled in the sexual implications of Genesis 12, and the punishments of the cases are related.[13] The ground is cursed because of Adam, a clear negation of the "fertility" association of the earth obtaining to that point. Pharaoh's house is cursed with a plague because of Abram and Sarai. The version of the deception of Genesis 20, involving Abraham, Sarah, and Abimelech, suggests a more specific form of curse—all of the women of Abimelech's house are made barren (Genesis 20:17–18). Genesis 12 is not so specific, but the idea of plague is sufficient to remove the fertile bounty which is the implied reason for Abram's trip to Egypt (Genesis 12:10). Like the character developments of Abram and Jacob, these stories develop a similar structure toward parallel and opposite images. The narratives thus present logical homologies of great importance to themal oppositions of fertility/barrenness, blessing/curse, poverty/wealth, and deception/justice. They also set the themal tone for the later situation of Israel in an Egypt where the Israelites are not allowed to leave, so richly described in the Deuteronomic oath (Deuteronomy 26:5–10):

> My father was a wandering Aramaean. He went down to Egypt to find refuge there, few in numbers; but there he became a nation, great, mighty, and strong. The Egyptians ill-treated us, they gave us no peace and inflicted harsh slavery on us. But we called on Yahweh the God of our fathers. Yahweh heard our voice and saw our misery, our toil and our oppression; and Yahweh brought us out of Egypt with a mighty hand and outstretched arm, with great terror, and with signs and wonders. He brought us here and gave us this land, a land where milk and honey flow. Here then I bring the first fruits of the produce of the soil that you, Yahweh, have given me.

Adam and Abram

Taken together, Genesis 1–3 and 12–14 posit strong associations between the land promised in Canaan to the descendants of Abram, and the primeval Garden. The promised land is the return of Eden to the righteous. The treatment of territory is given near genealogical form in the narrative. Just as Abram's blessed line represents the true descendants of Adam, carefully spelled out in the lineages presented within Genesis 1–14, Canaan is the true "descendant" of Eden, a fertile place where bounty exists without toil, God's presence is felt, and human misery is undone. The death of the mythic world in the flood enables the birth of the historical world in which a new "garden of the Lord" can be placed.

Genesis 4 and 11

The story of Cain and Abel and the genealogy of Cain is opposed to the tower of Babel story and the genealogy of Shem. The genealogy of Cain also appends the brief segment reporting the births of Seth to Adam, and Enosh to Seth. The last part of Genesis 11, as we have already seen, connects the stylistically distinct genealogy of Terah to the priestly list from Shem to Abram, Nahor, and Haran. Thus, each chapter includes two distinct genealogical reports following a story. Substantive parallels are found in the two stories. Cain's murder of his brother over their different treatment by God brings about a punishment of banishment "from the soil"—Cain is made a "wanderer on earth." Cain's offering to God was not noticed either because of his intent during the act of sacrifice, or simply because of an inexplicable act of divine preference.[14] There is little in the story to suggest that Cain was unduly prideful, although the name Abel *can* be interpreted as "vanity."[15] But Lamech's boast brings to the name of Cain a clear association with arrogance (Genesis 4:23–24):

> Adah and Zillah, hear my voice;
> Lamech's wives, listen to what I say:
> I killed a man for wounding me,
> a boy for striking me.
> If Cain is avenged sevenfold,
> then Lamech seventy-sevenfold.

This parallels the story of Babel, in which arrogance is interrupted by God who scatters the people over the earth and confuses their language. In both cases the subjects of punishment are disrupted from their place, and in both cases they are physically transformed. The mark of Cain is not specified, but it is apparently intended to allow others to recognize him (Genesis 4:15): "The Lord said to him, 'Therefore, if anyone kills Cain, sevenfold vengeance shall be taken on him.' And the Lord put a mark on Cain, lest anyone who met him should kill him." The change of the people of Babel is the disruption of their ability to recognize each other's speech. Pride and punishment are used as vehicles for differentiating the "unrighteous" in each story. In the genealogical segments, then, the families of Adam through Seth and the descendants of Terah among the Shemites occupy comparable positions. While the basic story development in Genesis 4 and 11 is about severing of human social ties and ties to God, the genealogical segmentation provides the key in each case to seeing the chosen people.

Genesis 5 and 10

Genesis 5 is the genealogy of Adam. It is opposed to the lists of descendants of Shem, Ham, and Japeth in Genesis 10. As previously noted, these genealogies are of different form, and relate to different social purposes in the broader text. From the point of view of chiastic opposition, however, the units are clearly comparable.

Genesis 6 and 9

The opening and closing segments of the Noah story are related by opposition of actions. Genesis 6 commences with the "disgrace" of God's spirit in human flesh—an eight verse segment that has been the subject of diverse interpretations. The remaining fourteen verses of the chapter depict Noah as a righteous man, a lone obedient servant living among evil men who are cursed by God. Noah is promised a covenant and instructed to build the ark. The two chapter parts of Genesis 6 are neatly mirrored in Genesis 9. First, God blesses Noah and makes his covenant with all future generations. Second, Noah's son Ham disgraces his father by seeing his nakedness, resulting in the curse of Canaan. The "nakedness" of Noah is indicative of a sexual crime by Ham, a disgrace comparable to the "divine beings" or "sons of God" taking the daughters of men as wives.[16]

Genesis 7 and 8

The core of the narrative chiasmus is centered on the flood and bracketed by entry and exit from the ark. The function of Genesis 7 in the overall structure is to achieve a negation of the creation. It should be noted that the creation involves manipulation of the waters, a primal element coexistent with God and darkness: "When God created the heaven and earth—the earth being unformed and void, with darkness over the surface of the deep and a wind from God sweeping over the water . . ." (Genesis 1:1–2; see also verses 6 and 9).[17] This should be compared to the opening verse of Genesis 8: "God remembered Noah and all the beasts and all the cattle that were with him in the ark, and God caused a wind to blow across the earth, and the waters subsided." Hence, the apex of the flood in the closing of Genesis 7 sets the stage for a full recreation of the initial conditions of the narrative. The inversion of action from entry into the ark, gradual building of the flood, gradual decline of the waters, and the discovery of new land and exit from the ark, is accomplished by careful source manipulation, as has long been recognized. Chiastic organization within the Noah cycle, then, is relatively uncontroversial.

Adam, Noah, and Abram

The tension created and then dissipated in the Noah story is much more straightforward than many other points in this narrative analysis. But should we expect that this kind of nonlinear literary device would be applied to only select parts of the text? Perhaps from a very dogmatic documentary perspective we might say yes. But in view of the parallels and oppositions outlined above, I think the answer is clearly no. Whether the narrative of Genesis 1 through 14 is built up from unrelated original sources or not, the compilation shows a careful matching of themes and content in what might otherwise be considered unrelated documents. Many of the parallels and oppositions noted in my treatment of Genesis 1–14 have been outlined or detailed by other authors. The problem is to determine the extent to which a particular reading is compelling. Within the limitations of chiastic reading, most of the meanings are suggested by using allied chapters as background for each other. Thus, the idea of "disgrace of Noah," though clear enough in the Noah story, takes on specific meaning in the context of the stated situation of God's disgrace in the counter-unit.[18] But the structure provides only the initial clues, and fuller interpretation must be based upon a wider appreciation of the Genesis story and its functions in the Torah. The formality of this kind of reading yields understanding of the nature of God's promises to the patriarchs in the composition, and a renewed confidence that the transition between Genesis 11 and 12, though important, does not represent a disordered tacking on of myths to a literary or "historical" narrative formed on different principles.

My uses of structure provide clues for examining meanings. In fact, any structural reading should work in this way, whether based in chiastic principles or not. It is clear also that less formal readings allow similar interpretations, but free association approaches to the text do not allow as much possibility for reconstruction of the original bases of textual interpretation. If we want to answer questions about literary purpose, including possible functions of recomposition from written or oral material, then we must develop means to make sense of such features as plot repetition, story segmentation, source conflation, language play, character archetypes, and the wide array of other structure-producing textual elements. Sometimes the features of one system interrupt those of another, changing the whole sense of the narrative. Sometimes it is even impossible to attend to competing systems simultaneously and come away with a feeling of unified reading accomplishment. But we can often find several sets of meaningful features working in complementation and yielding a very rich appreciation of the literary depth of the text.

In this context, let me note that chapter divisions and other quite late additions to Genesis, including Jewish section marks and names, seem more complementary than interruptive to the underlying literary structure of the book. Though chapter divisions are not the only key to analysis, providing as they do mainly some conventional points of textual reference, they are significant corroborations of a tradition of reading. We should not then expect that the chapters will have little to do with the principles of composition. Such an assumption implies that the 19th and 20th century mind has superior understanding of the text. On some technical and historical issues this may be true, but in general our readings of Genesis are filled with cultural difficulties far greater than many of the generations preceding us. It is probably fair to say that the seven-unit chiasmus suggested by the use of Genesis 1 through 14 as a narrative block would have satisfied the aesthetic and numerological interests of the priestly circle most of us associate with the composition. I cannot help but think that Stephan Langton and other medieval readers were not far off in their appraisal of the work of the person or persons who gave Genesis form. No matter that we can recognize some twenty-five independent stories, vignettes, genealogies, poems, and textual fragments in the narrative sequence of Genesis 1–14.

This leaves us at a methodological juncture. Might it not be possible to develop a unified structure for Genesis along similar lines? After all, the fifty chapters of Genesis come close to a seven-times-seven formula. I will not unduly push the idea that the present chapter structure is a perfect algorithm of compositional intention. On the other hand, we have very little to lose by taking advantage of the units as a starting point. This is totally consistent with a search for narrative *order,* and the approach also provides the practical benefit of not having to control the details of two referential systems. This is precisely why ordinary readers, and many professional students of the Bible too, do not like to read redaction criticism. Much biblical scholarship is like reliving Genesis 11.[19]

Toward a Unified Genesis Structure

No one who studies the Bible will question the idea that there are many levels of meaning inherent in Genesis, no matter how reading is achieved. A unified structural analysis of Genesis does not guarantee discovery of satisfying, central, or (for us at least) important meanings. On the other hand, neither does such analysis yield merely superficial cultural details. The validity of a structural reading, although it requires consistency of cultural and theological premises, does not require wide popular acceptance. The *value* of a reading, indeed, may become a matter of individual preference. But my purpose is to produce a substantively informative view of how Genesis works as a composition, and a view partially retracing my steps toward a model of the text.

We start, then, with the assumption that chapter divisions offer a reasonably sound narratology, that medieval readers had good reason to see the text as they did. It is not surprising that the number seven should be prominent in the scheme, in the middle ages or at the time of composition. The number is manifest in word repetitions, genealogical structure, verse organization, and other kinds of direct references throughout the book.[20] For these reasons, let us consider the organization of Genesis as a series of seven-chapter blocks, concluded with a chapter isolated in Genesis 50. The blocks are as follows:

1	creation	—	7	destruction by flood
8	replenishment	—	14	warfare
15	promises to Abram	—	21	birth of Isaac
22	sacrifice of Isaac	—	28	Jacob's move north
29	Jacob's marriages	—	35	Jacob's return south
36	descendants of Esau	—	42	Joseph calls for Benjamin
43	Benjamin to Egypt	—	49	Israel's blessings
50	conclusion; burial of Israel			

The labeling of the list already suggests narrative symmetries. The central chapters of each block, however, are also worthy of special attention. These chapters would form the crossing points in a series of linked chiastic inversions. For example, as we have seen in Genesis 4 and 11, genealogies differentiate the lines of Seth and the family of Nahor, while narratives contrast evil men with the righteous. Continuing through the list, Genesis 18 and 25 begin the stories about Abraham (the transformed Abram) and recount Abraham's death and burial together with the death of Ishmael and the births of Esau and Jacob. They thus bracket Abraham's lifespan. Looking back between Genesis 11 and 18 we find the lifespan of Abram, and looking forward from chapter 25 to chapter 32 we have all of the stories about Jacob before he is renamed Israel. Continuing this line of association, Genesis 39 marks the beginning of Joseph's experiences in Egypt, thus the chapter marks also the end of narrative about Israel's family in Canaan. In Genesis 46 Israel arrives in Egypt, terminating the separation of Joseph from his father. It is noteworthy that in the following chapter Joseph's character enslaves the people of Egypt, suggesting the kind of transformation symbolized for Abram and Jacob in name changes, and the status changes developed in the stories about Cain and Babel. We shall return to this point shortly, but for the moment we can recognize simply that the central units in the proposed organization block out genealogical segments of narrative.

Section marks in the Hebrew Bible fall close to the beginning, middle, and ending points of the seven-chapter blocks. Four kinds of marks appear in the text, not always at chapter junctures and not in any immediately apparent pattern. The minor divisions are noted with a single *sāmekh* (ס) or *pe* (פ) character, while the major divisions are marked with character triplets of one of these two letters. The marks seem associated mainly with the sections of the text attributed to the priestly author; clusters of text divisions occur in Genesis 1, 5, 11, 35, 49, and the last part of chapter 3. Several of the major divisions conform to the locations of the *toledoth* formula in the text, with the exception of its occurrence in Genesis 2:4. The locations of the major marks, the *toledoth* feature, and the clusters of minor marks are shown in Figure 18.

Given that these marks represent a theologically independent reading of Genesis structure, their rough coordination with a chapter-based chiasmus is of particular interest. Figure 18 shows the "S" divisions of Genesis 28 and 44 in a very rough alignment with the *toledoth* point in Genesis 2. But since there is no section mark there, we must consider other possible pattern associations. Note that with an

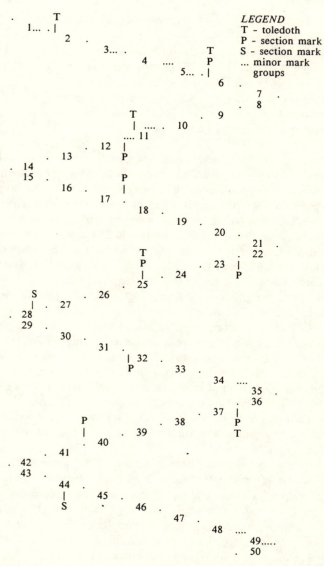

Figure 18.   Direct seven-level chapter chiasmus and section marks.

adjustment of one chapter, accomplished by compressing the material between Genesis 36 and 41, the "P" division at the end of chapter 40 comes into alignment with those of Genesis 11, 17–18, 25, and 32. If we slide the whole end of the text in this manner, then the "S" division of Genesis 44 falls into a better alignment with that of chapter 28, and chapter 50 no longer stands as an "extra" element.

Turning our attention now to the "P" divisions of Genesis 22–23 and 36–37, the adjustment of the Joseph cycle creates parallel placement of the two "S" division points, and a rough linear alignment to the mark in the Noah story. Note that the "P" and "S" points on the ends of the blocks differ not only by sign, but also by placement. The "S" points divide chapters, serving as sensitive indicators of the shifting narrative content. Thus, in chapter 28, the mark separates Jacob's conflict with Esau from his actual flight to the north; the division in chapter 44 marks Joseph's revelation of identity to his brothers. The differences between the "P" and "S" points, then, suggest differences in function and potentially of placement in an ideal structure.

Two alternatives for resolving the structure are immediately available. First, we might slide the "S" marks into alignment with the creation *toledoth,* matching the placements of the "P" marks on the other side of the graph. Second, we might slide the "S" points the other way, using them to form the turning points in the chiasmus. I favor the latter approach for several reasons. Placement of the "S" marks on the ends of the blocks conforms well with their functions in a continuing narrative, as opposed to the more decisive topical breaks at the beginnings of chapters 23 and 37. Also, if we think in terms of the central alignment, the end placement of the "S" marks yields a 3-3-1 vertical pattern for the whole structure. This is appealing because of the occurrence of that pattern in the creation story: God takes three days to create particular "habitats," three days to fill them, and one day for rest. This material appears in front of the first *toledoth* element, the only one not associated with a textual divider. Using a negative argument, I suggest that had the "S" points been intended to fall into alignment with chapter 2 in the final Genesis, the *toledoth* element there would have been marked. Of course, removal of the creation myth from its position in front of the stories of Eden would bring the *toledoth* formula into an initial position. Overall, then, the major textual marks look as if they were associated topically and structurally with the writing or editing process which linked the creation story to the stories about Adam and Eve.

My treatment of the right side of the structure, aside from sliding Genesis 50 into the final textual block, is more conservative. One could compress the Noah story to bring it into alignment with the other single-unit divisions, taking advantage of the story-genealogy combinations of chapters 4 and 11 to preserve the 3-3-1 vertical arrangement. Note, however, that the curses and blessings of Genesis 6 and 9 fall into vertical alignment with Israel's blessings in chapter 49. Other themal associations also derive from the alignment as it stands, and I see no particular advantage in tightly compressing the Noah narrative. We may read the structure either way in any event.

This leaves the question of how to achieve the compression of Genesis 37–40 to produce meaningful chapter alignments. My solution is based upon the underlying kinship parallels in the narratives of Genesis 38 and 39, to be discussed in detail in Chapter 4 of this book. The solution also relies on the symmetries of birth and death reports running between the story of Judah and Tamar, and the story of Lot's seduction by his daughters. These reports, shown with other significant birth-death symmetries in Figure 19, suggest that Genesis 38 must remain in the central position of whatever triplet units are developed. The question of whether Genesis 38 is intrusive to the Joseph story has been hotly debated in recent years. The comparison

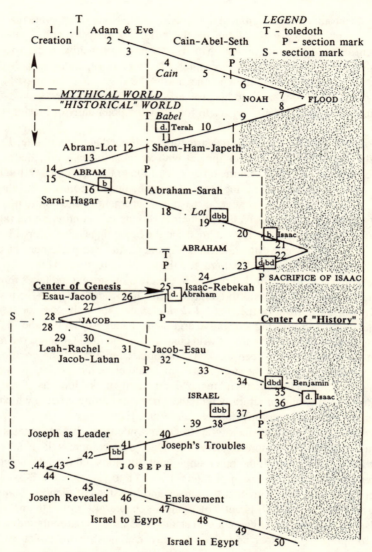

Figure 19. Symbolic genealogical associations of the adjusted chiastic narrative blocks in Genesis (cf. also Figures 4 and 5).

to the story of Lot is one more bit of evidence arguing that the Judah story is intrusive. Intrusive or not, I believe it is intended to be read in specific contrast to Genesis 39, and so I have placed the two chapters together in the central position of the structure. Finally, Genesis 39 and 40 could as easily be juxtaposed, since they deal with the condition of servitude and the causes of Joseph's ultimate rise to power. The new alignment of central chapters in the Joseph cycle creates a contrast between Joseph's own imprisonment and his later subjugation of the Egyptians. Genesis 39 also contains reference to a mark of status, the clothing kept by his master's wife as he flees from her advances. This links well with the notion of marking in the stories of Cain and Babel, other central units, as well as to the notion of slavery which was sometimes signified by marking (Exodus 21:6; Deuteronomy 15:16–17).[21]

Figure 19, then, moves toward an ideal recursive textual organization of Genesis, turning mainly on points of major life-cycle events. Thus, in many respects, we observed major aspects of the overall narrative plan in Figures 4 and 5. The ideal plan based upon chiasmus is supported by George Coat's discussion of the Joseph cycle.[22] John Gammie and others have replicated chiastic structures in the Jacob narratives from independent analyses.[23] Their analyses might resolve the stretching and compression of textual units differently from my solutions. Given the idea of "chapter" chiasmus, divisions still loosely based in the natural flow of the narratives, it is probably less important to achieve precise alignments at this point than to develop a general sense of the structure.

The implications of multiple recursive elements are also quite different from those in a simple opposition of two strands of text. In his essay "The Structural Study of Myth," Claude Lévi-Strauss outlined a method for vertical reading of narratives which is quite consistent with those implications.[24] His original treatments of myth, however, were faulted because one could never tell quite how the alignments and readings were implied in a narrative organization. The method employed here is to develop the narrative clues to structure, then perform a more general reading following the principles derived from the text. If I have imposed the "structure" of Figure 19, I am not the first to do so. When I read the structure, I shall probably engage in many kinds of interpretations which are quite specific to my background. Thus, the following readings offer only a beginning, an illustration of the potential of the method.

Themal Analysis

The overall symmetry of Figure 19 is striking, particularly in the division of chapter 25, but the distribution of births suggests that the first block of chapters is independent of the patriarchal life-cycle structure. The labeling of the figure formalizes some of the observations we have already made, but includes additional elements. The structurally "natural" division of mythic and "historical" worlds occurs with the flood. The original world is utterly destroyed, and the new world replacing it is one with placenames and regional associations we can locate on maps. As a literary construction, the mythic world is time before time, a generation in cosmology. The "historical" era replacing it is measured in human generations, specifically through the times of birth, death, and rites of passage or transformation of patriarchal characters. The earliest section of "historical" time, running beyond the usually recognized "mythic" section of Genesis to chapter 14, mirrors the events and formulations of the earlier intended mythic unit, as also do all of the following generational segments of the narrative structure. Thus, the most pertinent horizontal axis for reading narrative oppositions in "history" is defined by the "S" mark of chapter 28. The chapters dealing with the mythic world stand as a preface.

After the Noah story we become geographically focused on Mesopotamia until the death of Terah. This signals the beginning of territorial demarcations which we have already observed formally. In the structural symmetry produced by the center of "history," the Mesopotamian focus of chapters 10 and 11 stand in perfect territorial opposition to chapters 47–49, the time of Israel as a social group living in Egypt. Noah's drifting on the sea also mirrors the kinds of movements of Genesis 50, especially in its mention of places we cannot locate (Goren-ha-atad and Abel-mizraim). Similarly, Abram's trip to Egypt is mirrored by the ultimate arrival of Israel in Egypt.

The genealogical divisions of the book beyond Genesis 11, then, are an Abram cycle (12–17), an Abraham cycle (18–25), a Jacob cycle (25–31), an Israel cycle (32–40), and a Joseph cycle (41–46). The full Joseph story is divided into four parts, technically ending with Genesis 49 and the death of Israel. These divisions recount (a) the opposition of Joseph to his brothers and his period of low status and power, (b) the period of Joseph's leadership during which he is known to his family only as an Egyptian, (c) Joseph's revelation to his family, and (d) the period of Israel's occupancy in Egypt. Each of these divisions involves a transformation of Joseph's character. Mention of his sacred and mystical powers are most closely tied to chapters 37, 39, 40, and 41 and give way gradually to a more secular imagery. The transformation of Genesis 41 brings Joseph from slavery and prison to leadership. His emotional tie to his father and brothers is revived in the powerful narrative of chapter 44. Real force is given to Joseph's secular side in chapter 47, notable also for its juxtaposition with the arrival of Israel. My reading stresses this transformation and the possibility that Genesis is telling us that Joseph, not the Pharaoh of Exodus 1, brings Israel into the condition of slavery in Egypt. If nothing else, he certainly sets up the conditions for a retribution against the sons of his brothers after the death of Israel.

The chiastic oppositions of the Jacob cycle and its extensions to Genesis 22 and 35 are also strong. Genesis 23 involves the acquisition of land for a burial place at Mamre. This is paralleled by the acquisition of land by Israel at Shechem (the last part of Genesis 33) prior to the incident involving Dinah. Other minor points of detail form direct vertical links between the units. But the broad plan of the narrative opposes the four basic units: (a) replacement of Sarah with a new matriarch, Rebekah; (b) the conflict of Esau and Jacob; (c) the matrimonial service of Jacob to Laban, again providing a set of new matriarchs; and (d) resolution of the conflict between Esau and Jacob. The Jacob cycle and its extensions also spans the whole life of Isaac. Thus his character is given youth in chapter 24, and old age in chapter 27. His death is reported at the end of chapter 35 to close the section of narrative dealing with the conflict and contact of his sons. Jacob undergoes the counterpart transformation from a dependent youth (to Isaac in chapters 25–28, to Laban in chapters 28–31), to an independent patriarch at the opening of chapter 32.

Moving up to the Abram cycle, we again encounter direct lineal relationships running across several units between the flood and the expulsion of Ishmael after the birth of Isaac, but the most direct links are within the opposition of Genesis 10–11 and 18–19. The genealogies of chapter 10 seem to match the vertical association of other birth reports in chapters 19 and 38. On the other hand, the destruction of Babel and the destruction of Sodom and Gomorrah offer a more compelling parallel. As noted earlier, the genealogy-story-genealogy sequence of chapters 10 and 11 could be a basis for compressing the Noah narratives into a single unit's width. Babel interrupts the genealogies in the same way Sodom and Gomorrah shift our attention away from Abraham and Sarah. If one follows the column down the structure, it is apparent that chapters 24, 33, and 38 accomplish a similar interruption of narrative. Isaac's marriage is conducted by a servant of Abraham, taking us to Haran. The meeting of Esau and Jacob interrupts Jacob's travel between Aramea and Canaan. Judah's marriage narrative interrupts the Joseph story. Note that on the left side of the graph, similar functions occur in the centermost column, where chapter 12 takes us to Egypt, chapter 17 involves the detailed description of the Circumcision Covenant, and chapter 31 has Laban halting Jacob's progress toward the south. The reason for the difference in column associations of this kind will become apparent in the expanded analysis, which will also explain why I want to maintain the vertical associations of chapters 6 and 9. Suffice it to say at this point that direct vertical relationships are less impressive than the crossing functions of the four broad narrative blocks: (a) Babel and the creation of language differences, (b) separation of Abram and Lot, (c) the conflict between Abram's wives, (d) the final segmentation of Lot from association with the patriarchal line.

Viewing the associations of the three pairs of narrative blocks opening to the right side of the structure, an alternating focus is established. The two elements in the pattern are fraternal differentiation and matriarchal succession. Thus, beginning with Abram and Lot on the upper left, we follow the progression back and forth through the social differentiation of Abraham and Lot (18–20), the conflict of Esau and Jacob (26–28), the social differentiation of Israel and Esau the "Edomite" (32–34), and the negotiations of Joseph and his older brothers (42–44). Running counter to these blocks are the genealogy introducing Sarai (11), the conflict of Sarai and Hagar (15–17), the replacement of Sarah by Rebekah (23–25), the conflict of Leah and Rachel (29–30), the marriage of Judah and the incest avoidance of Joseph (38–39), and the revelation of Joseph to his brothers (44–46). I include the last block in this list because, as becomes more apparent in Genesis 48, Joseph is still treated as a "foreigner" by his family. He also maintains his role in Egyptian society, unlike Moses in the following elements of the Torah. We have already observed that Israel adopts *only* Manasseh and Ephraim, not Joseph's other children. In this sense, Joseph is treated as the eponymous ancestor of a Rachelite subgroup, and obtains a status very like that of the women in the kinship association.

The connection of "women" and "foreigner" is common in biblical literature, since women from outside the social group were often taken as captives but turned into wives (Genesis 34, Deuteronomy 21:10–14, Proverbs 2:16–19, 5:20). From the perspective of Canaanite territorial association, all of the women in Genesis except Dinah (and possibly Tamar and Lot's wife) are foreigners. The issue comes up in relation to foreign gods in Genesis 31, when Rachel seems hesitant to give up the spiritual symbols of her father's house. But the idea of Joseph as a *replacement* for Rachel (and perhaps also even Leah), structurally implied by the alternating chiastic blocks, seems to be given voice in Israel's words when he adopts Ephraim and Manasseh: "I do this because, when I was returning from Paddan, your mother Rachel died. . . ." (Genesis 48:7).

Considering the crossing pattern of block themes further, we should observe that the left-hand blocks introduce conflicts in general, while the right-hand units tend to resolve the conflicts or otherwise define the correct line of succession specifically. This puts special light on the status of the births of Perez and Judah. Tamar, by structural implication, is the right kind of woman (foreign or not), as opposed to Judah's first wife who is "wrong" because of her Canaanite status. Or at least that is one interpretation. The symmetry of the Judah and Lot episodes can also imply the segmentation of Judah from the other brothers for his inappropriate marriage. Considering Joseph's avoidance of relations with his master's wife, only to return later to marry the *daughter* of an official with a similar title, then Genesis 39 parallels the general theme of marriage on the wrong generation. But Genesis 41 forms a contrast placing Joseph in a better light. We will discuss these issues in my next chapter, and note now that the adoption of Manasseh and Ephraim is no mere whim. The blessing of Joseph's sons, taken alongside Genesis 49, resolves some of the conflict of Israel's original twelve sons.

These structural preliminaries underscore the carefully controlled association of genealogy, territory, and social conception in Genesis narrative. They also help us understand the parallel functions of the single right-hand elements in the proposed chiastic structure. All of the right-hand units are associated with "unknown" places or places where aimless wandering occurs. The sea of the deluge recommits the world to its primal formless condition, hence Noah's drifting is not controlled.[25] Similarly, we do not know where Moriah or Yahweh-yireh are located, since Genesis 22 does not specify a direction for Abram's travel. The movement of Hagar and Ishmael in Genesis 21 is more directly stated within the region of Beersheba, but Hagar is said to "roam aimlessly" and Ishmael is placed in a "wilderness." The places in the Edomite list, though intended to be in the southern district, are equally obscure. Only Genesis 35 provides relatively strong specificity, but Rachel's death and Benjamin's birth occur "on the way" rather than at Ephrath, and the point is a boundary between the two broad subterritories of Canaan. Finally, as noted earlier, the places in Genesis 50 are not locatable, and the process of burial for Israel does not involve direct movement to Mamre. It is as though the sons of Israel go to Canaan without being able to actually find the key points stressed in the rest of the narrative.

The right-hand elements, then, provide connection and emphasis of themes developed in each preceding block, much like the coda in a musical composition. For the Abram cycle and its extensions, we see the final resolution of the Sarah and Hagar controversy, accomplished through Isaac's birth, Ishmael's immediate expulsion, and Isaac's immediate transformation of status in a rite of passage where he is called Abraham's "only son." Similarly, the conflict between Leah and Rachel is closed with Rachel's death, and the sons of Israel are contrasted with the sons of Esau in Genesis 35–36. These resolutions look back to events toward the center of the structure, to the promise of a child to Sarah in Genesis 18 and the subtle announcement of Rachel's pregnancy in Genesis 31:35. This helps us find key connections for the flood episode and Genesis 50. The flood looks back to the first sins of men against God (chapter 3) and of man against man (chapter 4), while Genesis 50 looks back to the process of enslavement. We understand, then, why Joseph's brothers return with him to Egypt after burying Israel, instead of separating in the same way as Isaac and Ishmael or Jacob and Esau. We also understand why the mourning site is called "mourning of the Egyptians" or "water-course of the Egyptians" and lies beyond the Jordan. Israel too is "enslaved" by Joseph's administrative acts. Israel is, for the time being, thoroughly Egyptian.

We have not yet directly considered the counter-chiastic associations of the Abraham and Israel cycles, the units opening to the left side of Figure 19 and paralleling the Genesis 1–14 blocks. Direct comparison of the four blocks in each of these narrative units shows the clear parallels of Sarai-Hagar/Leah-Rachel, Abraham-Lot/Israel-Esau, Isaac-Rebekah/Judah-Tamar, and Jacob-Esau/Joseph-brothers. The last unit mainly contrasts Joseph to Reuben and Judah, but also specifically mentions Benjamin and Simeon. We have also already noted the counter-symmetries of the birth reports which link the two outer blocks, and we recognize the two inner blocks as the Jacob cycle. A more satisfying sense of the overall set of ties among all of the units is achieved by a slightly different themal diagram (Figure 20).

Figure 20 graphs the connections of stories running down the textual blocks within each cycle. Like the broader themal alternation of the cycles themselves, a crossing pattern emerges on each side of the central column of chapters. These associations link mainly the second through the sixth divisions of the text, leaving the mythic time and the time of the reunited "Israel" in Egypt as bracketing blocks. As the labeling of the outer units of the first two blocks implies, following my earlier analysis of Genesis 1–14, the pairs of adjacent divisions form an uninterrupted series of vertical associations. We will observe first the symmetry of the enclosed core of the diagram, then the outer and center columns of each chiastic level.

The crossing lines on each side of the diagram connect stories about marriage and stories of conflict-separation. In the conflict-separation sequence on each side is one unusual unit, the transformation of Abram and Sarai through the Circumcision Covenant on the left, and the negotiation for a tomb on the right. These units have just the opposite sense of the majority of the conflict stories, namely, a contractual negotiation which spells out precise terms of relationship and obligation. The feature also occurs in the separation of Abram and Lot in Genesis 13, the strict obligation of hospitality stated by Lot when he offers his daughters in lieu of the angels in Genesis 19:6–9, the mutual oath of Laban and Jacob in chapter 31, the

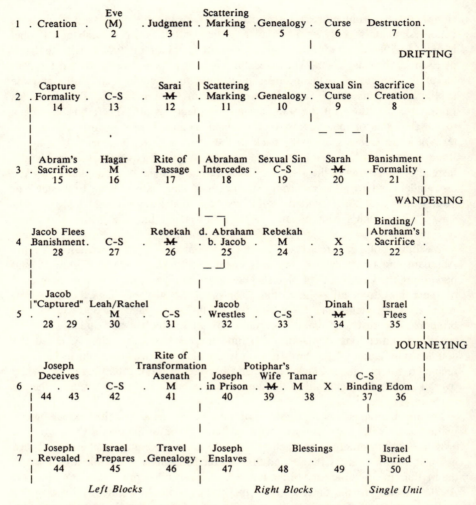

Figure 20. Symmetrical strands of alliance and segmentation stories suggested by vertical reading of a modified Genesis narrative organization.

formally polite treatment of Esau and Jacob in Genesis 33, and the conditions (though deceptive) placed by Joseph on his brothers in chapter 42. We may also think of Abram's circumcision as a formal separation from the Terahite connubium, though this is a weak argument given the continued marriages to Aramea following in the narrative.

The marriage sequences alternate between false negotiations, accounting for the symmetrical placements of Genesis 12, 20, 26, and 34, and validated marriages signified either by the birth of children or brideservice/brideprice and countergifts. The marriage sequence draws parallels for Hagar and Leah/Rachel on the left, and Rebekah and Tamar on the right. The false "negotiation" of Genesis 39 and the marriage of Joseph break the legal/illegal alternation in the vertical system, leaving us in a legal quandary about the status of Joseph's children. This feature is resolved by observing that the narrative order alternates between false and legitimate marriages, with Genesis 38, 39, and 41 conforming to the overall pattern. At the top of the structure, the creation of Eve provides the marriage precedent, while at the bottom the blessings of Israel, for reasons we amply observed in Chapter 2 (see pp. 49–52), can be reasonably linked to marriage circles.

Crossing associations similar to the creation-destruction/replenishment-warfare pattern of Genesis 1–14 are produced by each consecutive pair of narrative levels (numbered 1–7 on Figure 20). The second and third levels yield a parallel between Abram's sacrifice of animals and the sacrifice of Noah after his exit from the ark. On the other axis, Abraham swears an oath not to deceive Abimelech after their groups are involved in fighting over wells, an obvious contrast to the war in Genesis 14, and the formal dealings between Abram and the king of Sodom (this narrative follows the banishment of Ishmael). The sacrifice theme continues on the next level, as does the theme of banishment. This time Jacob is "sent away" because he has stolen the blessing of the elder brother. We recall that Isaac sends his son to the place his own father would under no circumstances allow him to go. But Jacob "flees" the wrath of Esau as much as he follows his father's direction to go north, and the notion of flight is carried across to the right hand unit of level five; Israel flees the potential anger of Canaanites living around Shechem after the killing of Hamor and the Shechemites by Simeon and Levi. In both these cases the flight is aided by divine action.

Returning to the themes of sacrifice running from Genesis 9 through 15 and 22, you will note on level five that Jacob's situation can be seen as a form of capture. He performs long periods of brideservice plus additional labor for Laban before his ultimate escape from Aramea. This stresses the distinction between the processes through which Isaac and Jacob obtained their wives. Even after all his time with Laban, Jacob is forced to take the women "like war captives." This is quite unlike the formal negotiations which brought Rebekah to Isaac. Thus, we see the echo of contrasts between contract and conflict/separation in the outer units of the pattern. The "capture" and "binding" elements from chapters 22 and 28–29 then are picked up again in the Joseph cycle. For this reason, the organization of chapters 36–40 in Figure 20 presents a refinement of the pattern observed in Figure 19. Genesis 37 is split between the right-hand block and the single unit formerly containing only the Edomite genealogies. Given the functions already cited for the single unit stories, we should note that Joseph's travel to Egypt as a caravan prisoner satisfies the themal connections of "wandering" or "non-directed" movement; he is not in control of his movement.

The adjustment of Genesis 37 pulls the Judah and Tamar story partially into the third position of the right block. This adjustment works well as a replication of the contractual negotiation theme. Judah engages in a marriage contract involving a legal obligation. The obligation is formalized and complicated by his negotiations with the disguised Tamar, culminating in a pledge. The pledge becomes the sign of contractual obligation which Judah recognizes, passing judgment on himself. The story also involves a character transformation, since Judah begins by marrying a Canaanite woman, then consorts with a supposed prostitute, but finally shows honor in his obligation.

Only the essential fact of marriage in Judah's case fits the matrimonial connections of the vertical reading, and this fact is brought into direct contrast with Joseph's honor toward his master in chapter 39. Genesis 38, then, is also split between the second and third positions of the right-hand block on level 6 of the diagram. These alternative readings point out the building complexity of the narrative by the time one reaches the Joseph story. What begin as relatively simply-stated themes in the stories of the myth cycle and Abram/Abraham narratives come together with a forceful counterpoint as one moves toward the conclusion. This is a good example of how structural hermeneutics should work. We can begin by guessing at a likely organization, but the overall set of associations drawn from analysis should force some pattern readjustments. In the end, we must never assume that a particular diagram or logical algorithm will do justice to the richness of the narrative, precisely because such heuristic devices are "well-defined."

The outer units of levels 6 and 7 present a superb set of oppositions. First, the capture and enslavement of Joseph is resolved through images of death and rebirth. Joseph is torn away from his father, and presumed literally torn by a beast. Calum Carmichael points out that Israel's blessing of Judah links this deed to Judah, the Hebrew of Genesis 49:9 reading literally: "Judah, like a lion's whelp, you have grown up on the prey of *my* son. . . ."

The major "S" division of Genesis 44 appears at verse 18, where Judah humbly implores Joseph to allow Benjamin to return to his father. Judah's speech brings about Joseph's change of character as he is at the brink of making Benjamin a slave, and incorporates the elements of tearing, and "binding" used in the sense of filial connection:

> So your servant our father said to us, "You know that my wife bore me two children. When one left me, I said that he must have been torn to pieces. And I have not seen him to this day. If you take this one from me too and any harm comes to him, you will send me down to Sheol with my white head bowed in misery." If I go to your servant my father now, and we have not the boy with us, he will die as soon as he sees the boy is not with us, for his heart is bound up with him (Genesis 44:27–30).

Judah also attempts to make good his promises to his father concerning Benjamin's safety, thus pronouncing a sentence on himself—he offers to be enslaved in Benjamin's place. Instead, he produces restitution. Not only does he save Benjamin, but he produces the return of the son "torn by a beast." The "tearing away" of Joseph by his brothers also constituted an act of banishment, a replay of the strife-banishment sense of Jacob's removal to the north in Genesis 28. Piled on these meanings is the notion of theft. Not only did the brothers in effect "steal" Joseph, but the Midianite caravan steals him from the brothers (chapter 37:28). If one prefers to have the Ishmaelites actually transporting Joseph to Egypt, as is implied in the text, then at least the sale of Joseph "steals" him again from Reuben (chapter 37:28b). Compare the situation, then, to the problems cited in the rules of the Mishpatim (Exodus 22:12):

> When a man gives an ass, or an ox, or a sheep, or any animal to another for safekeeping, if it dies, or is injured or carried off, without anyone seeing it, an oath before the judges shall decide between the two of them, whether he did not lay hands on his neighbor's property; the owner must accept the oath, and no restitution is to be made. But if the animal was stolen from him, he shall make restitution to its owner. If it was torn by beasts, he shall bring it as evidence, and he need not make restitution for the mangled animal.

The parallel of the rules is quite specific. Joseph was sent out to find his brothers, an act which effectively entrusts him to their care. This is specifically implied by Reuben's concern for his own fate when Joseph is lost to him. The brothers' act of taking him prisoner, because of the element of conspiracy, is a theft "without witnesses." If Reuben were to make the charge of theft against the other brothers, lacking witnesses, *he* would be responsible to make restitution because of a lack of witnesses against the others. The act of presenting Joseph's bloodied coat as evidence of his death, a false testimony in which all engage, protects Reuben from responsibility and hides the theft in general.

Recall now that it was at Judah's instigation that Joseph was sold to the Ishmaelites. This introduces the notion of a formal transaction, an actual act of theft and banishment by the brothers that we may see as more serious than simply stealing his coat and throwing him into a pit (taking him prisoner). The Mishpatim rules immediately preceding those just cited (Exodus 22:6–8) offer further illumination:

> When a man gives money or any article to another for safekeeping and it is stolen from the latter's house, the thief, if caught, shall make twofold restitution. If the thief is not caught, the owner of the house shall appear in the court of justice, to show whether he has not put his hand to his neighbor's property. In every case of offense, whether it concerns an ox, or an ass, or a sheep, or a garment, or any lost article, of which one says, 'This is it,' the case of both parties shall come before the court of justice; he whom the judges declare guilty shall pay double to the other.

In the narrative of Genesis 44, Judah and Joseph are immediately concerned with the punishment for a purported act of theft. After planting his "divining cup" in Benjamin's sack, Joseph arranged for the capture and search which results in the group's being returned to Joseph's house. The brothers plead innocence and offer themselves as "slaves" by their presence in honor. To this Joseph threatens only to take Benjamin as a slave. Judah then argues their case in an eloquent and humble presentation of the "facts."

The "thief" with whom Joseph is concerned, of course, is not Benjamin, but Judah. Judah has been brought to a court of justice, and has recounted to his victim the nature of the deception in which he and his brothers had engaged. Who better to relate the tale than Judah? And who better to stand with him as judge than the victim? We have seen Judah in this situation before, in the situation where his judgment of Tamar is shown to be incorrect by evidence she has "stolen" from him. We also know that he accepted that judgment honorably, accepting the idea that he had victimized Tamar more than she victimized him.

Thus, Judah is caught in his theft, becoming a victim in justice. The wording of Exodus 22:8 makes good sense of the situation. The theft could be of any article, but specifically listed are ". . . an ox, or an ass, or a sheep, or a garment, or any lost article. . . ." If the imagery of the rule is taken metaphorically, then we might see here "Israel" (an Ox) or a son of Rachel ("Ewe"); that is, we might see the favored son of Israel from the "father's" perspective and from the point of view of a matrigroup reference. The Hebrew forms do not allow such a reading, though the structural parallel makes such glosses tempting.[26] On a more literal level, the rule seems to cite a pregnant series of associations: animals, "a garment," or "any lost article, of which one says, 'This is it' . . ." As Genesis 44 unfolds, Joseph immediately identifies himself—he *is* the stolen brother; "this is it." The rule also cites the theft of his garment. But another implication can be found for the animals. Recall that when Joseph went to find his brothers, they were not where Israel thought they were, having moved from Shechem to Dothan. The man who found Joseph wandering in the fields said only that he heard the brothers say "Let us go to Dothan." From other elements of the narrative we believe that they clearly intended to go back. But from Joseph's perspective, could men who engaged in the theft of a son be trusted with the flocks? Read against Exodus 6–8, is there not in Genesis 37 an implication that Joseph could have accused his brothers of stealing the flock, an act for which he had a potential witness beside himself?

The location of the incident, Shechem, recalls the place where Simeon and Levi killed Hamor ("Ass") and took his goods and wives. This is the place Jacob had moved to after successfully stealing a blessing (Genesis 32), and his wives and flocks (Genesis 31). Given the blessings of Genesis 49 for Simeon and Levi, in which they are said to have "hamstrung an Ox and killed *a man* . . .", namely Hamor, the incident over Dinah was a clear breach of patriarchal authority.[27] Even the allegation of stealing the flocks, much less the fact of having stolen a son of one's own father, signals the depth of the political division between the Rachelite and Leahite groups. In the context of the rules of the Mishpatim cited here, I believe the opposition of units in Genesis 44 and 37 makes such an allegation.

The Exodus material concerning theft is generally supposed to be quite early, probably earlier than the Genesis narratives. Some of the rules, however, take a form suggestive of Deuteronomic legal forms.[28] Within the earlier form of rule statements, those beginning "When a man . . ." or "When an ox . . ." we may also make a distinction between those rules that include "the owner" in the formula for resolution (compare Exodus 21:33–36 and 22:45). Positioning of rules of these two forms in the collection of rules as a whole suggests that they may differ in historical context. I will not enter the debate over whether Exodus reflects on the Genesis narrative or Genesis was composed to incorporate the sense of the rules, though I favor the former view because of the complexity of the Genesis system. I suggest, however, that the interpretation across the two texts is in this case justified. Note, however, that the allegation of the theft of animals by Joseph's brothers, though derived from my cross-reading of Genesis and the Mishpatim, is clearly not without precedent in the structure of Genesis or the plot cycles of the Jacob/Joseph division of the book. Let us read forward, then, in terms of the punishment suggested by the rules.

According to the rules, a party declared guilty is to make twofold restitution. Judah cannot produce another son for Israel. His twin sons, in fact, amount to restitution by Tamar for her "theft" of the symbols of his authority, the signs of his kingship in Genesis 49:10. They provide not one heir but two, one representing the ancestor of David within the broader collection of Judean lines. Judah's saving of Benjamin merely fulfills his obligations to Israel, for he rather than Reuben was entrusted with Benjamin's care. Joseph, however, has two Egyptian sons. Thus Judah embarks with his brothers to bring his father back to a place where restitution can be accomplished. As leader of Egypt, Joseph is never properly returned to Israel. Instead, Israel adopts Ephraim and Manasseh, enhancing the Rachelite offspring by his own statements, but taking no more than just restitution for his loss of Joseph by excluding any other progeny Joseph might produce.

But Judah and his brothers are punished in other ways for stealing a sign of his status, his garment, represented again in the false charge concerning Joseph's cup. The punishment is enslavement, justified by another series of rules from Exodus 22:1–3 concerning theft and restitution:

> If a thief is caught in the act of breaking in, and is struck a fatal blow, there is no guilt of blood in his case. But if after sunrise he is struck dead, there is bloodguilt. The thief must make restitution; if he has not the means, he shall be sold for his theft. If the stolen animal is found alive in his possession, whether it is an ox, an ass, or a sheep, he shall restore two animals for each one stolen.

The item stolen in this case is the sign of Joseph's prominence. Joseph, destined for kingship as manifest in his dreams, and as indicated by his father's favor, ends up in power only as a minister of Pharaoh. His kingship in Israel is stolen. This is apparent in the blessings in two ways. First, Joseph is heaped with praise and, as we have already seen, his fruitfulness in Israel through Manasseh and Ephraim is assured. But Judah gets a somewhat back-handed blessing, one citing his culpability in Joseph's loss and "grudgingly" acknowledging his "royal" prominence.[29] At the point of the blessings, Judah is caught again with the goods, just as Benjamin was "caught" in Genesis 44. In the concern with the theft of Joseph's entitlement the discovery of the thief occurs long after the act, at a time when killing the offender would incur bloodguilt. Thus Judah must make restitution, but as we find in the other comparable case of "stolen" blessing, Judah "has not the means" to make restitution. Recall Isaac's words to Esau:

> Then Esau said: "Is it because his name is Jacob that he has twice supplanted me? First he took away my birthright and now he has taken away my blessing." Then he said: "Have you not kept a blessing for me?" Isaac answered Esau: "I have appointed him your lord, and I have given him all his brothers as servants, and with grain and wine I have sustained him. What then can I do for you, my son?" (Genesis 27:36–38)

There is nothing to be done, at least insofar as the blessing is concerned. In Esau's case, he could only weep aloud.

We find Joseph weeping too at his father's deathbed. The narrative clearly has this weeping stand as a sign of loss. But what is the loss? Has Joseph not also been twice supplanted, robbed first of his "birthright" (the favor of his father) and then of his blessing? Has not Judah's blessing been steeped in the images of wine, and have not his brothers been made his servants? And for his loss, what is the penalty? "If he has not the means, he shall be sold for his theft." Joseph, then, a powerful man in Egypt, has a claim on his brother Judah and all that he possesses. The crossing members of the final chiasmus show Joseph unrecognized by his brothers in Genesis 42–44; in fact, he is specifically seen as an Egyptian. In the counter-unit, Genesis 50, we find the whole of "Israel" unrecognized in Canaan, and specifically recognized as "Egyptians." Israel is captured, paralleling the earlier near-enslavement of Benjamin and actualizing the statement of his brothers that "they stand as his slaves."[30]

This reading is a start, I believe, toward a sense of the unified narrative potentials of Genesis. We find in the culmination of the book some powerful images, prefigured in the precise structural oppositions of stories involving conflict, enslavement, escape, theft, retribution, and blessing. All of these elements are woven together through symbolic uses of the "life cycle" as a metaphor for political succession. The social contract is also symbolized in the covenant promises made to Abraham, Isaac, and Jacob. But with God as with man, the bonds of the covenant are elusive. They are as elusive as the filial ties of fathers and sons, or the cooperative bonds of brothers and sisters. So the bonds of the covenant can be the result of formality and respect, or of conflict and strife. In the center of Genesis, in the elements of chapters 18 and 32, we find Abraham interceding for Lot and Jacob wrestling a man. Abraham talks to a God in human form, speaking as formally and carefully as does Judah to Joseph at the turning point of the conflict between the brothers. Abraham has just been given a special blessing, the notification that his wife Sarah will bear Isaac. Jacob wrestles a man who will not say his name; and he demands a blessing from the man before he will let him go. The man blesses him saying: "Your name shall no longer be Jacob, but Israel, because you strove with the divine and men, and have prevailed" (Genesis 32:29). Jacob "struggles against" God's strength, then, and for his trouble receives both a blessing and a disjointed hip. Some may be reminded of Oedipus, who prevails against his father, is called "swollen foot" and made lame by being hung by his foot in a tree, and who has sons brought into a deep conflict. We are reminded, then, that Genesis is a special kind of literary form, akin to myth but more developed, more complex, and more connected to the other traditions of which it forms a part. As readers, we are confronted with choices of our own, whether to tear the manuscript to pieces in analysis, or establish our own covenant with the text. Like the patriarchs, though, we must be prepared for the covenant to be an elusive one, sometimes held right before us and sometimes disappearing into a cloud of doubts.

Holism and Reductionism as Hermeneutic Principles

The human mind can accommodate a host of cues—more than we usually admit. But a document can precisely accommodate even more. The transformation from spoken to written tradition entails a kind of quantum leap in the human potential to create compelling, culturally-specific explanations of the world. What makes early written traditions such as Genesis last as "meaningful" experience is the way the symmetries of narrative structure work on the mind. Our contemporary history is content oriented, but the earliest histories were structure oriented. It is striking that the logical capabilities we associate with our most formal mathematics—topology and symbolic logic—are the hallmark of the human species. These capabilities have been with man since the evolution of our species—since the beginning. Only recently have we developed the arithmetic and probabilistic tools that help our minds work for us in more precise, not necessarily more refined, ways.

On a substantive level, a particular structure for the entire book of Genesis does not answer all our questions about meanings. No single model can even scratch the surface of "meaning." The skeleton of structure we have observed above demonstrates how rich are the interrelationships of genealogy, narrative, politics, law, and theology. The structure is "useful" to the critical pursuit we call form analysis. Biblical source criticism, an almost purely "reductionist" analytical direction, identifies pieces of scripture with different circles of theology, geographic association, and historical movements. Source critics also attempt to explain meanings through the interpretation of immediately juxtaposed segments, or sometimes with reference to blocks of text presumed to have a common origin in the editing process underlying Genesis.[31] These are important aims, deserving more careful attention by structuralist scholars studying the Bible.

A "structural hermeneutic," on the other hand, can pursue meaning without serious consideration of sources. When such analyses are completed, however, they often carry implications as to why particular sources appear where they do in narrative sequence. If structuralism can inform the Genesis construction debates in this way, it deserves more careful scrutiny by form critics. As a relative "foreigner" to the inner circles of biblical studies, I can appreciate the anxiety created by radical revisions of academic worldview. I realize too that my introduction of structuralist kinship orientation into the interpretation of Genesis is something of a radical departure from what are usually recognized as "anthropological" readings of the text. One must keep in mind that working with such a text, as opposed to oral tradition, is also a radical departure from Lévi-Straussian structuralism. It is not, however, a departure from the thrust of semiotics in general, nor are the form and content of the analysis inappropriate to the subject matter.

Our understanding of the world always profits from the tensions between our tendencies to generalize and operate holistically, and explanations which reduce a phenomenon to its component parts. It is therefore appropriate that as we move to understand the nature of minimal subunits of Genesis, employing an essentially reductionist method, we should always keep in mind the concept of the "whole" we bring under analysis. These two ends of inquiry should always serve each other. Each methodical reading of Genesis may still retain its unique potentials. Stress of the whole text certainly generates its own qualities and values, and its own problems. On other levels of textual organization, quite different cultural and historical concerns, quite different aspects of theology or cultural expression, may surely be discovered. Structural hermeneutics is merely one method of narrative analysis holding the potential to work in the directions of reduction and holism in one process. Let us remember that "parts" and "wholes" are fundamentally important concepts in the sciences. Marc Bloch eloquently stated the essential problem of paying too much attention to one line of analysis, and casts a proper parallel between the concepts guiding science and the humanities:[32]

> Science dissects reality only in order to observe it better by virtue of a play of converging searchlights whose beams continually intermingle and interpenetrate each other. Danger threatens only when each searchlight operator claims to see everything by himself, when each canton of learning pretends to national sovereignty. . . . we must beware of postulating any false geometric parallels between the sciences of nature and the science of man. . . . For in the last analysis it is human consciousness which is the subject-matter of history. The interrelations, confusions, and infections of human consciousness are, for history, reality itself.

Still, physicists cannot discuss the cosmos without reference to sub-atomic particles, and interpreters cannot discuss meaning without reference to structure, word, and event. In the science of signs, we must face the struggle with the balance between details of expression and the full potentials of the word.

IV

MYTHOS AND ETHOS

If Genesis forms experience for us through its larger structure, then we should expect the stories within Genesis to manifest carefully controlled features of cultural unity. Far from being a collection of loosely related independent writings, the exact substance of each element in the book serves some immediate purpose in the larger design. At least this is the effect of Genesis as a literary composition, regardless of how diverse the original sources of material might have been. One task of hermeneutics, then, is to examine the smaller patterns of organization which engage each other in the larger structure to produce our unified sense of text. On the level of individual story analyses, we encounter a very precise juxtaposition of what Aristotle called "mythos" and "ethos." These terms, forming the central elements of Aristotle's conception of tragedy, have in modern usage come to signify the *pattern* of basic values of a people and the disposition, character, or attitude peculiar to a specific culture or group.

Mythos in tragedy is especially concerned with the "structure of events." As Paul Ricoeur expresses this point:[1]

> Tragedy, as a poem, has sense and reference. In the language of Aristotle, the "sense" of tragedy is secured by what he calls the "fable," or the "plot" ($\mu\tilde{\upsilon}\theta o\varsigma$, *mythos*). We may understand the *mythos* of tragedy as its sense, since Aristotle keeps putting the emphasis on its structural characters; the *mythos* must have unity and coherence and make of the actions represented something "entire and complete."

We see in Ricoeur's statement something very similar to the idea of structural models as defined by Claude Lévi-Strauss, which "must make immediately intelligible all of the available facts."[2] Lévi-Strauss also makes the point that an effective structural model, in addition to presenting the immediate "sense" of facts, provides the basis of logical transformations—for each structural model there is an implied family of models functioning under a "law of the group."[3] It is not surprising that Lévi-Strauss would turn to Greek myths as part of the exposition of his basic concepts, since the mythic forms within Classical Greek culture show clearly the very relations of structure and transformation in which he is most interested.

The same, I believe, is true of many of the individual stories in Genesis. Unlike the diverse collections of plays, narratives, and poems comprised in Greek literature, however, biblical materials have been given to us in a set order, a macrostructure which gives us immediate appreciation of stories *as transformations* of each other. It is important to note here that Lévi-Strauss argues against the analysis of texts as myths, since texts are removed from the domain of spoken language (speech, *la parole,* or we might rather say "speeches" in the sense of rhetoric), while myths reside especially in the domain of speech and the unconscious structured aspect of language *(la langue).*[4] In the Aristotelian sense of mythos, designed as it is for literary analysis, the difference between an active myth tradition and literary art seems irrelevant. The Torah, because its reading is a central feature of Jewish religious observance, is not entirely removed from Aristotle's categories of "diction" (λέξις), "song" (μελοποιία), or "spectacle" (ὄψις), these forming the manner and media in which the text is brought to life.[5] We can analyze biblical literature as literature using Aristotle's categories, without bending them at all. As to the objects of tragic literature—"plot" (μύθος), "character" (ἤθη), and "thought" (διάνοια) in that order of importance—we find in biblical literature many of the precise elements of Aristotle's conception of aesthetic design.[6]

Ethos, the "things which make men what they are," has also been given special emphasis in modern anthropology, namely in the interests and expressive terms of configurationalist ethnologists. Ruth Benedict developed her ideas of cultural types around characters from Greek myth, attempting to show by way of unitary contrasts the full sweep of differences between cultures.[7] This ideally ordered, nearly "timeless" conception of difference is the core element in most definitions of "cultural pattern." It is no accident, then, that Clyde Kluckholn, for all the structural formality of his approach, chose to stress "character" as the endpoint of cultural analysis.[8] Nor is it unusual that he chose Greek culture to contrast with our own lifeways in some of his methodological essays; he was well-grounded in the classics, and, like Lévi-Strauss, highly sensitive to the relationships between structural interests and the exposition of the "manners and customs" of people.

We may use the cultural sense of *ethos* alongside its literary sense when approaching biblical stories, not only because the conventions of modern anthropological usage direct us along that path, but because both group and individual associations are inherent to the Aristotelian category. Both uses are also central to the biblical text, where we continue to encounter in the stories about individuals the passion, history, and social conception of Israel as a cultural ideal.

My interests in structure and custom, composition and theme, cause me to seek in Genesis stories the common features of plot which allow us to find the cultural order behind actions, words, and contexts. Among the features we have observed in Genesis stories so far in this book, kinship relations and place lie at the core of most of the narrative. I have attempted to show the structural sense in which these, along with the narrative structure itself, are a coextensive system. What happens through spatial reference has importance in kinship reference, and the two together *are* the narrative structure. This approach is not inconsistent with the study of myth proper, but it need not be confined to myth. Indeed, structurally homologous models are regularly generated from quite different cultural or natural phenomena. We now ask the questions, then: What kinds of patterns emerge when we apply kinship and themal models to several stories possessing common narrative features, such as

Genesis 12, 20, and 26? Do we discover differences of expressed sentiment or character? Do we discover systems of narrative (hence kinship) transformation? How do the results of such minute analysis relate to or inform the conception of overall structure in Genesis? Along the way we must also consider other questions of critical importance. How do the Genesis traditions compare with similar materials from other cultures? What can we say, for example, about the ethos of Israel in relation to the kinds of ethos portrayed in Greek tragedy?

Cross cultural comparison is necessary and appropriate on this level of reading, since some direct parallels will help develop the point that the kinship concerns of Genesis are not unique to Israel. Indeed, the patterns and concerns of kinship in traditional cultures show strong general tendencies, so that what at first appears to be a myriad of differences resolves into a relatively few key concepts and constructs.[9] On the level of the text, kinship relationships in Genesis display a specific pattern flowing from these generalities. Thus, in addition to direct comparison, we shall build an internal analysis elaborating on the particular "theory of the text" this book offers. A truly anthropological reading of Genesis and related biblical materials, a reading building "ethnographic" interests out of the literary artifact, will provide for us the strongest means of cultural comparison while it channels our appreciation of the immediate cultural case.

Kinship, Place, and Story Types

Typology, that is, simple differentiation, and *classification,* the organization of a series of types into a structured system based on features common to the group, are the principal bases through which George Coats developed his excellent treatment of narrative genres in Genesis.[10] These activities are fundamental elements of the analysis of mythos. Coats recognizes nine major types of narrative material, along with numerous minor types, assigning scriptures to the categories based upon structural, linguistic, contextual ("setting"), and intentional criteria.[11] To the major narrative forms may be added genealogy, yielding a list of ten kinds of key scriptural characterizations: saga, tale, novella, legend, history, report, fable, etiology, myth, genealogy. The classification of Genesis documents, then, proceeds through judgments placing units in a hierarchic narrative structure. For example, an etiological unit—one explaining the derivation of a cultural practice or the name of a patriarch or place—may form a substructure in a tale, legend, or some other higher-order unit. Through such classification, Coats's treatment of redactional questions in Genesis is particularly illuminating, as is also the force of his arguments for general structural design.[12] In the present analysis, I attempt to employ some cross-cutting typological notions drawn from general kinship theory, specifically some ideas about matrimonial alliance and group identification, while considering some of Coats's narrative units against my own structural divisions. Thus, I draw narrative structure or "plot" from my own and Coats's readings of units, consider the organization of events in terms of the social organization of the text (another aspect of *mythos*), and judge the features which may be attributed the status of "custom" or "character" for the group of units as a whole. The full analysis is a straightforward application of mythos and ethos, both in the sense of "narrative as stories about individuals" and the broader idea of "consistently applied customs and rules pertinent to a group." The material under analysis also draws into consideration the biblical texts associated with marriage and contract laws, as well as biblical parallels from other parts of the Hebrew Bible. A few direct parallels from Greek myth also cast light on the social intentions of some of the stories.

Matrimonial Alliance in Biblical Narrative

The larger structural depictions of kinship ties in Genesis, such as those seen in Figure 1, do not adequately show elements of pattern from particular marriage narratives. Family-tree diagrams are merely the background against which each individual story is read, and an overall design to which each story contributes. Marriage reports fall mainly between Genesis 11 and 41 and concern the central patriarchal marriages of Abram/Abraham, Isaac, Jacob, Esau, Judah, and Joseph. To these may be added the unsuccessful marriage attempts of Sarai/Pharaoh, Sarah/Abimelech, Rebekah/Abimelech, Dinah/Shechem, and Joseph (Genesis 39). These narratives and reports form the "alliance" connections we observed through vertical reading of chapter-based chiastic structure (see again Figure 20). One other story, the seduction of Lot, is associated with "sexual sin" and the conflict-separation connections of the text, and is not considered here in spite of the offspring produced.

Figure 21 presents the textual units of these marriages and alliance attempts, employing my divisions of Genesis and those of Coats. The figure underscores the difficulty of defining "how much" material from a narrative is pertinent to a particular incident, plot, or cultural concern. Because Coats's units are framed on genealogical reports and life-cycle structure, they correspond roughly to mine.[13] His effective use of narrative types showing the tiered patterns of story organization also provides some fine points explaining the placements of some of the minor reports, such as the marriages of Esau and the Egyptian alliance of Joseph.

The broader genealogical context makes Esau's marriage to Mahalath, the daughter of Ishmael, and Joseph's marriage to Asenath, the daughter of the Egyptian high priest, quite significant within the overall marriage system. Esau's Canaanite marriages are appended to the attempted alliance story involving Rebekah and Abimelech, and are not considered in this analysis. The brief report of his marriage to Mahalath accompanies Isaac's instruction to Jacob to seek a wife in Aramea, and so is linked as a preface to the Jacob marriage scenario. Note that the Esau reports fall at the beginning and end of Coats's "tale of strife" within the larger Jacob-Esau novella, while Genesis 38 and 41 stand in a roughly similar opposition in the Joseph Novella, the major part of what Coats calls the "Jacob Saga." The attempted seduction of Joseph is closely linked with Genesis 38 and includes information necessary to the full interpretation of the brief report of Joseph's actual marriage.

Thus, even minor marriage reports take on major functions in the overall narrative construction and alliance "meaning" system.

Scriptural references in the central column of Figure 21 are those I believe are critical to understanding the structural situation created by the account. Emphasis with the scriptural reading is on action, the genealogical connections being formed

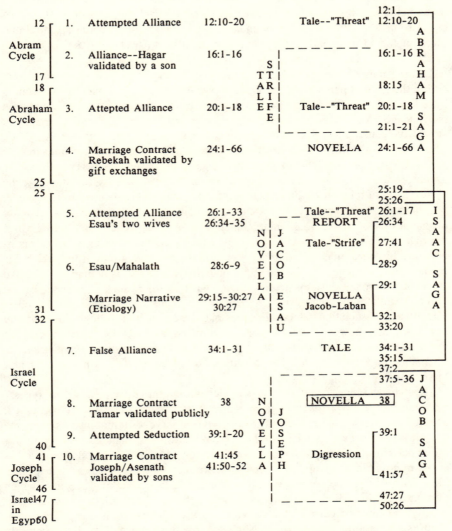

Figure 21.   Marriage reports, matrimonial alliances, and alliance attempts of Genesis 12-41, considered against the narrative genres and organization developed by George Coats.

mainly through the broader narrative. Our concern is with the movements of patriarchs or other characters along paths of social or territorial connection. Such movements may be one-way or two-way and may result in a permanent or temporary change in status. Status changes may involve (a) *territorial exclusion,* (b) *marriage,* (c) replacement of the previous generation, or *succession,* (d) *generation change* for marriage, (e) *servitude,* (f) *imprisonment,* (g) *alliance,* (h) *impoverishment,* including loss of material wealth or a spouse, and finally (i) *redemption,* including any rectification of a past reversal. Each of the stories speaks of at least one social or territorial boundary, the boundary often being an important place in the ideal geographic system now familiar to us (see again Figures 10 and 11).

Turning now to the general patterns formed by the cases, we should note that within the general pattern of Near Eastern patrilineal tribalism, maternal descent is traced in order to define alliance-forming groups. "Alliances" are formed when a patrilineage gives wives to another group, often involving a series of marriages in successive generations. Such wife-giving is usually one-directional, meaning that a group stands as *either* "wife-giver" or "wife-taker" toward another lineage, *not both.* The lineage to which a maternal reference looks in such cases is patrilineal. A group of men related to a common ancestor form an "agnatic" association. At the closest level of relationship, a lineage or group of lineages descended from brothers will possess strong social bonds founded in their common paternal ties. At more distant levels of agnatic association, men will see each other as potential allies through marriage. A man will distinguish, then, among three basic social associations: his own lineage or lineage group, the agnatic group from which his mother came, and the groups who might potentially take sisters in marriage. Unlike some of the social systems with similar marriage rules, no system-wide social groups regulate the marriage associations or degrees of agnatic affiliation.[14] The alliance associations among lineages may be quite fluid through time. At any point in time, however, very precise group and alliance designations may be in effect. The transformations of such nomenclature through the generations is often the subject of genealogical assertions of precisely the form we encounter in Genesis.

The marriage reports and narratives in Genesis fall into three basic "story types." I call these types: (a) *withdrawn woman* narratives, (b) *central marriage* narratives, and (c) *redemption* narratives. The three types serve different purposes in the overall set of social definitions in the text. Withdrawn woman stories account for group definition by citing instances of wife-giving which are thwarted or rejected as either impossible or invalid. The central marriage stories provide examples of an ideal form of alliance continuity. These are basically wife-taking accounts which turn out well, but which also point out some of the pitfalls of alliance negotiations. Finally, redemption narratives deal with issues of family obligation for different statuses within a household. As we shall see, the three types of stories are closely connected in form, such that some narratives fit into more than one of the categories simultaneously. We will view each of the types individually, then consider the more complex issue of narrative interpretation from the perspective of alliance principles.

Withdrawn-Woman Narratives

The most well-recognized cases of "withdrawn" women are found in Genesis 12, 20, and 26. The topical correspondence of these "deception" stories has long been noted, forming a rich field for analysis in most Genesis commentaries.[15] Three other stories in Genesis offer immediate parallels involving marriage. These are the union of Abram and Hagar (Genesis 16), the story of Joseph's near seduction by Potiphar's wife (Genesis 39), and the story of the "humbling" of Dinah (Genesis 34). The kinship homologies of the six stories are presented in the graphs of Figure 22. The four situations represented by the collection resolve to conflicts between groups, conflicts between husbands and wives, and conflicts of fathers and sons. In the basic form of the story type, a married woman is offered to a man of rank, but is withdrawn because of some intervention. The result in each case is the territorial or social exclusion of individuals left on the lower rank-generation position and a change in the material and/or blessing status of the individuals. In each case the status change of the woman is two-way.

Taking the situations individually, we may first note that Genesis 12, 20, and 26 also stress the "agnatic" connection of husbands and wives. This point serves as an important example of the difference between literal and social readings of the text. If we read Genesis 20 literally, then Abram and Sarai are brother and sister tracing through a biological father, but unrelated tracing through their mothers. Abraham's statement that Sarah is his "sister" can mean that they are related as parallel cousins, descendants of a common male eponymous ancestor from different patrilineages standing in a relationship of wife-takers and wife-givers. A more exact kin tie for Abraham and Sarah is only implied in the text, mainly in the parallel of Sarah to the Terahite alliances represented by Rebekah, Leah, and Rachel. Reading the statement of Genesis 20 literally, Abraham and Sarah could be direct parallel cousins—children of men in the same generation. But the more likely case is that Sarah is intended to be the sister of Bethuel, forming the generational difference between husbands and wives we find in the other central marriage reports.[16] This is the precise relationship obtaining between Isaac and Rebekah in Genesis 26.

Generation can be taken as a metaphor of rank or relationship of clientage, stressing the common practice in traditional systems of weaker lineages attempting to strengthen their position by marrying women into stronger lineages. This social feature is often accompanied by reservation of polygamy for elites.[17] Asymmetrical marriages based on rank also help support institutions of kingship or chiefdomship in many societies, as has been amply observed in royal dynasties throughout the world. Wife-takers, then, whether genealogically connected or not, are often of higher rank than wife-givers. This holds true for most marriages in Genesis. An important aspect of clientage in Genesis is "servitude" or "slavery." Such retainers, including the "handmaidens" of ranking women in the lineages, figure prominently in the dealings of the family. It is through this kind of familial association that the stories of Hagar and Joseph fit into this story pattern.

The union of Abram to Hagar, though only *temporarily* recognized as a valid

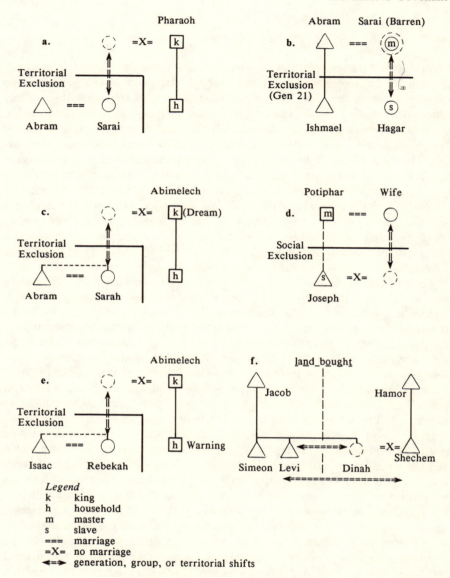

Figure 22.   Examples of the "withdrawn woman" story type from Genesis:
(a) Genesis 12; (b) Genesis 16; (c) Genesis 20; (d) Genesis 39; (e) Genesis 26;
(f) Genesis 34.

marriage, turns the rank formula of Genesis 12 around. In other terms, Abram's attempt to marry his wife "up rank" ends with his being given Hagar by Sarai; as wife-taker of an Egyptian woman, Abram is implied to be of higher status than Pharaoh, the source of the given woman. Of course, on the surface level of the story, Hagar is supposed to bear a child for Sarai. We must note, however, that the "given" woman never acts as a surrogate mother, and the child is never recognized by Sarai/Sarah. Thus, the expulsion of Hagar and Ishmael after the birth of Isaac is a reasonable parallel of the expulsion of the patriarchal couples in the deception stories. In each case the woman involved makes a two-way rank transformation, and the territorial exclusion of the lower rank "couple" is permanent. Note also that Sarai's barrenness is directly paralleled in the house of Abimelech in Genesis 20, and may even by implication be attributed to the "plagues" on Pharaoh's house in Genesis 12. This is joined by the blessing and fertility promised to Ishmael, part of an alternation of "wealth" and "blessing" themes seen when Genesis 12, 16, 20, and 26 are taken in narrative order.

The story of Joseph and Potiphar's wife presents the antinarrative of the first four cases. The woman attempts a conjugal relationship by moving "down" in rank/generation, the equivalent of approaching a "son" of her husband. Her temporary transformation of status is thwarted, and she returns to her husband who then excludes the man involved, sending him into further impoverishment, from slavery to prison. It is noteworthy at this point that Joseph's eventual marriage to the daughter of the "high priest" Potiphera is a strict parallel of alliance to Egypt found at the end of the Ishmael story (Genesis 21:21). For both Ishmael and Joseph, then, the apparent curse of exclusion from a promising family ends with alliance to the acknowledged power on the southwest of Canaan. Similarly, the union of Hagar to Abram, like Joseph's tie to Egyptian officialdom, involves both marriage and "non-marriage."

Genesis 34 is a thematically rich tale incorporating the "withdrawn-woman" pattern alongside principles of matrimonial "redemption." The story depicts Jacob as not moving with force when his daughter is "humbled" by Shechem, an act which amounts to marriage by capture.[18] Jacob had already entered into a contract for land, an indication of settling into the locality parallel to the other thwarted alliance scenarios, and we are led to believe that he might actually enter into a marriage alliance with Hamor. The story also includes the expressed patriarchal fear, after the killing of Hamor by Simeon and Levi, that other groups of the region will exterminate Israel. Like Abraham and Isaac, Jacob fears for his safety because the men of a place into which he has moved have found one of the women of his group beautiful. The fact that Dinah is a more marriageable token in the plot than the patriarch's wife does not change the social point that Israel, having newly settled in the territory, is placed in a "wife-giving" situation. The conclusion of the story in warfare and escape also parallels the territorial-exclusion themes of the other "withdrawn-woman" stories. Indeed, the killing of Shechem, Hamor, and their kinsmen actualizes the threats explicitly posed for Pharaoh and Abimelech in Genesis 12, 20, and 26.

The six marriage stories involving withdrawn offers of wives, then, are expressions of a common pattern of events, a common mythos. They also reflect several consistent themes about marriage alliance in general, most notably that failure of an alliance amounts to social, usually territorial, exclusion for the "offending" group. Further, a negotiation of alliance which is thwarted in process may result in a change of status and material wealth for both parties. These themes are inherent in the progressive theological stamp we view in the deception tales, as well as in the superb reversal of the surface narrative elements in Joseph's encounter with the evil Egyptian woman.[19]

Central Marriage Narratives

The marriage ties of the main line of Abraham, Isaac, and Jacob (Figure 23) show a strict genealogical parallel for the marriages of Isaac and Jacob. They also imply continuity of the pattern on the generation of Abraham. The major difference in the marriage accounts for Isaac and Jacob is in the manner through which alliance is achieved. In the first case, Abram sends a servant to the north to find a wife for his son. The servant must swear an oath to Abraham from which he will be released only if he cannot convince a woman to return with him. I have already commented on the contrast between Abraham's hesitancy to send Isaac north versus the long period of servitude Jacob spends before escaping with his wives and possessions back to Canaan. The escape theme incorporates a friendlier version of the territorial exclusion pattern we have observed in the stories of thwarted alliance. Thus, Abraham's action succeeds in maintaining an alliance tie without the risk of strife. By sending a representative, a "token" of himself, Abraham accomplishes the marriage through exchanges of brideprice (gifts to the allied line) and bridewealth (counter-gifts brought by Rebekah on her trip south). Even in the context of this negotiated marriage, some reluctance to send the woman is expressed in Laban's attitude.

The bridewealth of Rebekah is a counterpart of material possessions gained in the escape scenes of Genesis 12, 20, 26, and 34. In this context, we should note that of the principal matriarchs, only Rebekah does not encounter a problem with barrenness at some point. Rebekah is a close counterpart of Leah, whose barrenness is only an interruption of childbearing. Sarai/Sarah, by reason of her early barren status and the form of co-wife struggle in which she engages, is a counterpart of Rachel. The parallel of Sarai versus Hagar and Leah versus Rachel develops reversals of loved/unloved and fertile/infertile statuses. Rebekah's "loved" and "fertile" character development, then, places a stamp of approval on the *manner* of Isaac's marriage.

Rebekah's birth of twins gives emphasis to her fertility. The Jacob cycle (Coats's Isaac Saga) transfers the strife themes to the sons. Esau is loved but not blessed, Jacob is blessed but unloved, and their respective increases through procreation are differentiated. Esau's lineage is traced through five sons born to three wives (Genesis 36), with emphasis on the Canaanite origins of the women (Mahalath, indeed, does not appear in the lists). Jacob has twelve sons of whom two are dropped (Joseph and Levi) only to be replaced by Joseph's sons. Thus, though

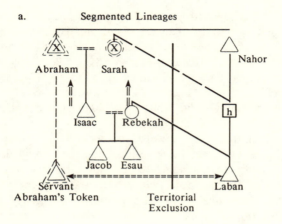

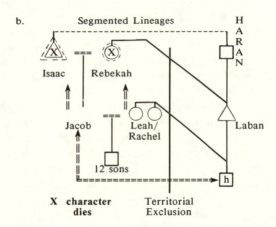

Figure 23. Central marriages of the patriarchal line in Genesis: (a) Abraham's servant obtains Rebekah for Isaac, and the couple replaces Abraham and Sarah; (b) Jacob goes to Laban for a wife, escapes with wives and sons, and replaces Isaac.

Esau's line is a "great nation" and is linked to kingship, Israel is increased by more than twice the measure of Edom and the Rachelites number as many sons as all the first-generation offspring of Esau.

We have already noted that the ties of Abraham and Sarah in Genesis 20 are identical socially to those of Isaac and Rebekah in Genesis 26. The text of Genesis implies an interesting reversal of rank of the Terahite sons. Not only does Abram leave the land of his father, and more specifically the territory of his brother Nahor, but he takes the generationally subordinate Lot with him. In marriage terms, this suggests that Abram's departure involves a similar segmentation to that of Laban and Jacob. This would explain why Abraham would not be quick to send his son back to the north; in Aramea Abraham's lineage is regarded as subordinate in rank, even though they are wife-takers from the line of Nahor. This interpretation draws a much more urgent comparison between Sarai and Hagar, women standing as independent tokens of alliance to higher-ranking lineages on the southwest and northeast. The status of the line of Abraham, then, like the apparently elevated status of Esau in Edom, is dependent upon maintenance of territorial separation. Continued marriages to the "high lineage" of Aramea on Jacob's generation represents the means through which final social segmentation is achieved and a new connubial order is established.

The final Aramean marriages, however, do not come without substantial risks. Because of his travel to Haran, Jacob suffers a temporary reduction of rank as he joins the household of Laban. Reading the genealogical connections in social terms, Laban is the ranking lineage leader within a "Bethuelite" or "Nahorite" alliance group. He is a true "individual" in the narrative, having *succeeded* to the position of paramount chief. This accounts for Laban's key involvement in the marriage negotiations for Rebekah, a background which makes his position firmly established when he encounters his direct parallel cousin Jacob. As a co-lineal subordinate from the perspective of rank, Jacob's marriages force him into a period of extended coresidence and servitude. This "brideservice" is brought to an end only by escape, a form of redemption through which Jacob reoccupies the territory of Abraham's exclusion, and succeeds to the position of ranking lineage leader in place of Isaac.

The two central marriage accounts in Genesis provide alternative forms of alliance behavior for a segmented group of relatively low status, negotiation from a distance and bride capture. Jacob's departure from Laban enacts a plot similar in several essential features to the story of Dinah and Shechem. In Genesis 34 Jacob's relatively mild, almost accepting posture toward the marriage offer of Hamor is based upon a careful assessment of his strength. Laban also judges his strength in a case of wife-taking running against his ultimate corporate interests. The killing of Hamor's lineage by Simeon and Levi is instructive, for it points out the danger of Jacob's final encounter with Laban. Jacob was accused, after all, of taking women and property belonging to Laban. The outcome suggests that Jacob's strength was sufficient to avoid bloodshed at the hands of Laban's household.

Overall, Genesis stresses the idea that genealogical distance produces greater probability of distrust among agnatic kinsmen, along with the need for separate residence because of lineage growth. The more extreme results of these tendencies take the form of separation to avoid strife. This feature is identical to the separations of more closely related kinsmen, "brothers" in conflict over succession. The textual juxtaposition of Jacob's separations from Laban and Esau affirms this point. The central theme of agnatic segmentation accounts for the literal weaving of conflict-separation stories with marriage stories shown in Figure 20. The ethos of the cases is consistent, but the mythos is different for the two kinds of stories. Separation of distantly linked or rank-determined groups is cast in terms of marriage potentials, while separation of closely-related men is stated in terms of strife over blessings. Genesis drives home the point that relationships between kinsmen *ought* to be close, but that even the ties of brothers are usually marked by competition and tension.

The narratives constantly reassert the idea that the transformation of a distant agnate or rank-equivalent male into an in-law, an ally by marriage, maintains social cohesion and political strength. The presentation of political tensions through kinship affirmations is not only realistic on this point; it is quite practical.

Redemption Narratives

Tales of redemption introduce cultural themes limiting or defining appropriate action of members of immediate households. As with the stories about withdrawn women, the redemption pattern displays close connections with the central patriarchal marriage patterns. The stories included in this group are the Dinah episode, the marriage of Esau to Ishmael's daughter, Joseph's marriage to the daughter of Potiphera, and the novella of Judah and Tamar (Figure 24). I have provided two graphs of Esau's marriage (Figure 24, b and d) which underscore the overall pattern similarities of the group. One graph links the Esau marriage report to the plot of Genesis 34, and the other ties it to the structure of Genesis 41. My rendering of the Judah and Tamar plot is also accomplished in two graphs, one depicting the initial rejection of Tamar's marriage contract, and the other showing the resolution of Tamar's marriage to Judah's lineage. Positioning of the patriarchal lineage on the graphs also reflects the difference between the "southern" or "western" alliance pattern represented by the marriages of Esau and Joseph (and also Ishmael, who married an "Egyptian" woman) versus the Canaanite territorial association of Judah's marriage.

The Joseph, Esau, and Dinah stories illustrate well how rank and generation influence matrimonial situations. Note that if we leave Esau on his original generation with respect to Ishmael (Figure 24b), then his marriage to Mahalath becomes a structural counterpart to the graph for Genesis 34 (Figure 24a). Because Esau to an extent rivals his brother by virtue of territorial exclusion, and because Jacob replaces Isaac, the alternative graph (Figure 24d) is probably a more accurate rendering of the textual intention of Esau's Ishmaelite alliance. Because of the stated social interactions of Genesis 34, such manipulation of the Dinah story structure is impossible. Regardless of how we interpret the "narrators point of view" graphically, the three stories are clearly variants contrasting wife-giving and wife-taking episodes pertinent to the line of central patriarchs.

The marriages of Esau and Joseph show correspondence in movements of the married couple "up rank." This is textually signified by Esau's ultimate association with "kingship" in Edom, and in Joseph's elevation from prisoner to overseer of Egypt. Esau and Ishmael constitute "great nations" developed after segmentation from the main line. Unlike Jacob, who becomes tied to Laban's household, the narrative implication when Esau goes "to Ishmael" for a wife is that he maintains territorial association with Isaac for the moment. His ultimate territorial placement in Seir puts him on equal rank level with Ishmael, accomplishing the transformation from Figure 24b to 24d. Mahalath, then, moves up a generation and out of territorial association with her father's lineage, producing the successful marriage structure stressed in the central patriarchal marriage narratives.

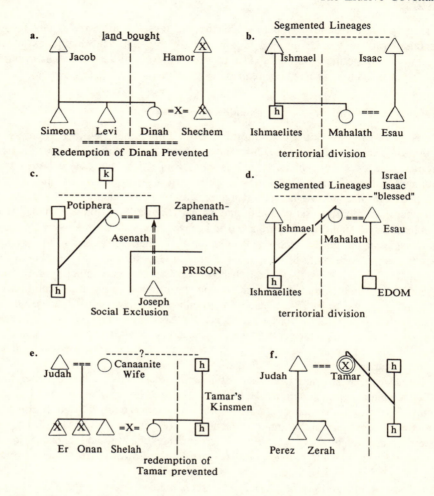

Figure 24.   Examples of the "redemption" story type from Genesis: (a) Genesis 34;
(b) Genesis 28, unsegmented Esau; (c) Genesis 41; (d) Genesis 28, segmented Esau;
(e) Genesis 38, Tamar rejected; (f) Genesis 38, Tamar redeemed.

My comparison of Esau's marriage to Joseph's redemption places Israel on the
same rank level as Pharaoh. This is warranted by Jacob's blessing over Esau, and
the attendant succession of Israel to Isaac's position as lineage leader. This produces
for Ishmael and Esau a rank equivalence comparable to that of Potiphera and the
redeemed Joseph *(Zaphenath-paneah)*. The equation is significant given the reduction of Israel's status produced by the move to Egypt in the conclusion of Genesis.
Once again, the text carefully defines rank transformation through territorial movement.

Joseph's elevation of rank is more straightforward than Esau's. In the process he
is redeemed from the injustice of his imprisonment, reclothed, renamed, and given

the daughter of "the high priest," a man who stands as his religious counterpart in the kingdom. The social division between Joseph and Potiphera is one of lineage and political function, and is stressed again in Genesis 47 when the priests are excluded from the enslavement produced by Joseph's political administration. The marriage between the two lineages is the only example of lasting coresidential alliance in Genesis. The only nearly similar situation is the near marriage of Dinah to Shechem, a most interesting case because of its ties to the redemption theme. Simeon and Levi represent the "brother's" interest and control over sisters in matters of marriage, a parallel of Laban's influence in Rebekah's marriage and the expressed concern of Laban's sons over Jacob's acquisition of property in Laban's household. When Dinah was abducted ("humbled"), she was transformed into a *de facto* wife and the subordinate rank of Simeon and Levi was asserted. In structural terms, Shechem attempted to enforce a rank differentiation similar to the graphs of Figure 24c and 24d on Jacob's sons. The "married" status of Dinah is also evident in that the narrative leaves Dinah in the household of Hamor during the period of negotiations between the two groups.

When Simeon and Levi kill Shechem, they eliminate Dinah's husband. This does not eliminate the marriage, however, since other kinsmen could redeem the woman through application of a levirate rule. Thus, the brothers also kill all of the "able bodied men" of Shechem's group, including the patriarch Hamor. This assures that no man of Shechem's lineage living or forthcoming can legitimize Dinah's married status by producing offspring.

The levirate rule is usually discussed in terms of its provision of continuity of the male line, but it also has important connotations about the legal status of the woman involved. Recall that Jacob does not request permission to leave Laban until the birth of Joseph, the offspring unequivocally legitimizing his conjugal tie to Rachel. Note also that when Judah decides to reject Tamar's union with Shelah, he sends her back to the household of her kinsmen; she remains, in a sense, only betrothed. The circumcision agreement of Simeon and Levi with Shechem, in fact, offers them a means of identifying potential levirs within Hamor's household. The ritual enactment also symbolically reverses the rank assertions of Shechem's bride capture, for it suggests the taking of Hamor's line into the "circumcised" house as slaves. In the end, the men are not enslaved, but their wives are taken and Dinah is reclaimed. The penalty is not severe, as it is often read, when seen in the context of alliance withdrawal, rank assertion, and lineage continuity for Israel.

The levirate rule lies behind the text of Genesis 34, but is the explicit subject of the story of Judah and Tamar. Genesis 38 is structurally more complex than Genesis 34 and shows close connection to both the Dinah episode and the account of Joseph's marriage. The immediate parallels of Genesis 34 and 38 are striking. Simeon and Levi incur the wrath of Israel, just as Er, and more specifically Onan, are offensive to God because of their Canaanite status and because of Onan's breach of fraternal obligation. The wrath is differently motivated, however, since the action of Simeon and Levi may be construed as a "righteous" killing of Canaanites. In either case, Canaanites are "evil," but the affront to patriarchal authority by Simeon and Levi is merely taken to the level of debate with Jacob.

Structural positioning of Simeon and Levi as parallel to Er and Onan is by no means a superficial parallel, especially given other themal symmetries of the stories. The key female characters, for example, are quite precise analogs of each other, women "offered" as wives on the base generation of the patriarchal lineage. In each case the marriage contract is withdrawn, for Dinah by the wife-givers and for Tamar by the wife-taker. This withdrawal is accomplished by different generations, but in both cases the patriarch is victimized by the withdrawal. Whether Judah's action was correct depends, in great measure, upon our interpretation of the origin of Tamar. We know that Judah's first wife is a Canaanite, but Tamar's origin is not stated. Recalling the patterns of successive wife-taking from a single line in the central genealogies, Tamar is by implication a Canaanite. This is probably the preferable reading of the text, though as noted before an "unidentified" woman takes on a special status in Genesis. We should also note that the parallel story of Ruth continually stresses the Moabite status of Ruth. The key to resolution of Tamar's status, then, is structural, relating to the difference between wife-giving and wife-taking as actions of the Abrahamic central lineage. That is, *all* of the cases of a woman from the central line being offered as a wife are thwarted, while the descendants of Abram take wives from Aramea, Egypt, the Ishmaelites, and even from Canaanites. Recall that even if Simeon and Levi would not give their sister to Shechem, they certainly had no problem with taking Hamor's women and converting them into wives. Thus, even if Tamar is a Canaanite, her status as a potential wife rests more on her "personal character" than on her background.

The structural reversal of Dinah and Tamar is similar to the reversal of "killing" and "killed" posited for Simeon and Levi against Er and Onan. Dinah "went out to the women of the land to visit," an action suggesting that she might become like them in custom. When the women of Shechem were brought into Israel, Jacob gave instructions to "his family and all the others who were with him: 'Get rid of the foreign gods that you have among you; then purify yourselves and put on fresh clothes' " (Genesis 35:2; cf. Deuteronomy 21:10–14). Tamar also changed her garments, from the widow's costume to the clothing of a temple prostitute, an image playing to Judah's Canaanite sexual association. Thus, Tamar moves the plot through her own "righteous act" disguised in treachery and deceit. Her act strikes the blow of redemption, just as Simeon and Levi violently cut off the redemption of Dinah. In having Judah perform her redemption, Tamar makes the genealogical shift which parallels the marriage movements of the central genealogies. She then symbolically affirms her "in-group" status by changing into her widow's clothing immediately after the conjugal enactment with Judah. Tamar is not an evil woman, but one willing to accept her obligations to the patriarchal line to whom she has been given, with the result that Judah is blessed with progeny, his fertility reaffirmed and his household brought from danger of extermination.

The parallel of Israel and Judah in Genesis 34 and 38 is an excellent example of what Aristotle called "thought" ($\delta\iota\acute{\alpha}\nu\iota\alpha$) in tragedy. He described the kernel of difference between "thought" and "ethos" as follows:[20]

> The third property of tragedy is thought. This is the ability to say what is possible and appropriate in any given circumstances; it is what, in the speeches of the play, is related to the arts of politics and rhetoric. The older dramatic poets made their characters talk like statesmen, where those of today make them talk like rhetoricians. Character ($\ddot{\eta}\theta\eta$) is that which reveals personal choice, the kinds of thing a man chooses or rejects when it is not obvious. Thus there is no revelation of character in speeches in which the speaker shows no preferences or aversions whatever. Thought, on the other hand, is present in speeches where something is being shown to be true or untrue, or where some general opinion is being expressed.

Confronted by his sons' actions, Israel states the obvious: "You have brought trouble upon me by making me loathsome to the inhabitants of the land, the Canaanites and the Perizzites. I have so few men that, if these people unite against me and attack me, I and my family will be wiped out" (Genesis 34:30). This is a statement about possibilities, what is to be expected from the situation. The response of Simeon and Levi is a manifestation of the ethos of the story: "Is our sister to be treated as a harlot?"

Harlot? To be sure, the reference makes sense of the Judah and Tamar plot, where Tamar must specifically be treated as a harlot in order to redeem herself. And the response of Judah when confronted with his personal signs of patriarchal status is parallel to Israel's statement to his sons, though not in the form of complaints we might expect him to have. He says, "She is more in the right than I am, since I did not give her to my son Shelah" (Genesis 38:26). Here we find a statement of what is appropriate, the recognition that Judah's personal choice in the situation was wrong. Thus, what has been interpreted as a negative treatment of Judah yields one of the finest examples of his personal honor, just as the portrayal of a weak Israel in Genesis 34 plays on the themes of honor and obligation.

Turning to the parallels of Genesis 38 and 39, we find two examples of an action pattern common to Genesis narrative, but developed with special emphasis for the characters of Judah and Joseph. In each story the brothers have the symbols of their status taken from them, then used as evidence against them in a judgment. Judah surrenders his "seal, cord, and staff," and when he cannot redeem them fears being made a laughingstock. The counter image has Joseph running naked from the clutches of a seductress, she grasping his clothing, the only real "possession" he might claim as his own. These farcical situations are to be compared with the portrayal of an Isaac so blind and old that he cannot tell the difference between the young Jacob and the true Esau, saying: "Ah, the fragrance of my son is like the fragrance of a field that the Lord has blessed . . ." (Genesis 27:27).

Hebrew stories, at times, make a laughingstock of the patriarch in order to drive home the serious point that the line is blessed. Such comedic elements, a "dumb luck" sense of the text, is in stark contrast to the effects of fate in Greek tragedy. In the Oedipus story, for example, the plot includes a violated patriarch, twin sons who struggle, a thwarted marriage alliance, and threats to lineage continuity; and in the end, everybody dies except Oedipus and Creon, the lineages come to an end, the marriage alliance is dashed, and every other sinister turn of events is enacted. The plots of the Dinah and Judah stories kill only those necessary to furthering the story development or social premises of alliance, and end with validations of lineages or kingly lines rather than termination. Indeed, aside from Genesis 38, no character in the Joseph cycle meets a tragic death.

Overall, the three story types pertaining to marriage in Genesis yield a highly consistent series of genealogical, rank, and alliance affirmations. The many vignettes contribute to a whole social conception, in the process resolving many elements of narrative action which otherwise might appear mystifying or contradictory on casual reading. The power of these structural elements is brought to full force through their interweaving and themal connection. It remains for us to observe some of the more refined sense of story development through formal analysis. In this task we may seek a provisional closure to a genealogically grounded reading of the "founding" book of the Torah.

Mythos of Patriarchal Succession

Claude Lévi-Strauss devised his notion of the "atom" of kinship through wide cross-cultural analysis of traditional systems of family reckoning.[21] The atom recognizes first that kinship rests upon ties of alliance represented in the relationships of husbands and wives and of men of lines married to one another, either a man and his wife's brother or, more usually, a man and his mother's brother. Second, kinship rests on modes of filiation running between generations, from either father to son, or again, from a man to his sister's son. The "atom" then, consists of key links expressed in the diagram:

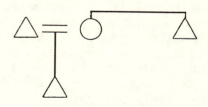

Individual cultural systems are distinguished by the way each of the relationships of this diagram are expressed in particular patterns of behavior, obligation, respect, and corporate identity. We should not be surprised, then, that the essential framework of kinship relations in Genesis should expressly reflect the basic unit of kinship. Of greater importance is our ability to construe the specific ethos, or cultural configuration, created for the unit by the Genesis narratives. In order to accomplish this task, it will be helpful to identify specifically how the basic structure is expressed throughout the text, as well as in some related texts from Hebrew and Greek literature. We may begin by observing that the central genealogies stress a one-generation difference between husbands and wives, such that a man is seen as occupying the same generation as his mother's brother. This convention recognizes the relative ranking of wife-givers to wife-takers, as we have seen, and sets up the potential discord between agnatically related uncles and nephews.

Three other points of discord are found in the Genesis texts, in each case associated with one of the other kinds of relationship of the elementary structure. That is, fathers and sons, husbands and wives, and siblings all engage in different kinds of struggle. Genesis handles sibling rivalry through pairs of brothers *or* sisters, producing the general kinship structure for stories shown in Figure 25a. The graph shows the relationships of husband and wife on the upper generation, the sibling relationship as sons of the primary line, and the other two relationships as a link between wife-giving and wife-taking groups, the actual wife-giver being on the lower generation.

Comparing Figure 25a to Figure 22, it will be immediately apparent that the central patriarchal marriages present an ideal situation of rank and marriage equations. The patriarch brings in a woman or women from the allied line, has "two sons," resolves the competition of the sons with blessings, and is then replaced by a son who starts the process again. Isaac provides the case of *direct* sibling rivalry, the competition of twins, while Jacob presents the case of *general* sibling rivalry, the sons of two competing mothers.

Additional development of the same ideal structure finds expression in several other Genesis stories, as well as in the book of Ruth and the Oedipus cycle of Greek literature (Figure 25, b–f). In wife-taking stories, the structure includes a third male sibling, while in wife-giving versions of the structure the third sibling is a female (cf. Figure 25, b and d against c, e, and f). The "third sibling" position is sometimes occupied by a true brother or sister (Er-Onan-*Shelah,* Simeon-Levi-*Dinah,* Eteocles-Polynices-*Antigone*), but more often involves a conflation of generations created by succession of a patriarch (such as *Oedipus*-Eteocles-Polynices-Antigone, Perez-Zerah-*Shelah, Joseph*-Manasseh-Ephraim). Stories about the redemption of women produce complex conflations of descendancy. Obed, for example, might be counted as "Mahlon's son" if we consider Ruth's redemption to be a levirate performance for Mahlon. Ruth's redemption, however, is linked to the land of Elimelech. In this sense she replaces Elimelech's wife, Naomi, in a marriage arrangement similar to the surrogate tie between Sarai and Hagar. Under these conditions Naomi is redeemed and becomes the child's "nurse," so Obed becomes a "brother" of Mahlon and Chilion. A similar situation emerges in Genesis 38 for different reasons. Tamar's generational movement to Judah for redemption replaces a dead wife, bypassing redemption through Shelah. Perez and Zerah, then, become Shelah's brothers, replacements for the dead Er and Onan. A third variation on this theme is seen in the Oedipus myth. Oedipus moves "up rank" and "up generation" to replace his father and redeem his (now childless) mother. He thus replaces himself through Eteocles and Polynices, and becomes the brother of his own children. Joseph's structural parallel with Oedipus is based on pure rank assertions, the narrative distinguishing between Potiphar and Potiphera. Thus, though Potiphar's wife represents the risk of an "incestuous" breach, Joseph successfully avoids the situation and replicates the "two son" birth pattern.

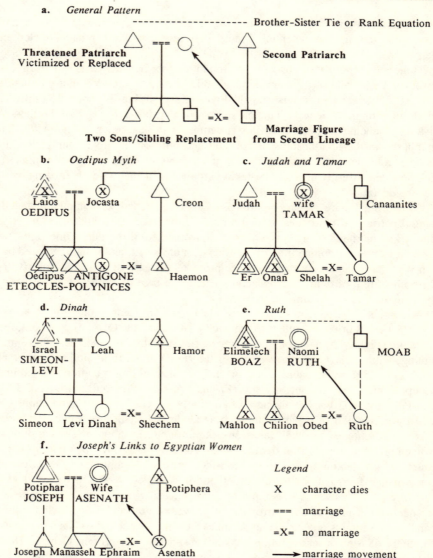

Figure 25. Variations on the "threatened patriarch" pattern in mythic narrative.

Reference to the genealogical structure moves the plot in each of the stories under consideration. In the Jacob marriage narratives, for example, it is noteworthy that mention of Laban's sons prompts Jacob's move toward separation from his uncle (Genesis 31:1). What is usually termed the conflict of Jacob and Laban, then, is actually a conflict between Jacob and the rest of his allies in the household. Recalling the hierarchy of textual units suggested by George Coats (Figure 21), we find that most of the Isaac and Jacob saga divisions entail fraternal strife, sororal strife, rank conflicts of allies, or father-son conflicts. This does not mean that discord is the only potential of the family links, but that discord is a potential which surfaces periodically as a feature of plot. Thus, Isaac "loves" Rebekah, but she intervenes to help Jacob deceive the patriarch at the time of blessing; Jacob favors Joseph, but political blessing is given to Judah in accordance with a strict recognition of Leah's superior rank over Rachel. These features of the text give the narratives literary tension and expose the underlying "legal" sense of the premises affirmed by patriarchal or other character actions.

The patterns of conflict resolution in Genesis, then, are the primary target for a study of ethos. I see four themal currents running through the narratives pertinent to these interests: (a) threats to lineage continuity, especially threats to the patriarch or matriarch; (b) violations of patriarchal authority by members of the household, (c) lineage validations through women and children, (d) justice in the final resolution of familial disputes. As we view the development of these themes we will stress the Genesis texts, then compare them to the two outside cases of Ruth and Oedipus.

Threats to Lineage Continuity

The central patriarchal narratives reflect various kinds of threats to lineage continuity. This is an explicit theme in all of the deception tales concerning Sarai, Sarah, and Rebekah, since the patriarch identifies his wife as a "sister" out of fear for his life (Genesis 12:12; 20:11; 26:9). A second kind of threat is also developed in these stories, the problem of barrenness, brought into explicit statement in Genesis 15:2–3: "But Abram said, 'O Lord God, what good will your gifts be, if I keep on being childless and have as my heir the steward of my house, Eliezer? . . . See, you have given me no offspring, and so one of my servants will be my heir.' " We can also argue more broadly that the long brideservice of Jacob and the enslavement of Joseph constitute endangerment of a lineage. Viewing the stories of Figure 25, we find that the highest ranking lineage representative in each case feels subject to a threat against continuity of his line.

The specific fear has different sources and enters the plot in different ways, but is usually tied to some action within the immediate household. Judah's fear is linked to his interpretation of the deaths of his sons; he believes Tamar is responsible for the losses, and so he sends her back to her kinsmen under the false pretense that Shelah is "too young" to perform the levirate duty. That he had no intention of giving Shelah to Tamar is indicated by his thought: "He must not die like his brothers" (Genesis 38:11). This is reinforced by his self-judgmental statement, "She is more right than I, since I did not give her my son Shelah to be his wife" (Genesis 38:26).

Joseph's master suffers fear from a different kind of misconception. He believes his slave has violated his wife, a breach of domestic authority with the connotation of "incest." Though Joseph is not a son, as a ranking servant in his master's household the violation of the patriarch's bed would constitute a grave sexual sin against Potiphar's family. Joseph's punishment also threatens his lineage, since as a prisoner he would lose any hope of marriage. Though Joseph's avoidance of sexual sin is successful, then, it produces the nadir of his personal experience in Egypt. Potiphar's reaction to his wife's allegation can be understood as motivated by fear of "replacement" by a member of his household, a very similar fear to that of Laios in the Oedipus story.

Such fear is also weakly developed in the story of Dinah and associated texts. The deception of Shechem and the killing of Hamor and his household by Simeon and Levi can be read as a bold and righteous act, but it places the brothers in the position of acting with patriarchal authority. The text is reasonably clear in disassociating Jacob from the negotiations or killings. His reaction, as the truly responsible individual in the household, is to fear that other people in the vicinity will band together and exterminate him and his lineage. This threat, and the threat posed by the unruly sons, are resolved in different ways. Israel escapes extermination by movement, and then "scatters" the brothers in their blessing, removing their tribal status. Loss of lineage identity in name is an appropriate punishment for a crime which threatened the continuity of Israel's "whole" social interests.

The stories of Ruth and Oedipus reinforce the idea that patriarchal concern with continuity can take extreme forms. The elder potential levir in Ruth, for example, publicly acknowledges his concern that he will "depreciate his own estate" should he redeem Ruth in order to exercise his claim to Elimelech's land. Read against Deuteronomic law, the Elder is brought to shame:

> If, however, a man does not care to marry his brother's wife, she shall go up to the elders at the gate and declare, "My brother-in-law does not intend to perform his duty toward me and refuses to perpetuate his brother's name in Israel." Thereupon the elders of his city shall summon him and admonish him. If he persists in saying "I am not willing to marry her," his sister-in-law, in the presence of the elders, shall go up to him and strip his sandal from his foot and spit in his face, saying publicly, "This is how one should be treated who will not build up his brother's family!" (Deuteronomy 25:7-9)

Whether such public shaming actually ever occurred is difficult to say, but the strength of the images is stirring.[22] The sandal-stripping is much milder in Ruth, consisting of a sign of binding agreement between two men. But the overall effect of narratives and rules about the levirate is emphasis of the seriousness of this familial obligation. In the case of Onan, the levirate obligation is clearly linked to responsibilities of obligation to both the father and the dead brother. This underscores the tension existing between fathers, like Judah and Jacob, who think in terms of their own reproductive increase, and sons who must defer to these patriarchal interests until such time as they can in fact assert their own authority. In Genesis as elsewhere, this comes only upon the death of the father, unless the son is banished from his kinsmen.

The Oedipus story gives the threat to lineage continuity its most extreme form, wherein Laios attempts to kill the son in order to avoid the son's patricide and ruin of the lineage by defilement of the mother. Once his plan is thwarted, the myth plays out the tension of father and son in a "blind" scenario in which the worst fears of the patriarch are actualized. The Joseph story enacts a similar turn of events. Joseph is presented as a righteous member of Potiphar's household, a man who must endure unjust consequences because of the evil wife's defilement of the patriarch's honor. Potiphar's action, however, creates the very "replacement" he is trying to avoid. Joseph is brought out of prison by Pharaoh and elevated to a position superior to that of Potiphar, and is given a highborn woman as a wife.

A wide array of instruments for termination of a lineage derives from the narratives: retribution for bloodguilt, failure to fulfill fraternal obligations, disrespect for patriarchal authority, incest, and the loss of sons through natural or divine causes. From the point of view of a patriarch, the loss of violating members of the household, no matter how trusted they might have been before generating the threat, is preferable to having the household brought to ruin or extermination. A patriarch may even be willing to face personal "shame" rather than face what he regards as a serious threat to his lineage. Such shame might come from public pronouncement, as in Ruth, or through breach of a contractual obligation, as in Judah and Tamar. Each story in Genesis seems to develop a new variation on the sources of patriarchal fears and possible means of countering them.

But Genesis also makes clear that patriarchal fears are not always warranted. The distinction between the premises of family responsibility and individual motivations is strongly developed in each case. Thus, Judah and Potiphar display correct motivations but wrong perceptions of events. The conflict of Israel and his sons demonstrates that pragmatic actions may be incorrect when considered against the assumptions of responsible action within or between corporate groups. Although the narratives seem to move in terms of crisp pronouncements of "right" and "wrong," on a deeper level the narratives blur our potential to unequivocally judge action. Unlike the Greek development of these themes, where the plot almost mechanically plays out the most extreme actions and consequences, the Hebrew narratives give a sense of "real-life" situations. The interplay of theme and countertheme is even given voice through the characters, such as Judah, who ends up weighing the merit of his case against that of Tamar, acknowledging his error, and going on with his affairs.

Violations of Patriarchal Authority

I have already amply noted that Simeon and Levi violated their father's authority. Violations of the patriarch were also carried out by Potiphar's wife and Tamar. The three stories provide a rich expansion on the themes of acceptable and unacceptable infringements on the patriarchal honor. Joseph's honor, given his status as a slave, would not be a major concern for the unfortunate Potiphar, and so he is left with a wife who clearly dishonors him. But we know that Joseph's redemption sets the matter of his honor right, and at least metaphorically accomplishes the replacement Potiphar feared. We may also understand the wicked wife's actions as a violation of Joseph which could have ended his lineage possibilities. Joseph comes to power because of his abilities as a "seer," and also because the plot of Genesis 39 spells out his honor in a familial matter. In other terms, the attempted seduction of Joseph is an essential ingredient in his total character development, a means of establishing for him an image commensurate with the taking of responsibility. As we shall see, this is also the critical link between Genesis 39 and 38. But let us recall that Joseph's dreams in Genesis 37 cause him to flaunt his position among the brothers, and even raise questions in Jacob's mind:

> Then he had another dream, and this one, too, he told to his brothers. "I had another dream . . . this time, the sun and the moon and eleven stars were bowing down to me." When he also told it to his father, his father reproved him. "What is the meaning of this dream of yours? . . . Can it be that I and your mother and your brothers are to come and bow to the ground before you?" So his brothers were wrought up against him but his father pondered the matter. (Genesis 37:9–11)

Other stories in the central genealogies involve the violation of the patriarch by wives or sons. Jacob steals the blessing of Esau by deceiving his father with his mother's help. Jacob is deceived by Leah at their marriage. Jacob tricks Laban out of his possessions, and Rachel steals Laban's household gods. Deception also flows in the other direction, along with the mistrust and fear characteristic of the patriarchs. In other terms, "violation" is the counterpart of "fear" in a system of mistrust running up and down the family rank structure, manifest through textual features of deception, reversal of blessings, escape, banishment, incest, and open confrontation.

Tamar's violation of Judah, for example, displays a balance of family interests offsetting Judah's fear. Tamar was "justified" by her motivation toward removing an injustice to her. But she proceeded very carefully. Judah was not brought to ruin or extreme public humiliation, suffering a milder tarnish to his pride because he was forced to admit his culpability. When Judah acknowledged the signs of his authority honorably, he actualized to an extent his fear of "being made a laughingstock." Because Judah was allowed in the narrative to pronounce his own guilt, he is shown to manifest the kind of judgment worthy of a leader. His "character" is exposed in such a way that the contrast drawn with Joseph in Genesis 38 and 39 is not one of "bad" versus "good," but instead one which places the two brothers on similar levels of potential.

It is again helpful to observe the notion of violation through the stark images of the Oedipus story. When Laios lost his life to the stranger on the road to Delphi, he also lost his kingdom. The young Oedipus moved on to Thebes and solved the riddle of the Sphinx. Through his action Oedipus is given the kingdom and the queen, Jocasta. Jocasta was, in effect, a sign of kingly authority. But the relationship she established with her son also violated her family's honor, specifically the honor of both father and son. Thus, Jocasta stands as a symbol of a tragic family fortune, in contrast to Tamar, the daughter-in-law who bears twins as her own curse but her husband's blessing. The struggling twins of the Oedipus cycle represent the ultimate violation of the father, since in the Greek religious tradition their deaths deny Oedipus a Theban afterlife.[23] Struggling twins in the Hebrew traditions yield kings, like Esau, Jacob, and Perez, the ancestor of David. In the balance of violation and fear, then, the Hebrew narratives develop a specific theme of providence, given voice through Joseph's statement to his brothers: "Have no fear. Can I take the place of God? Even though you meant harm to me, God meant it for good, to achieve his present end, the survival of many people" (Genesis 50:20).

Validations of the Lineage

The covenant promises of God to the central patriarchs especially include fertility. For Abraham and Isaac, fertility extends beyond the immediate lineage to the creation of parallel lines, the "nations" of Ishmael and Esau. For Jacob, fertility means the culmination of the promises, the creation of a powerful "chosen" people. In order for this new social identification to be achieved, the potential fraternal strife and paternal challenges by sons must be overcome, and the brothers brought under a lasting social canopy. The final promises of the brothers to each other in Genesis 50, whether Joseph actually enslaves the others or not, accomplishes this end, for it guarantees the continuing social identification of Israel through generations.

We must note, however, that the life of Jacob and his sons is more beset with strife, deception, and difficulty than either of the two preceding generations. In this context the signs of lineage validation take on critical importance. The *form* of validation is established in the central narrative patterns, specifically in the households of Abraham and Isaac, then brought to logical conclusion in the story of Jacob. In each generation the form of validation is the same, consisting of the elements of proper marriage and fertility. Wives and children, then, are the signs of lineage success, more important than access to land or material possessions.

Proper marriage involves the pattern asserted throughout the marriage narratives, union with a woman one-generation down from a colateral lineage. Agnatic association is not the essential feature of successful alliance, but most of the structural and symbolic information in Genesis and other biblical sources suggests that agnatic association is preferred. This is consistent with the reconstruction of ancient Jewish social organization presented by Norman Gottwald (see pp. 55–56), where lineages *(beth-'avoth)* are collected in alliance groups *(mishpāhāh)* functioning as agnatic associations within larger agnatic units, the tribes (shēvet). We must remember, though, that the actual genealogical link between men of different alliance groups might not be any more traceable than the relationship between men of different cultural confederations in Canaan. Because the "tribal" associations of Genesis are discussed as agnatic ties, Genesis presents an ideal model for what was in fact a much more fluid social system.

A proper marriage, then, is mainly dependent upon the production of offspring who honor the elders, manifest strength of character, and display a sense of corporate responsibility toward members of their household as son or as patriarch. The two-son formula is employed widely in biblical and world traditions to express these validating aims. Sons who do not conform to the patterns of corporate responsibility are removed and passed over in blessings, while sons fitting the ideal succeed their fathers as patriarchs.

In the central genealogies the removed sons are Ishmael and Esau. Ishmael is invalidated through three mechanisms. First, he is circumcised *with* Abraham. This makes him something of a rival to his father, a highborn man among the initial circumcised group. In contrast, Isaac is the first son of a circumcised patriarch who is brought into the covenant on the eighth day of life, in accordance with God's directions—Isaac is a more perfect symbol of the validating aspect of circumcision than is Ishmael. Second, after Isaac's birth, Sarah sees Ishmael "playing with" her son (Genesis 21:9). The Hebrew has a negative sense, that Ishmael was "mocking" or "making fun of" Isaac. This is the first indication of fraternal discord and, as such, disrespect also for the father. Finally, Ishmael's mother was disrespectful of Sarah's rights toward Ishmael and Abram, so Ishmael was never legitimized by unified parental recognition. In the end, after his banishment, we find Ishmael "set against his brothers."

Esau also shows disrespect for his parents through his marriages. His Canaanite wives draw negative comment from Rebekah, and his Ishmaelite alliance through Mahalath adds insult. Esau marries in the "wrong direction" and so faces territorial exclusion. But the strife between Esau and Jacob does not leave the younger brother without culpability. Jacob "buys" the birthright under a form of duress.[24] Jacob also deceives his father under the direction of his mother. I have pointed out that Isaac's instructions to Jacob to seek a wife in Aramea have a negative sense similar to banishment, but we must also recognize that the trip validates Jacob in terms of proper marriage. Rebekah's part in the deception of Isaac places her in a direct parallel with Sarah: the mothers act to determine the blessings of their sons, shifting succession from the natural inclinations of the fathers. The central cases of succession are instances of "mother knows best." In each case the narratives provide the supplemental validation of blessings from God, first through the sacrifice of Isaac and later through Jacob's theophany at Bethel (Genesis 28:10–19).

Turning to the stories graphed in Figure 25, in each case we again find the validation of lineage accomplished through births of "two sons" and action of a woman. The woman's role in each of the biblical cases, moreover, involves violation of the patriarch through a form of deception. The deceptions of Tamar and Potiphar's wife have already been discussed in detail; we may merely note again that each enables the birth of two sons, Tamar directly and Potiphar's wife in an indirect way. We should also recall that the blessing of Manasseh and Ephraim are reversed, just as the birth order of Perez and Zerah is confused. Treatment of the sons of Judah and Joseph involves the subtle replay of important themes of validation. Asenath, because of her Egyptian status, lies as outside the connubial range of Israel as do Ishmael's wife and daughter. Manasseh and Ephraim must be legitimized by adoption, the act being precipitated by the memory of Rachel's death. The two sons thus replace the lost sons, Levi and Joseph, in the context of later genealogical reckoning. In their original context Manasseh and Ephraim may have been intended to be replacements for Levi and Simeon, the brothers scattered in the blessings of Genesis 49. In any event, generational replacement of the two boys is a formal recognition of succession to Joseph's honored position, and provides a closer balance between sons of Leahite and Rachaelite heritage. Because of his Egyptian wife, Joseph never regains full social inclusion in Israel.

Perez and Zerah revive the predicament of twin sons, the "resolution" being the confusion created by a midwife who marks the hand of the elder with a red thread, only to have it withdrawn and the other brother born first. Because Perez is linked to the genealogy of David we know he is the primary successor of Judah, but he and his brother remain signs of the fertility of Judah rather than being elevated to the status of named lineages at the top of Israel's social organization. Thus, Perez and Zerah replace Er and Onan, Judah's sons killed by God. The most significant fact in the story is that Perez and Zerah are allowed to live. This must derive from some sense in which Tamar is "correct" as a wife of Judah. The most likely textual sign of her correctness is the generational status established for her in the plot of the story, taken together with Tamar's action in the face of injustice. Looking back to the central marriage accounts, we should note that Tamar reconstitutes the same kind of deception which gave Jacob Leah instead of Rachel. Her "veiled" face prevented Judah from recognizing the woman presenting herself to him. Recall also that Rebekah veiled her face when she first encountered Isaac (Genesis 24:65), but that Rachel was embraced on her first contact with Jacob (Genesis 29:11). Seeing a woman's beauty, indeed, is fully associated with less desirable unions throughout Genesis, as in all of the deception stories and the tale of the humbling of Dinah.

The same themes permeate the book of Ruth. Naomi directs Ruth's encounter with Boaz at the threshing floor. When Ruth is discovered, Boaz cannot tell who she is. Ruth does not resort to a clear deception, but Naomi's use of Ruth to assure her own redemption is a more "active" parallel with Tamar's drastic measures. Naomi, after all, represents the case of a woman who might well not be accepted back into the group. Her husband had discontinued residence with his kinsmen, and the letter of the levirate rules in Deuteronomy (chapter 25:5) concerns brothers "who are living together." Naomi had already produced sons, and hence could not claim redemption under the levirate rule. The fact that her sons died complicates her situation. These confusing aspects of the Ruth story have been much discussed, but not in the context of an overall Genesis marriage formula.[25] My reading of Ruth sees the plot as a levirate deception in which the Elder levir is not adequately informed of Ruth's status. In the end, Ruth's union to Boaz is a simple contract marriage which is validated by a birth pertinent to the kingly line of David. Because of this topical thrust and the close pattern parallels of Ruth to Genesis 38, the story reaffirms my interpretation of Judah and Tamar as an "honor tale" showing Judah's patriarchal strengths, and Tamar's correctness as a wife.

Comparison of Genesis 38 and 39 with the Oedipus cycle also supports this view, as noted in the preceding section. The Oedipus story works on the theme of validation through a reverse logic, however, citing the circumstances where the status of a "validating" woman can produce lineage termination. The ancient Greeks would certainly have appreciated the mythos of Genesis, though they might not have liked the "character" of biblical patriarchs. What is clear in both traditions is that lineage validation is not a simple matter of patriarchal choice. It is based instead upon the strict adherence to rules of proper behavior, proper marriage, and proper assessments of situations. This brings us to the last prominent theme of conflict resolution, justice in domestic relations.

Justice in the Resolution of Conflict

Genesis resolves each of the major lineage oppositions it presents through application of a pattern of judgment. The pattern involves the elements: (a) a call for judgment, (b) human action, and (c) justice confirmed by divine blessing or curse. Consider, for example, Sarai's complaint to Abram in their confrontation over Hagar: "Then Sarai said to Abram: 'The wrong I suffer falls on you! I put my maid into your arms, and as soon as she found she had conceived, she looked with disdain on her mistress. May the Lord decide between me and you!' " (Genesis 16:5). The call for justice incorporates the idea of God as witness and judge. The implication of Sarai's last statement is that God *knows* who is correct, and will act against the offending party in the dispute. This feature is more explicitly developed in the honorable separation of Jacob and Laban, where Laban says:

> . . . May the Lord watch between you and me, when we are absent one from the other. If you mistreat my daughters, or take other wives besides my daughters, even though there is no man with us, remember, God is witness between you and me. . . . Note this heap and this memorial pillar I have set up between you and me. This heap is a witness, and the pillar is a witness, that I will not pass over this heap to you, and you will not pass over this heap and this pillar to me, for harm. May the God of Abraham and the God of Nahor, and the God of their father, judge between us.

In these two instances, opposite resolutions of the call for justice occur. Abram returns Hagar to Sarai's control, resulting in Hagar's mistreatment and escape; Laban and Jacob go their separate ways in peace, ending their long pattern of mutual deception. Divine validation of these "solutions" to conflict comes in the form of blessings.

The case of Hagar is complex, for, as we have already observed, Abram is in a difficult double-bind over the status of his wives. His return of Hagar to Sarai is only a short-term solution, heeding the complaint of Sarai. Hagar's escape prestates the ultimate solution, but is incorrect because it removes from Abram the opportunity for just patriarchal action. The promise to Hagar of Genesis 16:7–14 is accompanied by a direction for her to return to Sarai, but Ishmael's birth on the way precludes Sarai's opportunity to recognize Ishmael. The plot carefully moves toward the final "just" solution in Genesis 21. After the birth of Isaac, Sarai again calls for justice, but Abraham is distressed over his son Ishmael. He receives an immediate promise of blessing for the boy, and so finally discharges Hagar and Ishmael to fully resolve the marriage strife for both women. Once the separation is accomplished, the blessing of the boy is repeated for Hagar and a well is miraculously provided to sustain Ishmael. The double resolution of the problem is characteristic of the Genesis narratives, as can be seen from the list of conflict resolutions shown in Table 3.

Returning to the case of Jacob's separation from Laban, we find an even more complex statement of resolution. The oath of Laban and Jacob just observed is the call for justice enunciated by Laban, the functioning patriarch in the story, but

Segmentation	*Call for Justice*	*Action*	*Divine Validation*
a. Abram-Nahor		Separation 12:1-6	Promise 12:7
b. Abram-Lot	Honorable Discharge 13:5-9	Separation 13:10-12	Promise 13:14-17
c. Abraham-Lot	Intercession 18:16-33	Segmentation 19:1-29	Sexual Sin 19:30-38
d. Sarai-Hagar	Sarah's Charge 16:5	Mistreatment/Escape 16:6	Promise 16:7-14
e. Isaac-Ishmael	Honorable Discharge 21:9-11	Separation 21:14-16	Promise 21:12-13 21:17-21
f. Jacob-Esau	Blessing Request 27:36-40	Banishment/Escape 28:1-5	Promise 28:10-19
g. Jacob-Laban	Release Request 30:25-27	Denial/Deception 30:27-31:2	Promise 31:3
		CHIASTIC SEQUENCE	
h. Jacob-Laban	Jacob's Charge 31:36-42	Escape/Deception 31:4-35	Promise 31:3
i. Jacob-Laban	Honorable Discharge/ Oath 31:10-13	Separation 32:1-2	Angels at Mahanaim 32:2-3
j. Israel-Esau	Prayer 32:10-13	Subordination/Gifts (Deception) 32:4-7; 32:14-22 33:1-17	Struggle 32:23-33
k. Brothers-Joseph Israel-Joseph	Reuben's Plea 37:21-22	Theft/Imprisonment 37:23	Redemption 39--41
l. Brothers-Joseph	Judah's Plan 37:25-28	Theft/Deception Enslavement 37:28-36	Redemption 39--41
m. Joseph Resolution	Joseph's Charges 42:8-17; 44:1-13	Judah's Plea 44:18-34	Joseph's Promise 45:9-10 50:19-21

Table 3. Repetitions of the conflict-separation narratives in Genesis, showing the patterns of calls for justice, action, and divine validation (also see Figure 20).

constitutes the third search for resolution in the Jacob-Laban novella. This call is immediately followed by separation of the two kinsmen and an appearance of angels: "Early in the morning Laban arose, and kissed his grandchildren and his daughters and blessed them; then he departed and returned home. Jacob also resumed his journey, and angels of God met him. When Jacob saw them, he said: 'This is God's camp.' So he named that place Mahanaim" (Genesis 32:1–3).

This final resolution and validation are preceded by a chiastically organized narrative in which Jacob makes two different requests for justice from Laban, centered on the divine promise of Genesis 31:3. Jacob's first request presents his case for release after the birth of Joseph, and his second request charges Laban to prove any wrongdoing of which he is accused. His first request is justifiable under the legitimizing function of Joseph's birth, but is met with refusal and an agreement for additional service to Laban. Jacob's deception of Laban in this instance results in most of the flocks being transferred to Jacob's ownership. The "magical" means Jacob uses for producing spotted, streaked, and speckled kids introduces the idea of hidden knowledge used against Laban—we need not engage in an argument giving Jacob knowledge of selective breeding. Jacob's culpability is increased by his selection of "hardier" animals over "weaker" ones.

The second charge of Jacob follows his divine instruction to leave Laban and incorporates his escape plot and the theft of Laban's household gods by Rachel. When Laban overtakes Jacob with a force of kinsmen, he charges Jacob with the theft and is deceived by Rachel during his search. Thus, Jacob's second charge for justice is actually a false one, placing Laban in a more sympathetic position for the reader. The whole narrative underscores the tensions of wife-giver and wife-taker relationships founded in brideservice, and prepares us for the honorable discharge of the final separation.

Viewing Table 3, it is apparent that the Jacob-Laban struggle and resolution are neatly punctuated by the Jacob-Esau controversy. The two resolutions of Jacob's primacy over Esau accomplish the transformation of the brothers from quarreling youths to individual patriarchs fulfilling the blessings of their father. Not only does Jacob obtain (and maintain through struggle) a divine blessing, but the individual calls for justice of Esau (Genesis 27:36–40) and Jacob (32:10–13) nicely oppose to show the anguish of their relationship. Jacob's subordinate presentation to his brother at their final meeting fulfills Esau's blessing promise that he would "throw off his yoke" to gain independence. Consistently with Esau's character, he does not seem to realize what is happening. He accepts Jacob's gift (a tribute? a price for the birthright?) but seems to actually expect his brother to follow him to Seir. For Jacob's part, the presentation is a ruse, a diversion allowing his return to Canaan as Israel. In spite of the deception, if it is deception rather than honorable agreement, the brothers fulfill their blessings and leave each other on good terms. Each has his share of justice.

I include at the top of Table 3 the cases of Abram's separations from Nahor and Lot. The Abram-Nahor separation is not accompanied by a call for justice, but the promise to Abram in Genesis 12:7 parallels the promise to Jacob of Genesis 31:3. This, together with Abraham's reluctance to send Isaac to Haran, suggests that the initial movement of Abram prestates the general pattern of conflict resolution. The theme of conflict is explicit in the Lot stories, and is again resolved in double scenarios. First, Abram honorably discharges Lot, they separate with Lot taking the apparently most desirable area, and then God makes his promise to Abram. The second resolution accomplishes the kinship segmentation of Abram and Lot by killing Lot's wife, likely a woman from Abram's household, and bringing the younger kinsman into sexual sin.

The narrative of the second Abram-Lot segmentation presents the only central patriarchal example of "curse." The scenario opens with Abraham defending Lot's honor to God, and God honoring Abraham's request by sparing Lot and his family from the destruction of Sodom and Gomorrah. In the process of Lot's escape, the angels visiting him are demanded by the evil people of the city. His solution is to offer his daughters to the crowd, an action we may reasonably count as an unfortunate error of judgment. Thus, in the validation of Lot's lineage, his blessing of fertility, he is given to the very daughters he would have victimized. Lot is reduced to the sin of incest. The event is marked by the absence of the divine, and located in a cave.

The conflict development of the Joseph novella incorporates a subtle differentiation of "character" and "motive" for the key sons of Jacob. The novella is characterized by independent calls for justice by Reuben, Judah, and Joseph. The Reuben and Judah contrast is interwoven between chapters 37 and 44, with the ultimate resolution of the conflict concentrating on the characters of Joseph and Judah. The general conflict between Joseph and his brothers involves his "bad reports" about the sons of Bilhah and Zilpah, his dreams which are interpreted by his brothers and father as involving unreasonable aspirations, and the general favor shown to him by Jacob. Genesis 37 quickly brings these conflicts to a head in the complex events at Dothan. In Dothan, when the brothers plot to kill Joseph, Reuben issues the first call for justice, suggesting that the boy be thrown into a pit so he might then restore the lad to his father. Reuben's concern is as much for himself as for Joseph, but his planned rescue is thwarted by the first in a series of redemptions. Joseph is taken from the pit by Midianites even as the counterplan of Judah is unfolding.

The plan of Judah to sell Joseph represents a second call for justice, but involves taking the matter of judgment against Joseph to the brothers. Judah cites the potential of bloodguilt and the obligations of agnatic relationship as justifications for sparing Joseph's life. Thus, Judah's motive, to rid the brothers of the favored rival, is bad, but his justification is consistent with themes of lineage obligations and is openly stated. The plan is a clear infringement on patriarchal honor, as evidenced in the deception of Jacob after the crime is committed.

Reuben, in contrast, has a stronger motive, but sets himself against his brothers by his deceptive means. He is ultimately drawn into the plot of deception to save himself. The actions in both sequences involve theft, first of Joseph by the brothers and the Midianites, then of an animal which is killed to provide blood used in Jacob's deception. The subtle difference between imprisonment and enslavement brings emphasis to the general rejection of Joseph's attitude by all of his brothers.

We have already discussed the general resolution of this family conflict in detail. Here we may add simply that Joseph's charges of espionage and theft are, like Jacob's charge to Laban in Genesis 31:36–42, categorically false. As we have seen, the false charges bring forth Judah's formal pronouncement of the true issue. The resolution by divine validation comes from Joseph's own lips, both in his initial revelation of identity and in his final promise to his brothers. These statements, moreover, refer to the redemptions of Joseph's rise in Potiphar's house and his final elevation by Pharaoh, both of which are accomplished with copious references to divine intervention in Joseph's affairs.

We find in these scenarios the counterpart of validation through marriage and fertility. Because fertility brings with it the necessity of differentiating offspring, God and the patriarch are continually called upon to resolve conflicts. Patriarchal action which is just results in validation by God, while the wicked and unjust are brought through divine action to some form of justice. Justice, in each case, seems to be structurally commensurate to the infraction. Thus, Lot is delivered to his daughters, Hagar is given her freedom because of her mistreatment, Sarah is given a son because Ishmael was denied her, Jacob is banished into brideservice for his theft, and Esau is given gifts and kingship for his loss of birthright and blessing. Justice, then, is the restoration of honor when family rights are violated, and so it cannot be discussed at all in the absence of violation.

This helps us understand why the text is the way it is. I recall a conversation I had several years ago with an ancient historian about my study of Genesis. When I spoke of the moral themes in the Torah he sneered: "What moral system is in Genesis—Adam and Eve lie to God, Cain kills his brother, Noah gets drunk, Abraham gives his wife to other men, Lot commits incest with his daughters, women cheat their fathers and husbands, Jacob and Joseph. . . ." My response to such viewpoints today is the same as it was then: I see the question of morality in Genesis as a matter of interpretation. But biblical interpretation is no easy matter. Most modern readers are equipped with only a few of the conceptual tools to begin reading. We encounter language barriers, cultural difference, editorial and theological bias of translation, and most of all, constant limitations of our willingness to meet the text on its own terms. *My* reading of Genesis is not *the* reading of Genesis, for it is never quite the same on each encounter with the text. I also know from the work of my colleagues that their experience is similar.

These comments move us far from Aristotle's essentially static view of literature. After all the models, graphs, and charts, we find that interpretation is not simply a matter of structure, but is instead that activity wherein we allow our minds to move beyond structure to implication, and from implication to a total experience. Genesis is a book about signs, beautiful expressions of how God signified a relationship of commitment to human beings, a covenant with the patriarchs and their descendants. Genesis is an allegory of semiotic, a text which continually prompts our "reflections upon the role of signs in structuring experience."[26] Encounters with the text lead us toward the elusive covenant. The signs of the covenant appear, only to be defiled, then transformed into new appealing images loaded with the contradictions of the evolving narration. We must be constantly aware of the tenuous covenant between writer and listener, with the text as its signifier, its potentials and realized meanings leading the two apart. The graphs on the page may be fixed, but Genesis shimmers before us. Its meanings are illusions of our own flickering consciousness.

V

SEMIOSIS

Each of the preceding chapters offers a different notion of structure, and hence a different orientation to the reading of Genesis. Scripture was viewed throughout the presentations—no matter what level of text was involved—as a stable and well-organized whole. Interpretations of the whole depend upon culturally astute readers, readers sensitive to some of the formal metaphors, political concerns, literary structures, and cultural backgrounds which make Genesis meaningful in immediate, but for modern readers perhaps unusual, ways. Such an orientation to the text is not inconsistent with biblical scholarship in general. Many of the standard critical strategies of readers outside the discipline of anthropology figure prominently in my analysis. The anthropological content of the readings in this book, indeed, only touches lightly upon the formal models and language of kinship and structural analysis.

This chapter does not purport to fill the gaps of theoretical background supported in my occasional citations. Instead, we will briefly concentrate on the meaning of "semiosis" in the context of biblical reading, reasserting and redeveloping some of the points about interpretation theory offered in my substantive presentation. To this end, let us again recognize that no privileged interpretation of Genesis can exist. Genesis persists through its continual reinterpretation—the constant recreation of those who experience it formally or informally. Jewish critical and liturgical tradition surrounding the Torah reinforces this point. What happened, after all, as the Torah became a fixed document, independent of the flexible oral tradition from which its particular stories were partially derived? Were not the original functions of myth and folklore replaced with a written critical medium, the Talmudic documents, thus referring centuries of real-world problems back to the immutable documents of the law?

Our awareness of the relationship between scriptural law and critical tradition is an excellent departure point into the theory of signs, or "semiotic." If there is no privileged interpretation of law, except in the immediate sense of socially approved interpretation, then a text like Genesis has no particular meaning. The static physical medium we call the "text" is a complex of signifiers imbued with potentials, a set of "promiscuous signs."[1] Moreover, the meaning potentials of the text are partitioned, not only along the lines of linguistic hierarchy, but also along the lines of the history in which the text as object resides. Thus, the formal structure of the book and the lifeplay surrounding us constantly recreate the effect we call "interpretation of the law."

Genesis specifically satisfies conditions allowing structural interpretation of myth, set down by Claude Lévi-Strauss decades ago in the widely read and critiqued paper "The Structural Study of Myth." Lévi-Strauss concluded his powerful essay with the following remarkable passage:[2]

> Prevalent attempts to explain alleged differences between the so-called "primitive" mind and scientific thought have resorted to qualitative differences between the working processes of the mind in both cases while assuming that the objects to which they were applying themselves remained very much the same. If our interpretation is correct, we are led toward a completely different view, namely, that the kind of logic which is used by mythical thought is as rigorous as that of modern science, and that the difference lies not in the quality of the intellectual process, but in the nature of the things to which it is applied. This is well in agreement with the situation known to prevail in the field of technology: what makes a steel ax superior to a stone one is not that the first one is better made than the second. They are equally well made, but steel is a different thing than stone. In the same way we may be able to show that the same logical processes are put to use in myth as in science, and that man has always been thinking equally well; the improvement lies, not in the alleged progress of man's conscience, but in the discovery of new things to which it may apply its unchangeable abilities.

Here, Lévi-Strauss teaches by example, for he employs the distinction of qualities between objects represented in signs as a means of dashing the quality distinction between the minds of people creating signs. The signifying behaviors of a Kariera man in Australia, or Mozart, or "Moses," were not founded in a different kind of intellect than that of Lévi-Strauss. But in pointing out a false distinction between "primitive" and "scientific" consciousness, Lévi-Strauss affirms the human ability to create signifiers for objects which do not "exist" otherwise. Of this "unreal" part of culture John Deely has recently stated:[3]

> It is true that the unreal relational components of human experience only exist through the cognitive functioning of living individuals, and in this sense the cultural system does have actuality only in and from social interaction. But this "unreal" dimension of experience recognizable as such . . . is in itself something distinct from even though immanent within social interaction and social system. It is then this unreal dimension which is the ground of the cumulative transmission of learning that makes human society as enculturated different in kind from animal societies that cannot jump the links of individuals connecting the generations.

We entertain two broad assertions. First is the idea that the quality of human mind, at least insofar as language is concerned, is constant. Second is the idea that a critical aspect of human mind is the "unreal" component of thought, whether in the form of theory construction or myth construction, a quality capable of forming and modifying experience. The two ideas not only complement each other, but produce the giant leap away from the idea of inherent "meaning" in nature.

Numerous recent essays speak of universal qualities of thought, while questioning the value of purely mechanistic approaches to structure. As Paul Ricoeur observed of text analysis in his essay "Explanation and Understanding":[4]

> I understand full well that structuralism, remaining within the confines of the story, will not look elsewhere than in the signs of the narration for the mark of the narrational level. . . . But what motive does the analyst have in looking for the signs of the narrator and the listener in the text of the story itself, if not the understanding which envelops all of the analytic steps and places the narrative back into a movement of transmission, into a living tradition, as a story told by someone to someone? The story thus belongs to a chain of speeches by which a cultural community is constituted and by which this community interprets itself by means of narratives.

Structural analysis must serve a process of interpretation; and by interpretation we mean not simply a mechanistic application of *how* meaning occurs, but an enthusiastic approach to *what* meanings occur. Yet some texts are more appropriate to structural reading than others.

Genesis invites structural explanation more directly than the examples of Lévi-Strauss's original argument. Where is the independently demonstrable structure behind the presentation of the Oedipus myth of the French master? Where is the internal limitation of details which provides the formal bridge between Lévi-Strauss's understanding of the myth and his structural representation of the myth as narrative? In what way are Lévi-Strauss's wonderful interpretations of Greek and Zuni myth compelled? Certainly, his results are extraordinary as much for what they leave out as for what they tell.

We must note that the conscious structural interpretation of the Genesis text, far from leading us to an absolutely new theology or cultural reconstruction, reinforces and complements traditional viewpoints hermeneuticists have embraced for a hundred years. This suggests the critical question: Should structural treatment necessarily yield extraordinary understanding? Probably not. What makes structural interpretation work on conscious levels is the same set of principles that allows our subconscious experience of interpretation. After all, a structural analysis, to be wholly true to the linguistic model, is nothing more than a systematic and explicit set of statements detailing how meanings are produced in a particular instance, by virtue of signs juxtaposed in a syntax. Hence, the "inspired" or "received" view of the text should differ from a formal view mainly in being a product of unconscious associations.

Do we say that a grammarian has a better understanding of the sentence "May I have a slice of bread?" than the grocer? Certainly not. The grammarian may have more power to create meanings, if concerns for structure do not get in the way; at least this is implied in the ideal grammatical construct Noam Chomsky called "competence."[5] But the hearer of a particular sentence, each attentive reader of a particular story, is exposed to more or less the same structure and has an equal chance to create associations leading to meanings.

The difficulty with Genesis and modern readers is that we often simply dismiss some of the most important elements of text and never experience a whole structure.

If we encounter several different structures, then we may expect to arrive at somewhat different interpretations in each case. This is not to say that a perception of similar structure, consciously or unconsciously, must call forth identical meanings, whether for different readers or the same reader on successive scriptural encounters. We must expect at times to assert similar linguistic or syntactic evidence for quite different interpretations. Texts are simply rich, and reader backgrounds plentiful.

But the idea of "cumulative transmission of learning" is central to semiosis, the active process of experience through signs. Individual experiences in particular cultures remain products of both shared and individual potentials of meaning generation. In linguistics we call the individual potential "ideolect," emphasizing the uniqueness of the speech productions originating in collective association. In semiotics, we call this potential "the interpretant," giving emphasis to the absolutely unique set of associations which may be achieved for each individual experiencing the "sign." The world unfolds as we engage it, but our various avenues of engagement constrain the unfolding process. If we change process, our world changes. Nature, even when "shared" to a degree, is necessarily understood through such an individually changing structure.

A structural reading of Genesis can be rather like encountering geometry. The premises are relatively few, but the combinations of premises yield complex and ordered arguments. What could not happen, or would not likely happen, occurs purely, offering a *mimesis* rich in possibilities. We experience the story, take hold of the signs, concatenate them, and *know* the law of the group which creates their transformations. We are not surprised, then, as we would be in the informal reading based upon unconscious traces of connection, when the narrative turns to the very possibility we have already generated. Structural analysis is incapable of unlocking anything beyond this, yet we should not lack appreciation for a process which brings the artifacts of a reading into conscious representation. The formal experience of Genesis involves us in poetics and mythscape in such a way that we more precisely apprehend how the richness of text is created, even as we deprive ourselves of its effect.

For most contemporary readers such formal excursions may represent our most ready access to the text. For example, to conclude with a last comment on the beginning of Genesis, let us recall the compelling representation of a primal God. Amid darkness and void ". . . a mighty wind swept over the waters" or ". . . the spirit of God moved upon the face of the waters." How beautifully the image of wind works on our senses. It is something powerful which has no apparent substance. Wind is the perfect first stirring of an eternal Spirit. But some translations of the Hebrew do not force us to appreciate the image, even though "spirit" and "wind" are comprised in a single word, *ruach*. Even when the passage is rendered ". . . and a wind from God sweeping over the water" we may miss the unity of the sign.

I am reminded of the Zen story about two monks who argued over a flag waving in the wind. Was the flag moving or the wind? Their master resolved the question by observing that neither the flag, nor the wind, but instead the *mind* was moving.

So it must be with the reader new to the text, or old, be the reading in Hebrew or English. Translations are only interpretations of some defined original. Special though they are, they are no different from the process they promote by giving us first access to a foreign document. The original document is not more special, for it is merely an instrument guiding our thought. We are to an extent left to ourselves, and secondarily to the historical community surrounding us, in our attempts to ground our experience of the other minds in the text. In some ways we can never meet these other minds, but happily, in other ways we can touch across centuries of differences based in our common abilities.

NOTES

I. Genealogies

1. Readers who are unfamiliar with kinship studies in anthropology might wish to consult the excellent short work of Robin Fox, *Kinship and Marriage* (Baltimore, Maryland: Penguin Books; 1967). The two prominent orientations to the study of kinship are "alliance" theory, stressing how marriages link diverse groups and enhance access of each group to political and economic resources, and "segmentary" theory, stressing how populations maintain reasonable group size through generations while also maintaining political cohesion. These orientations underpin much of my discussion, although it will become apparent that I have made stronger use of the alliance perspective. Those who seek more formal introduction to the complexities of kinship should consult either R. Needham, *Structure and Sentiment* (Chicago: University of Chicago Press; 1962), or Claude Lévi-Strauss, *The Elementary Structures of Kinship* (Boston: Beacon Press; 1969 [orig. French ed. 1949]).

2. For the seminal exposition of this point by an anthropologist, see "The Legitimation of Solomon" *in* E. Leach, *Genesis as Myth and Other Essays* (London: Jonathan Cape; 1969). The importance of genealogy to hermeneutics has been strongly recognized in recent biblical scholarship; especially see R. Wilson, "The Old Testament Genealogies in Recent Research," *Journal of Biblical Literature* 94:169–89; R. Wilson, *Genealogy and History in the Biblical World, (Yale Near Eastern Researches),* vol. 7 (New Haven, Connecticut: Yale University Press; 1977); and R. Wilson, *Sociological Approaches to the Old Testament* (Philadelphia: Fortress Press; 1984). See also R. Oden, Jr., "Jacob as Father, Husband, and Nephew: Kinship Studies and the Patriarchal Narratives," *Journal of Biblical Literature,* vol. 102, no. 2 (1983), pp. 189–205; and R. Oden, Jr., *The Bible without Theology: The Theological Tradition and Alternatives to It* (San Francisco: Harper & Row, 1987). Wilson and Oden provide bibliographic entry to other sociologically based interpretations by biblical scholars. Also, the collection of essays by E. Leach and D. A. Aycock, *Structuralist Interpretations of Biblical Myth* (Cambridge: Cambridge University Press; 1983), includes an excellent survey of British anthropological works on biblical topics.

3. The "formula" association is called forth especially with the *toledoth* divisions, opening statements usually translated "these are the generations of." Cf. also Wilson, *Sociological Approaches to the Old Testament,* pp. 40–47. A large literature on related kinship representations for the Near East exists—many key papers appear in *Journal of Near Eastern Studies.*

4. The name Haran in Genesis is applied to a brother of Abram and as a place name in northwest Mesopotamia in which Abram's brother Nahor lives. Similarly, Canaan is applied in several dialectical variants as a personal name and as a region designation.

5. For an excellent treatment of political and kinship issues forming background to the biblical text, see Norman K. Gottwald, *The Tribes of Yahweh: A Sociology of the Religion of Liberated Israel, 1250–1050 B.C.E.* (New York: Maryknoll; 1979).

6. David Daube's work in biblical law spans over fifty years. Works of particular interest include D. Daube, *Biblical Law* (Cambridge: Cambridge University Press; 1947), and D. Daube, *Ancient Jewish Law: Three Inaugural Lectures* (Leiden: E. J. Brill; 1981).

7. D. Daube, *Ancient Jewish Law,* offers a wide range of examples of legal prestatement in Genesis narrative. See also C. Carmichael, *Women, Law, and the Genesis Traditions* (Edinburgh: Edinburgh University Press; 1979).

8. Wilson, *Genealogy and History in the Biblical World;* for examples see pp. 160–61 and 201.

9. Numerous authors describe the basic elements of "documentary theory" in commentaries on Genesis. The first three on the following list are the works I have consulted most often on source questions: Hermann Gunkel, *Genesis,* 3rd edition, (Goettingen: Vandenhoeck & Ruprecht; 1910 [subsequent editions unchanged]); G. von Rad, *Genesis: A Commentary* (Philadelphia: Westminster Press; 1972); Bruce Vawter, *On Genesis: A New Reading* (New York: Doubleday; 1977); Gunther Plaut, *The Torah, Genesis: A Modern Commentary* (New York: Union of American Hebrew Congregations; 1974). The last work is devoted to "whole text" analysis of Genesis, an approach more consistent with mine.

10. Oden, *The Bible Without Theology,* pp. 44–91.

11. G. Coats, *Genesis with an Introduction to Narrative Literature* (Grand Rapids, Michigan: W. B. Eerdmans; 1983).

12. N. Frye, *Anatomy of Criticism: Four Essays* (Princeton, New Jersey: Princeton University Press; 1957).

13. Carmichael, *Women, Law, and the Genesis Traditions.* See also C. Carmichael, *Law and Narrative in the Bible: The Evidence of the Deuteronomic Laws and the Decalogue* (Ithaca, New York: Cornell University Press; 1985).

14. See M. Buss, ed., *Encounter with the Text: Form and History in the Hebrew Bible* (Philadelphia: Fortress Press; 1979); D. Patte and A. Patte, *Structural Exegesis: From Theory to Practice* (Philadelphia: Fortress Press; 1978); D. Patte, ed., "Genesis 2 and 3. Kaleidoscopic Structural Readings," *Semeia,* vol. 18 (1980); G. W. Coats, *From Canaan to Egypt: Structural and Theological Context for the Joseph Story,* Catholic Biblical Quarterly Monograph Series, no. 4 (Washington D.C.: Catholic Biblical Association; 1976). Also see the entire series of the journal *Semeia.*

15. This theme was one of several pursued by the National Endowment for the Humanities Summer Seminar, "Biblical Law in Historical Perspective," offered by David Daube and Calum Carmichael at the University of California, Berkeley, between June and August, 1988.

16. I shall refer to the Priestly redaction circle and to the Yahwist and Elohist sources, following early source-critical practice. But my analysis, it should be noted, takes the premise that attempts to separate the conflated Yahwist-Elohist narrative into independent narratives have been, in the main, unwarranted and unconvincing. Thus, I see the text of Genesis in terms of a two-tier system involving a primary J-E narrative core in chapters 25–50 and a secondary manipulation of that core with addition of stories, some perhaps quite ancient and others consistent with the J-E material, to form Genesis 1–25 and the full final redaction of the book.

17. Vawter, *On Genesis,* p. 100. Although Genesis 4 is ordinarily considered a Yahwist document, Vawter suggests that chapter 4:25–26 is at least a modification of Yahwist materials by the redaction circle, and that the two verses can be linked to the Noah reference of chapter 5:29.

18. See M. Carroll, "Leach, Genesis, and Structural Analysis: A Critical Evaluation," *American Ethnologist,* vol. 4 (1977), pp. 663–67.

19. Cf. Vawter, *On Genesis,* p. 103. The two versions of the list are also dialect variants. Note as well that the priestly variant has Lamech live 777 years, while the other version speaks of the "seven-fold" vengeance for Cain, and claims that Lamech will be avenged "seventy-seven fold" (Genesis 4:24).

20. See Wilson, *Genealogy and History in the Biblical World,* pp. 138–66, for comprehensive analysis and comparisons to other Near Eastern traditions.

21. Wilson, "Old Testament Genealogies in the Biblical World," pp. 169–89. My argument recognizes the linking function of Genesis 11:27–32 cited by Wilson, but places greater emphasis on the organizing and theological functions such a linking genealogy may produce for the broader text.

22. E. Leach, *Rethinking Anthropology* (London: Athelone Press; 1966), pp. 124–36. See especially pp. 131–32. Leach's time essays represent one of the essential backgrounds to my analysis of social organization and textual construction in Genesis. The applicability of his

ideas, developed from a substance in Greek myth, underscores the nature of the biblical text as well as the importance of genealogical, social, and ritual elements in the text as parts of a potential overall structure.

23. Theophany involves the visible appearance of a god to a human bȩing. Alliance interests are represented in the availability of groups from whom wives may be taken.

24. As logical duals Abram and Jacob differ in such a way that they *call each other forth,* or stand as "signs" of each other. This is an application common to the structuralism of C. Lévi-Strauss, where a structural model immediately implies its transformations, in this instance offering, among other possibilities, two transformations in perfect complementation. Expanding on this notion of signs in "Structure, Word, Event," an essay in Reagan and Stewart, eds., *The Philosophy of Paul Ricoeur: An Anthology of His Work* (Boston: Beacon Press; 1978), Paul Ricoeur states (p. 110) that given the underpinning distinction of linguistic form and external substance: ". . . we must define the sign not only by its relation of opposition to all other signs of the same level but also in itself as a purely internal or immanent difference. It is in this sense that Saussure distinguishes the signifying and the signified, and Hjelmslev, expression and content." Thus, the personifications of Abram and Jacob may be seen on one level as signifying men in a historical narrative about society, and on another level as complementary elements in a structure which signifies a society and a covenant. The structural aspect of Abram vis-à-vis Jacob provides an "immanent" difference that accomplishes the critical shift from "individual" to "group" concerns.

25. The situation is a feminine version of that depicted for men in Genesis 38, when Judah's son Onan fails in his responsibility to produce an offspring for his brother Er. Hagar's action (and apparently also Abram's) defies her responsibility to produce a son for her mistress. In both cases the division of patrimony is at stake. See also Vawter, *On Genesis,* pp. 214–15.

26. Leach, *Rethinking Anthropology,* pp. 131–32.

27. On a political level we might well rename the Joseph story "the saga of Reuben, Judah, Joseph, and Benjamin," or better, "the saga of the Leahites and Rachelites," representing the relative contributions of the key sons of Leah and Rachel to the successes of Israel.

28. The formal oppositions emphasize the association of grandparent/grandchild, consistent with our starting point in Leach's essays and with the broader structural perspective on elementary kinship systems; the text bifurcates patriarchal society generationally in a manner similar to, say, Australian section systems.

29. See also J. Gammie, "Theological Interpretation by Way of Literary and Traditional Analysis: Genesis 25–36" *in* M. Buss, ed., *Encounter with the Text.*

30. See also the discussion of Ishmael in this chapter, pp. 27ff.

31. Coats, "From Canaan to Egypt"; Coats, *Genesis with an Introduction to Narrative Literature,* pp. 272–76, 307–11. See also J. A. Emerton, "An Examination of a Recent Structuralist Interpretation of Genesis XXXVIII", *Vetus Testamentum* 26:79–98 (1976).

32. Oden's "Jacob as Father, Husband, and Nephew" represents the first strong move by a biblical scholar into applications of alliance theory to Genesis, though Gottwald's *The Tribes of Yahweh,* working on a very different scale and with different sociological presuppositions, includes much useful direct social analysis of backgrounds pertinent to the specific tasks of interpreting Genesis.

33. Leach, "The Legitimation of Solomon" in *Genesis as Myth and Other Essays.*

34. For other treatments of kinds of associations see: K. Andriolo, "A Structural Analysis of Genealogy and Worldview in the Old Testament", *American Anthropologist,* vol. 80, no. 4:805–14 (1978); and T. Prewitt, "Kinship Structures and Genesis Genealogies", *Journal of Near Eastern Studies* 4:87–98 (1981).

35. This point is strongly argued by Leach, *Genesis as Myth and Other Essays,* but is worthy of further emphasis. In brief, when we approach surface genealogical content of Genesis as a unified "argument" we find sophistication in the wielding of what we would today call "social models." Cf. also my more formal version of these arguments in " 'Do

Dual Organizations Exist' Revisited: Semiotic Analysis of Cultural Expressions in Genesis",
Semiotica, vol. 59, no. 1/2 (1986), pp. 35–53.

36. In addition to the formal treatments of kinship theory cited previously, some readers
may wish to consult J. Goody, *The Character of Kinship* (London: Cambridge University
Press; 1973), or R. Marshall, "Heroes and Hebrews: The Priest in the Promised Land",
American Ethnologist, vol. 6 (1979), pp. 772–90. Also see J. Irvine, "When is Genealogy
History? Wolof Genealogies in Comparative Perspective", *American Ethnologist,* vol. 5
(1978), pp. 651–73, which offers an excellent contemporary example of how oral genealogy
is used in processes of political legitimation.

37. Needham, *Structure and Sentiment,* pp. 7–8, 97–98. Note that the connubium model,
because it is cyclical, does not imply differentiation of patrilineages by rank. In a large
system the circulation of women may actually occur, even when the native model is
noncyclical in expression. Genesis offers a noncyclical, ranked social order, while the
structure of kinship reports suggests the potential of cyclical closure. See also Gottwald, *The
Tribes of Yahweh,* p. 308. Detailed mathematical treatments of recursive and circular forms
of elementary kinship structure are to be found in F. Lorrain, "Social Structure, Social
Classifications, and the Logic of Analogy," *in* P. Ballonoff, ed., *Mathematical Models of
Social and Cognitive Structures: Contributions to the Mathematical Development of Anthropology* (Urbana: University of Illinois Press; 1974), and F. Lorrain, *Réseaux sociaux et
géométrie des structures sociales* (Paris: Hermann; 1975). Lorrain's work represents an
extension of the early definitions by Lévi-Strauss, and formal exposition of P. Courrege, "Un
Modéle mathématique des structures élémentaires de parenté," *L'Homme,* vol. 5 (1965), pp.
248–90. Other recent contributions to mathematical kinship theory include F. El Guindi and
D. W. Read, "Mathematics in Structural Theory," *Current Anthropology,* vol. 20 (1979), pp.
761–90; and F. E. Tjon Sie Fat, "More Complex Formulae of Generalized Exchange,"
Current Anthropology, vol. 22 (1981), pp. 377–99.

38. In this respect, my analysis is in accord with that of M. Donaldson, "Kinship Theory
in the Patriarchal Narratives: The Case of the Barren Wife," *Journal of the American
Academy of Religion,* vol. 49 (1981) pp. 77–87, and Oden, "Jacob as Father, Husband, and
Nephew," p. 198, concerning the specific relations of Sarai, Nahor, and Abram. However, I
do not see the marriage of Sarai and Abram as particularly "incestuous"—such a determination depends upon who their mothers are, and the nature of the descent principle through
which the relations are read. It should also be noted that preferred marriages in matrilineal
and patrilineal connubia are to the mother's-brother's daughter, so it is impossible to
determine filiation precisely from the marriage pattern data alone. See also C. Lévi-Strauss,
Structural Anthropology (New York: Doubleday; 1963), pp. 31–54.

39. Descent can be traced through either men or women or both. It is clear that the text of
Genesis intends to have the descent lines traced primarily through men, but underlying
features of the text and the general form of Near Eastern kinship systems as they are known
historically suggest that descent through women should be strongly considered. Note that if
Lot's wife is an Abrahamite and Isaac's sister, then the line of inheritance from mother's-
brother's to sister's-sons runs from Isaac through Lot to Bethuel, and finally, if Bethuel is
interpreted as the *mother* of Laban, to Laban via Bethuel's brothers and then to Jacob. For
detailed arguments on this implied matrilineal relationship see D. Gaston, "Matrilineal
Background of Genealogies in Genesis," *in* Deely and Lenhart, eds., *Semiotics 1981* (New
York: Plenum Press; 1982), pp. 505–19.

40. This notion also occurs in the relation of Joseph to his first Egyptian master (Genesis
39)—as first among the household servants Joseph's corporate responsibilities were like
those of a son. This is similar to certain stages in the practice of corporate authority and
delegation of authority in Greek and Roman family law; see N. D. Fustel de Coulanges, *The
Ancient City* (New York: Doubleday; 1873 translation [original French edition 1864]), pp.
90–94. Note the language of the Circumcision Covenant (Genesis 17) which refers also to
retainers.

41. Recall the alternative interpretation of Sarai's birth status, based upon the structural marriage implications shown in Figure 1, that she is the sister of Bethuel, a daughter of Nahor (see p. 13). In this interpretation "daughter of Terah" refers to a woman of a lineage in the Terahite association of lineages with different maternal background from that of Abram.

42. A comprehensive discussion of "covenant" concepts is found in D. R. Hillers, *Covenant: the History of a Biblical Idea* (Baltimore: Johns Hopkins University Press; 1969). Hillers's treatment of Genesis places emphasis on chapters 9, 15, and 17—sections dealing with Noah and Abram/Abraham. My inclusion of the Circumcision Covenant as a "stage" of social development supporting an unfolding, more perfect, association is not inconsistent with Hillers's view. However, my treatment is more deeply involved with Genesis as a unity, especially in the relationships of the covenant promises of the Jacob story and other narrative after chapter 25.

43. Vawter, *On Genesis*, pp. 248–49; von Rad, *Genesis: A Commentary*, pp. 195–97; Gunkel, *Genesis*, pp. 184–93, 226–29.

44. See Oden, *The Bible without Theology*, pp. 92–105, on the strong associations of clothing and status in biblical narrative.

45. Ibid., p. 109.

46. Ibid., pp. 127–29.

47. Cf. F. Barth, "Descent and Marriage Reconsidered," *In* Goody, ed., *The Character of Kinship*, pp. 6–7, 11–16.

48. For detailed presentation of this thesis see Gottwald, *The Tribes of Yahweh*, pp. 362–67; also see N. Gottwald, "Sociological Method in the Study of Ancient Israel," *In* Buss, ed., *Encounter with the Text*, pp. 69–81.

49. Gottwald, *The Tribes of Yahweh*, pp. 298–318, offers a comprehensive discussion. His objection (p. 309) to the analysis of J. Renger, *"marat-ilim:* Exogamie bei den semitischen Nomaden des 2. Jahrtausends," *Archiv für Orientforschung*, vol. 14 (1973), pp. 103–7, states that it is inconsistent to consider Abram, Nahor, and Haran heads of lineages while also considering them "brothers" born of Terah. This is true only if the system of kin reckoning involves patrilineal principles. In a purely matrilineal system Abram, Nahor, and Haran might be in quite different corporate groups, if their mothers came from different groups. In such a case their relation to Terah would not necessarily preclude intermarriage of their offspring.

50. See again note 39.

II. Polity and History

1. Oden, *The Bible Without Theology*, pp. 106–30, especially 106–12 and 130.

2. Ibid., 107–8, 113–14, 117–18.

3. See Wilson, *Genealogy and History in the Biblical World*, pp. 167–83, for a comprehensive discussion of genealogies in Genesis 36. Note, however, that he excludes verses 31–39 on the grounds that they do not constitute genealogy. This reinforces my use of the material as being more significant as a place list.

4. All of the point plots are based on H. May, ed., *Oxford Bible Atlas* (New York: Oxford University Press; 1984).

5. See especially, Lorrain, "Social Structure, Social Classification and the Logic of Analogy," and Lorrain, *Réseaux sociaux et géométrie des structures sociales*.

6. Tree-diagrams used by certain Jewish mystics rely on chaining processes which are similar to those used in kinship modeling, and in some cases apparently tap into the same elements of cultural or rhetorical structure.

7. See C. Lévi-Strauss, "Do Dual Organizations Exist," in Lévi-Strauss, *Structural Anthropology*. For technical development of some of these arguments see my " 'Do Dual Organizations Exist' Revisited."

8. For an example of how these references carry social meaning in Genesis, see Carmichael, *Women, Law, and the Genesis Traditions,* pp. 36, 47–48, 71–73.

9. The animal translation is considered dubious by many scholars. It appears in *The New American Bible* (Washington, D.C.: World Publishing Company; 1970) and a few other contemporary English translations.

10. Wilson, *Genealogy and History in the Biblical World,* pp. 187–88.

11. The analysis was part of an exploratory reading of Exodus 21–22 against several Genesis narratives in the National Endowment for the Humanities Summer Seminar on Biblical Law in Historical Perspective/University of California, Berkeley, summer 1988.

12. My renderings of names are based on the *New American Bible,* text and notes of pp. 38–40, 56; see also Plaut, *The Torah, Genesis.*

13. Gottwald, *The Tribes of Yahweh,* pp. 318–23.

14. Numbers 3:38 ends with the statement: "Any layman who came near the sanctuary was to be put to death." I take "layman" in the context to include Levites outside the Aaronite priesthood. I do not mean to imply that such a distinction necessarily applied in other biblical contexts, especially in the territorial context provided for in Joshua.

15. Gottwald, *The Tribes of Yahweh,* pp. 237–337.

16. Ibid., p. 340.

17. affine: i.e., *in-law,* or relative by marriage.

III. Structural Hermeneutics

1. Form criticism and the documentary hypothesis are closely related terms covering a very wide range of biblical studies. A large number of form critics emphasize the recognition of textual types, their primary interests being the construction of classifications relating materials stylistically. This orientation does not necessarily imply interests in dating the materials precisely or linking the recognized parts in historical reconstructions of editorial process. The historical questions permeate the documentary orientation so much, however, that it becomes difficult to speak of genre or style without creating implications about dating and the nature of editorial circles. Yet after a century of such criticism, debate still rages on questions of single versus multiple authors, the place of oral tradition in the formation of the texts of the Torah, and the classifications of literary forms in general. The uninitiated will find R. N. Whybray's *The Making of the Pentateuch: A Methodological Study, Journal for the Study of the Old Testament Supplement Series 53,* (Sheffield, England: JSOT Press—Sheffield Academic Press; 1987) most helpful. For Genesis, Coats's *Genesis with an Introduction to Narrative Literature* is the most definitive recent work.

2. Stephen Langton was an Archbishop of Canterbury whose chapter system for Genesis, reflecting the culmination of several competing strands of thinking about textual organization in the 13th century, has become the standard in the modern Bible. Much earlier traditions of chaptering and verse citation were introduced by the Masorites, basing divisions on ancient appreciations of biblical material and the scriptural reading system forming the core of Jewish education in the Torah. Among the divisions are the parashah (paragraphs or minor sections) and sidrah, major sections associated with weekly reading in the synagogue. In some Hebrew Bibles the sidrah are marked with a triple ‏ס‎ or ‏פ‎ . The divisions created by these marks also have names, usually derivations from words in the first line of the division. All of the named sections in Genesis except *Vayyehi,* beginning at Genesis 47:28, are so marked. Jewish reading of the Torah since at least the 9th century has been aided by signs of vocalization, texts with signs for vowels added to the original consonantal characters. Earlier vocalized texts are likely to have existed, though the standards of pronunciation were carried through oral readings originally. Other marks introduced into the text at a relatively late time control the melodic sense of the reading. The Hebrew Bible, then, provides an ancient system of divisions which has undergone considerable elaboration in form related to religious practice.

For a fuller discussion of these forms, including association of the *Haftarah* recitations with reading, see Philip Birnbaum's introduction in *The Torah and the Haftarot* (New York: Hebrew Publishing Company; 1983); cf. also the introduction and text provided by Plaut, *The Torah, Genesis*.

3. See C. Kluckholn, *Anthropology and the Classics* (Providence: Brown University Press, 1961), pp. 43–68 (especially pp. 47–50); and Lévi-Strauss, *Structural Anthropology*.

4. In addition to his initial article "Themes as Dynamic Forces in Culture," *American Journal of Sociology*, vol. 51 (1945), pp. 198–206, the essay defining the general notion of cultural themes within the configurationalist perspective, Opler extended his ideas in the following key articles: "An Application of the Theory of Themes in Culture," *Journal of the Washington Academy of Sciences*, vol. 36 (1946), pp. 137–66; "Some Recently Developed Concepts Relating to Culture," *Southwestern Journal of Anthropology*, vol. 4 (1948) pp. 107–22; "The Context of Themes," *American Anthropologist*, vol. 51 (1949), pp. 323–25; and "Component, Assemblage, and Theme in Cultural Integration and Differentiation," *American Anthropologist*, vol. 61 (1959) pp. 955–64.

5. See the philosophical introduction to semiotics of J. Deely, *Introducing Semiotic: Its History and Doctrine* (Bloomington: Indiana University Press; 1982), the technical exposition of U. Eco, *A Theory of Semiotic* (Bloomington: Indiana University Press; 1979), and the many applications of semiotic perspective which cut across our appreciation of texts, space, and action; for example: J. Bunn, *The Dimensionality of Signs, Tools, and Models; An Introduction* (Bloomington: Indiana University Press; 1979); T. Sebeok, *The Sign & Its Masters* (Austin: University of Texas Press; 1979); R. Barthes, *S/Z*, R. Miller, trans., (New York: Hill and Wang; 1974 [original French edition 1970]); A. Greimas, *Semiotique. Dictionnaire raisonné de la théorie du language* (Paris: Hachette; 1966) also as *Semiotics and Language—An Analytical Dictionary*, L. Crist, D. Patte, J. Lee, E. McMahon II, G. Phillips, and M. Rengstorf, translators, (Bloomington: Indiana University Press; 1982).

6. My initial feelings that Genesis includes prefigurements of law have been bolstered by the lectures of David Daube in the NEH Summer Seminar on "Biblical Law in Historical Perspective" (1988). This does not mean that Genesis itself includes codes or straightforward legal examples or legal precedent, but that the legal codes, legal proverbs, and legends associated with contracts and obligation form a rhetorical system that takes nonlegal scriptures into account. On the level of rhetorical or literary practice, narrative supplements law in much the same way it supplements genealogy. Some striking examples of how complex the relationships can be are given in Daube's many writings, among which I shall cite but a few: see in particular "Nathan's Parable," *Novum Testamentum* 24 (1982), pp. 275–88; "Codes and Codas in the Pentateuch," *Juridicial Review* 53 (1941) pp. 1–20; and *Witnesses in Bible and Talmud*, Oxford Centre for Postgraduate Hebrew Studies (1986); these all in addition to his *Biblical Law* and *Ancient Jewish Law* noted earlier (note 6, chapter 1); also see "Rabbinic Methods of Interpretation and Hellenistic Rhetoric," *Hebrew Union College Annual*, vol. 22 (1949), pp. 239–64; "Texts and Interpretation in Roman and Jewish Law," *Jewish Journal of Sociology*, vol. 3 (1961), pp. 3–28; and "How Esau Sold His Birthright," *Cambridge Law Journal*, vol. 8 (1942), pp. 70–75.

7. For example, G. Plaut states in *The Torah, Genesis*, p. xxii: "In general, our commentary favors the position just outlined, namely, that Genesis (with which we are here concerned) is essentially the repository of centuries of traditions which became One Tradition and One Book. At what time it was set down as we have it now will likely remain a matter of conjecture; what is important is to treat the book as an integral unit rather than a paste-up amalgam."

8. See D. Patte and A. Patte, *Structural Exegesis: From Theory to Practice* (Philadelphia: Fortress Press; 1978); also D. Patte, ed., "Genesis 2 and 3. Kaleidoscopic Structural Readings," *Semeia*, vol. 18 (1980); and Coats, *From Canaan to Egypt*.

9. The *toledoth* divisions occur at Genesis 2:4, 6:9, 11:27, 25:19, and 37:2.

10. John Gammie, "Theological Interpretation by Way of Literary and Traditional Analysis," pp. 120–24; and M. Fishbane, "Composition and Structure in the Jacob Cycle (Gen.

25:19—35:22)," *Journal of Jewish Studies,* vol. 26 (1975), pp. 15–38. Both papers employ chiastic analysis of subchapter blocks as a means of expanding the theological interpretation of the Jacob Cycle. See also A. Ceresko, "The A:B:B:A Word Pattern in Hebrew and Northwest Semitic, with Special Reference to the Book of Job," *Ugaritische vorschungen* (1975), pp. 73–88; A. Ceresko, "The Chiastic Word Pattern in Hebrew," *Catholic Biblical Quarterly,* vol. 38 (1976), pp. 303–11; and A. Ceresko, "The Function of Chiasmus in Hebrew Poetry," *Catholic Biblical Quarterly,* vol. 40 (1978), pp. 1–10.

11. My analysis of Genesis 1–14 was developed with strong critical input by John Gammie, and additional comments by Daniel Patte and Jean-Claude Choul concerning the integration of chiastic representation and my application of Greimas's "semiotic square." See also D. Patte, "Greimas' Model for the Generative Trajectory of Meaning in Discourses," *American Journal of Semiotics,* vol. 1 (1982), pp. 59–78; this article prompted my treatment of Genesis 1, 7, 8, and 14. An earlier version of the structure presented here was discussed in a symposium on biblical analysis at the 1983 meeting of the Semiotic Society of America in Snowbird, Utah.

12. Cf. Carroll, "Leach, Lévi-Strauss, and the Garden of Eden," *American Ethnologist,* vol. 4 (1977), pp. 672, 675.

13. Plaut, *The Torah, Genesis,* p. 35.

14. Ibid., p. 46.

15. Ibid., p. 41.

16. Ibid., p. 85.

17. Ibid. Translation is the New Jewish Version.

18. Ibid., p. 55, note 3, points out that "disgrace" is tied to an uncertain translation which can be rendered "My spirit shall not *shield* man forever, . . ." (emphasis added). Note also that Shem and Japeth, in their protective action toward Noah, cover his nakedness with a cloak.

19. I make this statement at considerable risk of being accused of complicating, rather than simplifying, our view of the text. Let me point out again, then, that Whybray, *The Making of the Pentateuch,* and Coats, *Genesis with an Introduction to Narrative Literature,* offer highly readable, straightforward, and informative views of what can be a treacherous subject.

20. Vawter, *On Genesis,* pp. 61–62; also Plaut, *The Torah, Genesis,* p. 11.

21. Oden, *The Bible Without Theology,* pp. 98–105, treats the subject of clothing and status with specific reference to several stories in Genesis.

22. Coats, *From Canaan to Egypt,* especially pp. 53–54 and 80–89. Although on the analysis of political themes I have come to many different conclusions than Coats, his view of the text as a coherent and well-developed structural whole is not that different from the one being developed here. See also Coats, *Genesis with an Introduction to Narrative Literature,* pp. 263–65 and his following detailed analysis of the Joseph story.

23. Gammie, "Theological Interpretation by Way of Literary and Traditional Analysis." Fishbane, "Composition and Structure in the Jacob Cycle (Gen. 25:19—35:22)."

24. C. Lévi-Strauss, "The Structural Study of Myth," a chapter in *Structural Anthropology,* but better read in its context *in* T. Sebeok, ed., *Myth: A Symposium* (Bloomington: Indiana University Press; 1958—originally 1955), pp. 81–106.

25. Carroll, "Leach, Lévi-Strauss, and the Garden of Eden," pointed out the "drifting" parallels of these stories quite independently of any "whole-text" structural considerations. The broad structure of the narratives helps make sense of why Carroll's parallels rest among "intended" meanings of the text.

26. Calum Carmichael is quick to stress that metaphorical readings must be justified with detailed textual support in word-forms and meaning-generating contexts. Those metaphorical readings cited here derive from other relationships between the Mishpatim and Genesis, specifically readings of rules in the form "Thou shalt not . . ." which bear morphological similarities to names in Genesis 31, 34, and 37–38, and a few other segments of the Jacob/Joseph cycles. See Carmichael's *Women, Law, and the Genesis Traditions* for several

of the animal/name correspondences. Carmichael's warning is consistent with the Jewish reading tradition emphasizing the most careful forms of textual support for interpretation. I have strong sympathy with this view but see also structural opposition of broader narrative units as carrying more general "meaning pattern" correspondences and important literal connotations. My readings of legal material from Exodus, though they imply relationship between the processes of production of the texts, are used here mainly to draw points of general legal concern from the Genesis text.

27. See Carmichael, *Women, Law, and the Genesis Traditions,* pp. 33–48.

28. The laws involved have the form "Thou shalt not . . ." but are not clearly Deuteronomic. The interweaving of laws of different form is common in the codes of the Near East in general, and is attributed by most scholars to the gradual addition of material over long periods of time. Calum Carmichael has noted correspondences of rule sequences and narrative development, especially Genesis narrative development, with regard to some of the Deuteronomic material, and for those rules of "similar" form in Exodus. David Daube's more traditional view of the rule forms and patterns recognizes, even if many narrative correspondences to Genesis are not totally convincing, that the material of Exodus 21–22 is not the consistent work of a single legal circle. From the point of view of structural analysis, the origin and redaction of the rules is less important than their pertinence to the narrative situation.

29. Calum Carmichael's reading of Judah's blessing stresses diverse metaphorical slurs on Judah's character. This is not inconsistent with a provision for Judah's kingship, and given the broad nature of elder/younger blessings in Genesis is not a surprising feature. It is apparent that the text "cleans up" many of the rougher confrontations of paternal interests and political antics of sons, as in the account of Jacob's blessing and departure north and the confrontation of Jacob with Simeon and Levi. Such features support the idea that the political "reality" behind composition of the text is distant from some of the original narrative intent of elements in Genesis. Another example of how complex the political intrigue of narrative can be is to be seen in Daube, "Nathan's Parable."

30. The brothers' fear of Joseph is handled in the text in verses 14–21. Philip Birnbaum's note for this section reads: "Joseph, who reiterates his belief that his brothers' intentions were overruled by God for his own beneficent purposes, freely forgives them, and reveals his high moral and religious character. The selling of Joseph had been a sinful action, but through his coming to Egypt, God brought about a great blessing to many. God often brings good out of evil, though Evil is not to be done in order that good may come. Joseph himself demonstrates this great lesson in his life, so far at least as his brothers are concerned" (Birnbaum, *The Torah and The Haftarot,* p. 83). Compare the comments by Coats, *Genesis with an Introduction to Narrative Literature,* pp. 312–13, which point out that Joseph's brothers' fear is in contrast to their lack of request for forgiveness in Genesis 45, and that Joseph's response refers to the "saving of many people" rather than to the preservation of Israel. The theological interpretation supporting Joseph's high moral character is built, in spite of its obviously positive tone, on the undercurrent of mistrust and potential discord, a process which must continue in the lives of the characters. Thus, we have a further justification for the process of enslavement. Bloodshed has been averted in the constant intergroup rivalry, but coordinated action by the brothers as tribes must await their deaths, just as the entry of Israel into Canaan under Joshua must await the deaths of the generation born in Egypt. In this sense the "political" and "historical" intent of Genesis is maintained. Recalling that we may read the sons of Israel as individuals in the narrative or tribes in a political array, there is room to see both the positive and negative senses of Joseph's character as a key to interpretation of political and historical formulae.

31. Compare, for example, Vawter, *On Genesis,* or G. von Rad, *Genesis: A Commentary,* both of which preserve the narrative order, and Gunkel's *Genesis* which sorts the text into blocks destroying the original order. Yet each style of commentary accomplishes a restructuring, inasmuch as material inserted between blocks of text, or subordinated to the new narrative, breaks the experience of reading. Structural analysis has the potential of

channeling the order of reading into new orders while maintaining some sense of the original linear whole. It is therefore not too radically different from other forms of commentary, except in the formality of its models.

32. M. Bloch, *The Historian's Craft* (New York: Random House; 1953), pp. 150–51.

IV. Mythos and Ethos

1. P. Ricoeur, "Metaphor and the Main Problem of Hermeneutics," in Reagan and Stewart, eds., *The Philosophy of Paul Ricoeur,* p. 146.

2. Probably the best, and most difficult, essay in Lévi-Strauss's *Structural Anthropology* is "Social Structure." This essay systematically develops the notion of "structural models" in a manner consistent with the full sweep of Lévi-Strauss's work, and hence for structuralism in general.

3. This point runs through all of Lévi-Strauss's writings, but is explicitly stated in his essays on linguistics in *Structural Anthropology.*

4. See "The Structural Study of Myth" *in* Sebeok, ed., *Myth,* pp. 84–85; or *in* Lévi-Strauss, *Structural Anthropology.* I consider much more of the content of Genesis and other parts of the Torah to be "mythic" than most biblical scholars—that is, I believe oral narratives functioning as myth served as sources for many of the stories. The literary construction which has come to us, however, probably represents a radical reshaping of these original stories, and cannot be placed in the literary or folkloric categories of myth per se. For a more restrictive idea of myth in Genesis see Coats, *Genesis with an Introduction to Narrative Literature,* p. 10. Also see the discussion of myth in Oden, *The Bible Without Theology,* pp. 40–91.

5. See Aristotle, "Poetics," chapter 6 (sections 1449b:21–1450a:14), *in* R. Kassel, ed., *Aristotelis de Arte Poetica Liber* (London: Oxford University Press; 1965), pp. 10–11.

6. Ibid., chapter 6 (section 1450a:15–1450b:20), pp. 12–13.

7. The most direct expression of this approach is found in the very well known book *Patterns of Culture* (Routledge & Kegan Paul Ltd.; 1934), in which Benedict developed her famous "Dionysian" and "Apollonian" categories.

8. General readers may want to see Kluckholn's *Mirror for Man* (McGraw-Hill; 1944), although *Anthropology and the Classics* is a readable and informative technical application of configurationalist principles.

9. See Lévi-Strauss, *The Elementary Structures of Kinship,* Lorrain, *Réseaux sociaux et géométrie des structures sociales.* Continuing development of the mathematical and cultural principles of kinship is to be found in the literature of French and Dutch anthropology, especially in the journals *L'Homme* and *Current Anthropology* (see again note 37 for "Genealogies" in this volume for several key articles). It should be stressed that these principles are fully integrated into Lévi-Strauss's approach to myth, such that kinship structure and myth structure constitute a coextensive system.

10. Coats, *Genesis with an Introduction to Narrative Literature,* pp. 3–10; pp. 317–22.

11. Ibid., pp. 3–4.

12. Ibid., pp. 13–34 and individual treatments following throughout the work.

13. Ibid., pp. 30; also continuing references, as in pp. 35–36.

14. As Gottwald, *The Tribes of Yahweh,* effectively demonstrates, no *clans* or other formal marriage-defining categories are clearly evident through the analysis of biblical usages of social categories. Certainly no marriage systems such as those found in Australia were in use by ancient Israel, nor do agnatic groups seem to have the formal "sib" status we observe in some patrilineal societies. We must clearly distinguish between the "mechanical" ideal presented in the text, and the "statistical" marriage system operating through shifting alliances; see also Lévi-Strauss, *Structural Anthropology,* for a full discussion of "mechanical" and "statistical" models within his "Social Structure" chapter.

15. Coats, *Genesis with an Introduction to Narrative Literature,* pp. 109–13, 149–51, 188–92, provides a commentary overview and excellent bibliography.

16. What is clear is that the term "sister" is not intended to contradict the laws of incest. It is also somewhat parallel to Abram's use of the term "brother" for Lot.

17. A wonderful modern treatment of Near Eastern polygamy is to be found in E. Fernea, *Guests of the Sheik: An Ethnography of an Iraqi Village* (New York: Doubleday; 1965).

18. See also E. Neufeld, *Ancient Hebrew Marriage Laws: With Special References to General Semitic Laws and Customs,* (New York: Longmans, Green and Co.; 1944), pp. 77–88.

19. Coats, *Genesis with an Introduction to Narrative Literature,* pp. 151, 190–91.

20. Aristotle, "Poetics" (section 1450b:4–13), pp. 12–13; translation from T. S. Dorsch, transl., *Classical Literary Criticism,* (New York: Viking Penguin Inc.; 1965), pp. 40–41.

21. The most comprehensive formal treatment of the "atom" principles introduced by Lévi-Strauss is P. Courrege, "Un Modéle mathématique des structures élémentaire de parenté." The kernel idea is presented in *Structural Anthropology* and served as a basis for much of *The Elementary Structures of Kinship,* all work accomplished by Lévi-Strauss before the 1950s.

22. David Daube draws our attention to this and a few other Torah scriptures as examples of "shame culture" (see also, for example, Deuteronomy 22:13–19, 23:10–15, 24:4, 24:10, 25:3). Calum Carmichael, on the other hand, brings emphasis to the metaphorical sense of the "sandal" and "foot" in Deuteronomic treatment of the levirate and in Ruth. These elements can be read as references to the female and male sexual organs, giving the notion of a woman stripping a man's sandal and spitting in his face strong sexual force.

23. Fustel de Coulanges, *The Ancient City,* presents a functional treatment of ancient Greek and Roman religion. The early chapters outline his general thesis involving the idea of ancestor worship and the definition of family, drawing heavily from Greek myth.

24. See also D. Daube, "How Esau Sold His Birthright," *Cambridge Law Journal,* vol. 8 (1942): 70–75.

25. Neufeld, *Ancient Hebrew Marriage Laws,* pp. 23–55, especially pp. 37–38.

26. J. Deely, *Introducing Semiotic,* pp. 65, 107–23.

V. Semiosis

1. The notion of the "promiscuous sign" was introduced in a paper read at the annual meeting of the Semiotic Society of America in 1983 by Philippe Desan, "For a Promiscuity of the Signifier," *in* Jonathon Evans and John Deely, eds., *Semiotics 1983* (University Press of America, 1987) pp. 605–12. Although I did not care for the wording originally, I have become increasingly impressed by its descriptive efficacy for matters of listening/reading.

2. Lévi-Strauss, "The Structural Study of Myth," *in* Sebeok, ed., *Myth,* pp. 105–6; or in *Structural Anthropology.*

3. Deely, *Introducing Semiotic,* p. 122.

4. Ricoeur, "Explanation and Understanding," *The Philosophy of Paul Ricoeur,* p. 154.

5. "Competence" may be thought of as the "ideal" grammar of a hypothetical "perfect" speaker of a language. Since the notion was introduced in Noam Chomsky, *Aspects of the Theory of Syntax* (Cambridge: MIT Press; 1965), it has undergone a number of sinister transformations in psycholinguistic and educational psychology circles. I do not particularly recommend reading "Aspects" or its derivative literature; it is not as much fun as reading Genesis, nor is it likely to be as informative about the nature of language.

INDEX

F designates a figure and T a table on the page cited (e.g., 45T indicates a table on page 45).

TERRY J. PREWITT teaches in the Anthropology Department of the University of West Florida. He has published articles on semiotics and anthropology in numerous scholarly journals and edited volumes.